Write to the Point

Write to the Point

A Master Class on the Fundamentals of Writing for Any Purpose

SAM LEITH

THE EXPERIMENT

NEW YORK

WRITE TO THE POINT: *A Master Class on the Fundamentals of Writing for Any Purpose*
Copyright © 2017, 2018 by Sam Leith

Originally published in the UK by Profile Books Ltd. in 2017.
First published in North America by The Experiment, LLC, in 2018.

The Experiment, LLC
220 East 23rd Street, Suite 600
New York, NY 10010-4658
theexperimentpublishing.com

Many of the designations used by manufacturers and sellers to distinguish their products are claimed as trademarks. Where those designations appear in this book and The Experiment was aware of a trademark claim, the designations have been capitalized.

The Experiment's books are available at special discounts when purchased in bulk for premiums and sales promotions as well as for fund-raising or educational use. For details, contact us at info@theexperimentpublishing.com.

Library of Congress Cataloging-in-Publication Data

Names: Leith, Sam, author.
Title: Write to the point : a master class on the fundamentals of writing for any purpose / Sam Leith.
Description: New York, NY : The Experiment, LLC, [2018] | Includes bibliographical references and index.
Identifiers: LCCN 2017052670 (print) | LCCN 2017059369 (ebook) | ISBN 9781615194636 (ebook) | ISBN 9781615194629 (softcover)
Subjects: LCSH: English language--Rhetoric--Handbooks, manuals, etc. | Rhetoric--Handbooks, manuals, etc. | English language--Style--Handbooks, manuals, etc. | English language--Errors in usage--Handbooks, manuals, etc. | Composition (Language arts)
Classification: LCC PE1408 (ebook) | LCC PE1408 .L4113 2018 (print) | DDC 808/.042—dc23
LC record available at https://lccn.loc.gov/2017052670

ISBN 978-1-61519-462-9
Ebook ISBN 978-1-61519-463-6

Cover and text design by Sarah Smith

Manufactured in the United States of America

First printing August 2018

10 9 8 7 6 5 4 3 2 1

For David Miller

Contents

1

Surviving the Language Wars

Most public discussion of how language is used—and certainly the most vociferous public discussion—is concerned with mistakes. Should that be a capital letter? Is it "different from" or "different than"? Where should that comma go—inside the quotation marks or outside them? On questions such as these, we're encouraged to think, rests the difference between civilization and barbarism.

These arguments have been characterized as "language wars"—and they can look like that. The sound! The fury! To one side, the Armies of Correctness mass behind fortifications made not of sandbags but of secondhand copies of *Fowler's Modern English Usage, Gwynne's Grammar,* and Strunk and White's *Elements of Style.* Here's Lynne "Deadeye" Truss, of *Eats, Shoots & Leaves* fame, her sniper rifle loaded with apostrophes, taking potshots at mispunctuated grocery advertisements; and there's the William Safire platoon, preparing a shock-n-awe offensive involving the word "decimate," which they hope will reduce the enemy forces by a tenth.

On the other side, equally well dug in, are the Descriptivist Irregulars: a curious fighting force in which hippy-dippy school-teachers battle shoulder-to-shoulder with austere academic linguists. There are a lot of cardigans. Someone has just pulled the pin and lobbed a split infinitive over the barricades. Now they're sticking their tongues out and flashing V-signs and laughing. And, yes, I can just make out the linguist Geoffrey Pullum, looking peevish and tinkering with the controls of a devastating secret weapon they call only "The Corpus."*

At issue is whether there is a correct way to write. Are there, or should there be, rules about the meanings and spellings of words, the use of punctuation marks, and the formation of sentences? And if there are, or should be, who pronounces on them? Like the conflict in George Orwell's *1984*, this war has been going on for as long as anybody can remember. In the introduction to his *The Sense of Style*, the linguist Steven Pinker writes, "Complaints about the decline of language go at least as far back as the invention of the printing press." He quotes William Caxton (who set up the first printing press in England) in 1478 beefing that "certaynly our langage now vsed veryeth ferre from what whiche was vsed and spoken when I was borne."

Both sides—because all armies have their propaganda wings— will tend to caricature the positions of the other. Descriptivists see the Armies of Correctness as snobbish amateurs, obsessed with a set of prohibitions half-remembered from their own school days and essentially mistaken about how language works. Prescriptivists, meanwhile, see their opponents as smart-assed ivory-tower types who, in trendily insisting that anything goes, actively collude in the coarsening and eventual destruction of the language they purport to study.

Intellectually, the Descriptivists are right. Nobody made the English language up. It isn't an invention, like tennis or a washing machine, where there's an instruction manual to which we can refer. It is not a fixed thing. It is a whole set of practices and behaviors, and it evolves according to the way it is used. One hundred

---

* Not a corpse, i.e., a human body, but a body of language, valuable to linguists wanting to study usage in the wild.

years ago, "wicked" meant "evil"; now, in many contexts, it means "excellent." Nobody decided that; it just—to use a technical linguistic term—sort of caught on. And if it just sort of catches on that "gay" is understood to mean "homosexual," or "decimate" is understood to mean "annihilate," no number of indignant letters to the editor will prevent that from happening.

Does a language have rules? Yes, in one sense it does. It would not work if it didn't. But it doesn't have an umpire. It has rules in the same way that the acceleration of a body through space under gravity or the formation of a fetus in the womb have rules. The rules of language are a property of the system itself. And that system is a property of its day-to-day users.

You may think you don't know any grammar—because, perhaps, you weren't taught at school what a gerund is, or the difference between a conjugation and a declension. But every sentence you utter is grammatical; if it were not, nobody would be able to understand you. You conjugate—I conjugate, he conjugates ... hell, we all conjugate—like a champ, and use gerunds without even thinking about it. The grammar that is taught and written down in books is not a manual for language users; it's a description of what they do.

That is where this book starts from. I take the part not of the Armies of Correctness nor of the Descriptivist Irregulars, but of the huddled civilian caught in the middle, cowering in the shelled-out no-man's-land somewhere between them. And I want to try to present a practical way through. I hope to acknowledge that there is real value in knowing where to put a question mark or how to spell "accommodate"—and that the armies of proofreaders, copy editors, and schoolteachers who think about these questions are not laboring in vain. I'll have plenty to say in later sections about correct (or, more precisely, standard) usage—and about the pointless myths that have grown up about it, too.

But I also want to get the language wars in proportion. Language is a social activity—which is why these things matter. And yet it's precisely because language is a social activity that these things change over time. Knowing your audience is always more important than knowing a set of rules and prohibitions. Correctness is part of the picture, but it's not the whole or even the most important part of the picture.

Good writing is about much more than knowing how to frame a restrictive relative clause. It has to do with how you get a voice down on paper, how you make a sentence easy for your reader to take in, how you attend to the prose music that makes it pleasurable to read, how you make it fresh in idiom and vivid in image, and even how you present it on the page.

Almost all of us need to put pen to paper or stubby finger to keyboard daily. We write memos, emails, reports, presentations, CVs, blogs, tweets, and letters of complaint, congratulation, or supplication. Our working lives and our working relationships are shaped by how and what we write. To write clearly is an essential courtesy, and to write well is to give pleasure to your audience. You are not only making a case or imparting information; you are cultivating a relationship.

That's an important point. It's worth pausing for a moment to think about why prescriptivists and proud pedants—the sort driven to apoplexy by signs that say "Five items or less" rather than "fewer"—feel as they do, and why they mind so much. Oddly, this has more to tell us about language than any of the rules they cherish.

The arguments people tend to make in support of "correctness" are of four kinds:

1. **Appeals to tradition.** They will cite the authority of previous style or grammar manuals, or the evidence of distinguished writers who seem to fall into line with their rules.

2. **Appeals to logic.** They will argue that the correct sequence of tenses, or the proper agreement of a modifier with its subject, is essential to the clarity of a sentence.

3. **Appeals to efficiency.** They will argue that nonstandard usage blunts the precision of the language. If "enormity" is allowed to mean "bigness," or "wicked" is allowed to mean "excellent," confusion and, possibly, rioting will follow.

4. **Appeals to aesthetics.** They will denigrate certain constructions as ugly or clumsy or even "barbaric."

There is some merit, on the face of it, in all these arguments.

"Authorities" on language are often not only careful users but careful observers of the way language is used. The usage of distinguished writers tells us something about the norms of the language at the time they were writing. And yet: What either tells us is not always straightforward. Writers serve their own ends; authorities have their own axes to grind, and themselves often refer to previous authorities. Which writers? Which authorities? And what are we to do when they contradict one another?

It is indeed possible to use logic or analogy to make some of your writing consistent—and you will usually benefit in terms of clarity if you do. But not always. English was not designed as a logical system. It was not designed at all. It evolved—jerry-built by millions of users over hundreds of years—to do its job. In the old children's TV series *The A-Team*, there was typically a scene in which our heroes were locked into a shed by the villains. Rummaging through the shed, they would discover a collection of old rubbish and would use their ingenuity to knock up some improvised device to mount an escape. Before long, out through the doors of the shed would crash a three-wheeled tank made of plywood and dented paint cans, powered by an outboard motor and flinging tennis balls and old potatoes at the enemy from a rear-mounted trebuchet. The English language is that three-wheeled tank: No amount of wishful thinking will make it a Maserati.

In infancy, our language-hungry little brains vacuum vocabulary out of the air, and not only that, they very quickly figure out the grammar that makes sense of it and start bolting the two together with a facility so efficient that theorists believed for a long time we must have an innate "language organ" in the brain. By four months, children can recognize clauses; by ten months, they're getting the hang of prepositions; by a year old, they have the noun/adjective distinction down; and by the time they're three, they've mastered the whole of English grammar. It's staggering—like deducing the rules of chess by watching a handful of games, or like figuring out the workings of the internal combustion engine by standing next to a busy intersection for half an hour.

Languages evolve in communities and they therefore bind communities. Americans don't aspirate the *h* in "herb," for instance, because in standard spoken English at the time their ancestors boarded the *Mayflower* it was pronounced *erb* (it came in from the French, which didn't aspirate the *h*, either). At some point between now and then, British English underwent a trend for pronouncing words as they were spelled and so, as the British comedian Eddie Izzard put it, "We say *herbs*—because there's a fucking *h* in it." But is that rule applied consistently? No, because it's not a fucking rule. We both call the thing with which we chop our *herbs* or *erbs* a *nife*.

The difference between *herb* and *erb* is what's sometimes called a shibboleth: a word or pronunciation that distinguishes one language community from another. "Shibboleth" was a shibboleth. If you needed to tell an Ephraimite from a Gileadite, a millennium or so BC, you'd ask him to say "shibboleth," a Hebrew word that has something to do with corn. The Ephraimites didn't have the *sh* sound in their language, so if he said *sibboleth* you had your man, and could get straight to the business of slaying him with the jawbone of an ass, or similar.

When we talk about "language," everyone knows we're not talking about just one thing: There are about seven thousand languages spoken worldwide. Less attention is paid to the fact that when we talk about "English," we are not talking about a single thing either; we're talking about a huge, messily overlapping mass of dialects and accents and professional jargons and slangs—some spoken, some written—that have their own vocabularies and grammatical peculiarities and resources of tone and register. The sort of "legalese" you'll see in the small print of your car insurance is English; as is the Russian-inflected "nadsat" used in Anthony Burgess's *A Clockwork Orange*; as is the abbreviated text-speak burbling through your SMS or Twitter feed. They share a common ancestor, they share almost all of their vocabularies and grammars, and they are, more often than not, mutually intelligible. It takes a while for a standard English user to "tune in" to *A Clockwork Orange*—but not all that long.

On the other hand, a language is not only a set of practices. It is also, in its broader sense, a set of ideas about those practices. And the fact is that a very large number of people do believe that there is a right and a wrong way to speak or write. Those ideas are bound up with identity. Sometimes they are explicit—as in books written by proud pedants deploring the corruption of the language. Sometimes they are implicit—as in the suspicion with which one community of dialect users might regard an outsider. The former of these two things is, at root, no more than a elite variant of the latter.

By adopting a pragmatic, rhetorical approach, we can come at this from a third direction. How? Suffer fools gladly. God knows there are a lot of them about, so you're going to be suffering them anyway. If you can't do so gladly, it's your gladness that will suffer, not the fools.

Yes: If someone believes that it's not English to split an infinitive, they are, technically, quite wrong. But you're not interested in proving them wrong; you're interested in getting them on your side. Indulge them. If that's the sort of person you're writing to, *or even if there's a decent chance such a person will be in your audience,* leave that infinitive unsplit with a good grace and an inward smile.

We should also recognize that we have, and are entitled to indulge, a whole set of stylistic preferences. Every time you speak or write, you are trying to form a connection with your audience, and that connection depends on speaking that audience's language. This book is primarily interested in standard English. One of the sociological features of standard English is that many of its users place a high value on getting it right. So, as I'll be repeating, you go to where the audience is.

That means that, as we make our way across that battlefield, it's worth knowing where the shell holes are; better to step into one knowingly and carefully than to stumble over it in the dark and break your silly neck.

Furthermore, knowing the rules of standard English can help give you something that is vitally important to any writer: confidence. Many people, sitting down to write, feel apprehension or even fear. How am I going to fill this white space? How am I going to say what I mean? What if I get the punctuation in the wrong place? What if I end up sounding stupid? Even the most fluent speakers can freeze up so that the voice that falters onto the page is not, somehow, their own.

That fear is responsible for more bad writing than anything else. Fear, more often than self-regard, is what makes people sound stiff and pompous in print, and fear is what makes people cling to half-remembered rules from their school days.

Writing, then, is in some respects a confidence trick. I don't mean that writers are in the business of hoodwinking their readers. Rather, that in the best and most fluent writing, the writer not only feels but instills confidence. The writer is in command and projects that— meaning the reader feels in safe hands. You are confident that the writer knows what he or she means and is expressing it exactly.

I don't say that there is one, and only one, form of good writing. This book is not a list of rules or instructions, though it contains many suggestions and opinions. It does not pretend to contain a magic formula. What it hopes to do, rather, is to walk you companionably around the question of what it is we're doing when we read and write, and how we can do it better and more confidently.

I'll talk about the basic bits and pieces that make up a sentence, and how you fit those sentences into paragraphs and larger units of thought and argument. I'll talk about why sentences go wrong and how you can fix them. I'll talk about specific types of writing, the conventions of grammar, and common mistakes and irregularities. I'll talk about the difference between writing for the page and writing for the internet. And I'll discuss some of the tricks that can be used to make prose livelier and more immediate.

But I'll also look at the bigger picture. Most of the writing we do is intended, one way or another, to persuade, so I want to consider how persuasion itself works. What will make someone read your words and adopt your point of view? How do you capture someone's attention and keep it focused? How do you step back and see your words from the point of view of your reader? There's a body of knowledge on this subject that leads us from the ancient world, where Aristotle first set out the principles of rhetoric, to the laboratory of the modern neuroscientist.

Right. Out of the shell hole. Let's see what it's like up there. One, two, three, HUP!

2

The Big Picture

You Talkin' to Me? Speaking, Reading, and Writing

Many years ago, I interviewed the writer Julian Barnes for my school magazine. Imagine an eighteen-year-old me, settling my tape recorder nervously on the North London coffee table of the great man. I was armed with a list of overwrought and pretentious questions. I was eager to please. But just as I set my tape recorder running, he said something that disrupted me completely. He said, with a sphinxlike Barnesian smile, that he insisted on only one precondition for the interview. I was not to quote him verbatim.

I was confused: Wasn't being misquoted the complaint that every interviewee made of every journalist? Yet here was someone—who could see my tape recorder on the table as an earnest of my good intentions—positively insisting on inaccuracy. "You can make anybody look like an idiot by quoting them verbatim," he said.* And, of course, he was right. None of us speaks in complete and well-formed sentences.

What I have come to think of as the Barnes Principle is a good way to consider something that we don't pay enough attention to.

---

* Well, he said something like that. Under other circumstances I'd hesitate to put that in quotes, but here . . .

Speech and writing are different things; more different than we often notice. And reading is different, too, from either. In fact, the ways in which people read—on a computer screen, in a book, on a smartphone—are themselves different enough to need thinking about.

In this chapter I'd like to offer some hints as to how this might affect your practice.

One of the commonest pieces of advice you hear is: "Try to write as you speak." But it's a piece of advice that needs to be treated with real caution. In one way, it's sensible. All of us, in conversation, improvise fluently and grammatically. We speak with unthinking confidence—at least until we're asked to do so in front of a room full of people, or to a stranger who intimidates us—and that confidence is the heart of effective communication. You can learn as a writer from the way you speak, and you can seek to capture your speaking voice on the page.

But to write as you speak is much more easily said than done. Speaking is natural; writing is artificial. You cannot write exactly as you speak, nor should you. I just tried, for instance, to dictate the next paragraph without preparation into my iPhone.

The spoken language tends to be redundant. It tends to contain a whole lot of things that, um, that aren't features of the written language. It's much more freely and openly structured ... you find that sentences run on into each other, a whole lot of little things like, voice, intruding, you'll say a lot of things, fillers, filler phrases that will, um, interrupt and give the listener time to react and time to digest what you've already said. You'll tend to find that you stop halfway through sentences and break off and, um, basically the spoken language is much more slippery than the written one and readers can go back in the written language which they can't in the spoken language, so if you transcribe exactly how someone speaks, even if they speak,

well, more eloquently than I'm doing now, um, you'll still end up
with something that in no way looks fit for the page.

Ending up with something in no way fit for the page is certainly what I've done (what was all that guff about "like, voice, intruding"?) by quoting myself verbatim.

What I was trying to get at in that ramble was that the written and spoken languages have different formal properties and slightly different grammars. There's nothing in my spoken voice that tells me how to punctuate the above, for instance—already, I've started to tidy it up by inserting spaces and periods and commas and an ellipsis, according to the grammar of standard written English. But as phoneticians will tell you, the spoken voice doesn't usually leave gaps between words—there's no exact spoken equivalent to the semantic difference between a period, a colon, a comma, or a dash. Already, I'm falsifying it for the page.

Accordingly, literary writers will often use nonstandard style to capture a speaking voice. Here's a bit from Marilynne Robinson's novel *Gilead*, for instance.

> *I wrote almost all of it in the deepest hope and conviction.*
> *Sifting my thoughts and choosing my words. Trying to say*
> *what was true. And I'll tell you frankly, that was wonderful.*

Grammar sticklers would probably allow the first sentence. They'd object to the lack of a main verb in the second and third, regarding them essentially as modifying clauses. They might tut-tut over the fourth, too, on the grounds either (if they were particular asses) that it begins a sentence with the word "and," or that the comma after "frankly" wants an opposite number to isolate the adverb as a parenthesis ("I'll tell you, frankly, that was wonderful"), or perhaps that the comma would be better as a colon ("I'll tell you frankly: That was wonderful").

The sticklers would miss the point. Here the punctuation is being used not as a grammatical signpost but solely as a score for the cadence. Read it aloud. It's expressed perfectly. The periods and the comma tell you exactly where the pauses in the spoken language come. And—though this isn't a precise science, as I'll discuss in more detail in the section on punctuation—those pauses are the length of a period where Robinson puts a period and the length of a comma where Robinson puts a comma.

Why the difference? Speech does not have to be learned in the same way as writing. Normal children, in their first six years of life, will acquire a full competence in the grammar of the language and a passive vocabulary (that is, a list of the words they understand) of something like twenty thousand words. All you have to do is surround a baby with other language users and leave it to do its thing.

But forming letters, stringing those letters into words, and applying the rules of punctuation . . . these have to be painstakingly taught and practiced. Writing is an arbitrary and artificial code for representing a natural behavior. It assumes a theoretical or imaginary reader: When you write, you are creating a sort of message in a bottle. That's odd. It's not an intuitive thing to do. It's a learned behavior.

As I fumblingly put it in my straight-to-Dictaphone paragraph on page 11, the spoken language tends to be much more loosely packed and less structured than the written version. Sentences run together, break and change direction, or circle back. Speakers say "um" and "uh," and insert empty phrases. This not only helps them catch up with themselves: it helps the listener digest what's being said without suffering cognitive overload. For the same reason you'll see much more repetition, too. To state the obvious, readers can go back and reread a sentence, or refer to an earlier paragraph. The listener can't press rewind.

So writing and speech are profoundly different animals. There are several ramifications of this. One is that writing obeys more precise, conscious, man-made rules. There are conventions that apply to particular forms of writing, and those conventions are much of what those in the language wars fight about. So when you sit down to write, however well-trained you may be, you're conscious of doing something artificial, something formal, something unnatural. And more often than not you stiffen up.

Take an extreme example: the policeman. No real cop alive would, returning to the precinct and being asked about his afternoon over a cup of coffee, tell a colleague: "As I was continuing my westerly patrol along East Forty-Fifth Street, I became aware of an altercation between two males. Upon their disregarding a verbal warning to desist, I proceeded to engage them. I apprehended one suspect. The other suspect escaped on foot and remains at large."

He would be more likely to say something like: "I was cruising down Forty-Fifth and there were these two guys getting up in each other's faces, so I told them to stop. They weren't listening, so I went in, but by the time I cuffed one of the bozos the other guy had taken off."

You can be sure, though, that it's the first version that will be read out in court. The tone of formal notes for testimony in court *should*, of course, be different from the one that you'd use when telling the story to your colleague in the precinct. But my imaginary cop is doing an extreme version of something that very many of us tend to do: He's overcorrecting. He's not just representing speech in a formal way; he's representing a form of speech that never existed. And you'll find cousins to this sort of thing in any amount of official and formal writing.

The question of what you might call tone of voice, of the right level of formality, is what's known as decorum or, sometimes, register. Getting it right—finding a style appropriate to the communication—is at the very heart of effective writing. To get it wrong is to make the prose-equivalent mistake of messing up the dress code for a party. In the precinct, you're in jeans-and-sneaker mode; in court, you're aiming more for suit-and-tie. Our policeman has presented himself in an ill-fitting tuxedo with a badly knotted bow tie. This is one of the things behind that idea of writing as you speak: You're trying to capture the spontaneity and directness of spoken communication on the page without sounding stiff or pompous.

But as I say, writing is a representation of speech, not a transcription of it. You're translating something that lives in sound into something that lives on the page. That is a more radical transformation than we're used to noticing. It's not less of an illusion than the representation of a physical object in oil paint. You can tell the difference between a painting that looks like a pipe and one that doesn't. We're so used to assuming the equivalence between painting and subject that if someone shows you a painting of a briar pipe and asks you what it is, you'll probably say: "A pipe." But as René Magritte reminded us: "Ceci n'est pas une pipe" ("This is not a pipe").

When you're writing, you're trying to produce the *illusion* of your best speaking voice, in the most apt register, in written form. As I've started to suggest, the way the spoken language works is shaped by the way in which it's received; it adapts to its audience. The same is true of the written form. Reading and hearing are related, just as writing and speaking are related, but they are not the same thing.

One of the ways this manifests itself is pace. A fast writer will be able to knock out something between five hundred and one thousand words in an hour. A fast reader can take those words in in approximately a minute. We read tens of times as fast as we write, in other words. So we experience the text differently: Hours of agonized concentration at the keyboard translates, at the other end of the process, into a few minutes of interested attention on the page. That means that the writer won't have a natural sense of the pace of the finished product.

Imagine shooting a feature film in stop-motion, moving a Plasticine model or redrawing a cell minutely differently, for each frame. In order to see how it's going to flow for the viewer, you'll need to run the rushes back at normal speed. So you'll only really get a sense of the pace of your work on revising; you need to try to experience it as a reader, not as a writer. And in practice, this means rereading. Indeed, you'd be astonished by how different a text you've written feels when you experience it as a reader.

If you have time, leave it for a couple of days. When you reread something you've just written, you're still bruised by the experience of composing it; you'll be too aware of the joints, the awkward transitions, the hidden architecture. This paragraph or that paragraph will distract you because you're conscious of the specific labor you spent composing it. Something that felt arduous to compose will feel heavier on the page, and, if you've been busy with cut-and-paste, you'll have a sense, as no reader would, of how it used to connect to a separate part of the text altogether. Leave it a bit, and those scars heal. When you return to it as a reader, you'll have a much better sense of how it reads to someone coming to it cold. It may well read better than you imagined.

It's worth thinking, too, about another thing: What happens when we read? We learn a language, it is now generally accepted, in much the same way we learn anything else: Our clever, super-adaptable neurons develop the tools to do the job as our brains develop in childhood. But learning to read and write is not a natural process—it's a cultural rather than an evolutionary skill. Learning to read is more painstaking and more artificial than learning to speak or learning to listen.

The brain repurposes various other areas—those dedicated to the spoken language, to object recognition, motor coordination, sound, and vision—to cobble together a set of reading circuits. As the cognitive neuroscientist Maryanne Wolf puts it in *Proust and the Squid: The Story and Science of the Reading Brain* (2007), the brain is able to learn to read because of "its protean capacity to make new connections among structures and circuits originally devoted to other more basic brain processes [. . .] such as vision and spoken language."

Quite how this happens, it should be said, is not known in very great detail. We all love neurosciency stuff—publishers most of all—but we're still at a pretty rudimentary stage. You can use various devices to measure blood flow or electromagnetic impulses in the brain. Afterward you can point to a bit of the brain and say: "Something's definitely going on in there when X does Y, but we don't have much of a clue what it is."*

But this stuff at the very least offers hints and suggestions for the practical writer; you're working with the reader's brain, so a quick glance under the cranial hood has the potential to put you at an advantage.

By the time you're a fully competent speaker of the language, two areas of the brain in particular will have developed language specialisms. There follows, duly, a massive but intriguing oversimplification. Broca's area is associated with rhythm and syntax—with what you might call the structural features of the language. Wernicke's area specializes in words and meaning—i.e., the content.†

When we process spoken language, these areas work in association with the parts of the brain that deal with auditory input. And when we process written language, they also have to stir in the parts

---

* Apologies to neuroscientists if this explanation under-reads your good work. Consider it a corrective to the widespread tendency to over-read the same.

† These inferences have been made from observations of the behaviors of people who have been damaged in one or another of these areas. People with Broca's aphasia will often be able to utter a series of individually meaningful words, but will be quite unable to turn them into a grammatical sentence; people with Wernicke's aphasia, conversely, may spool out sentences of perfectly grammatical nonsense such as you might hear in an academic conference in the social sciences. That's suggestive, but to identify one as a grammar machine and one as a vocabulary store is, as Harry Ritchie puts it in his *English for the Natives: Discover the Grammar You Don't Know You Know* (2013), not much better than "phrenology in a lab coat . . . language happens all over the brain."

of our brain that deal with visual input. But it's a complex transaction. You can't just, as it were, unplug the input cable from the ears and replug it into your eyes when you stop listening and start reading.

Language is associated with the auditory centers of the brain—when you read silently, and particularly when you read an unfamiliar word that you are "sounding out" in your head, something's going on in the parts of your brain that usually govern hearing.

And our visual systems are not geared to abstraction, essentially abstract though words on the page may be. They are geared to recognizing things in the world: telling the difference between a nice brown tree stump that would be comfy to lean against while we eat our lunch and an angry brown bear that would not. Early writing systems seem to have been pictographic in nature—and a series of leaps took us to systems representing sounds and abstract concepts.

All this means that the process of reading is not as abstract and cerebral as you might think. We do engage with letters and words as material objects in the world, and we do "hear" the sounds they make in our heads. We live in bodies, and we experience the world, even the world of the imagination, through them. That, then, offers what looks to me like a neurological underpinning for two well-worn but useful pieces of advice to writers. You should prefer concrete language—visual images and real-world situations—to abstract language, because these ask less work of the reader's brain. And you should attend to the sound and rhythm of your words, because whether your reader reads aloud or not, sound and rhythm are a major presence in the way he or she takes in what you have written—which means, especially for less confident writers, reading your material aloud.

You also need to think not just about the concreteness of your language but about the physical format in which it will be read. A couple of stapled sheets of computer paper will give one impression and invite one sort of attention; a text message on an iPhone will give and demand something different. Consider the physical differences. You experience a codex book—that is, the sort of book you're reading now, in which a sheaf of paper is bound at one side to form a spine—as a series of two-page spreads. There's a certain physical punctuation to the process of reading—even if you're whipping through the continuous flow of Molly Bloom's four-and-a-half-thousand-word unpunctuated monologue at the end of *Ulysses*. You're turning the pages. You have a mental sense—even a physical sense, between your fingers—of how far through the text you are. In creating a mental map of the text, you are able to locate passages with reference to left-hand page or right-hand page, and roughly where on that page it comes.

And that's how you do it, right? Anybody who has ever studied a text for school, or who has wanted to read out a particular bit of a newspaper for someone, searches pretty efficiently by physical location. You will have a sense—even several hundred pages later—that this or that quotation is somewhere about a quarter of the way through the book, near the top of a left-hand page.

When I say "mental map," it's not an idle metaphor. You don't just read a long text; you navigate through it. Professional mnemonists from the ancient world to the modern one have used the "method of loci"—*loci* means "places" in Latin—to store memories: They create an imaginary architecture in their minds' eyes and populate it with the things they want to remember. This seems to be based on sound science.

So the codex book makes mental mapmaking easier. Something similar applies for a set of sheets of paper—a presentation or a company report or a handout. You might not have those left-side, right-side markers to steer by, but you might (if it's printed on both sides) have a sense of which side of the paper your quote is on. You'll probably have oriented yourself with regard to one of the four corners of each page, too. And you'll know roughly how far through the document your quote is.

Reading on an e-reader, things are a little different. You won't have the physical sense of how far through you are. Some digital devices mimic the codex—presenting a set of double-page spreads. Others give you a continuous downward scroll of text. In both cases navigation is, you might say, lower-tech than with print: The reader has less control. You can flip backward and forward with more ease in a physical book than you can in a virtual one. The sense of how far through a digital text you are can be given by a percentage, or a progress bar—but it's less readily, less physically, apprehended.

Does this matter? It seems to. A large number of studies over three decades have found that people reading on screens find the process more mentally taxing, and (perhaps consequently) that they less easily and less thoroughly remember what they have read. Some also suggest that the *way* in which we read on screen is different—that, essentially, we approach on-screen reading with less concentration than we do the dead-tree kind. We expect to be distracted; we expect to read less deeply—and so we do.

I don't raise these findings to denigrate online or on-screen reading. In the first place, these young technologies are changing; some of the cognitive load involved in on-screen reading can be attributed to issues that aren't necessarily intrinsic to the screen/page distinction. For instance, e-ink, which reflects light like a paper-and-ink book, is known to be less taxing than a tablet or a phone, which shines light directly into the reader's eyes.

The default mode of reading online has been given the name "continuous partial attention." I'm fond of quoting the science fiction writer and blogger Cory Doctorow's matchless description of the internet as an "ecosystem of interruption technologies." We are used to seeing visual movement, pictures, embedded links, wobbly GIFs, and what have you—and the characteristic activity on the internet has been described as "wilfing," from the acronym WWILF: "What was I looking for?"

There's no reason to suppose that that can't or won't change. But we are where we are. And the smart writer will bear all this in mind when thinking about how a long text will go over. As I will discuss in later chapters, there are useful tricks you can use to direct that "continuous partial attention," when writing for electronic media, to the important bits of your text.

Audience Awareness, or, Baiting the Hook

"When you go fishing you bait the hook, not with what you like, but with what the fish likes." This quote, variously attributed in various forms, captures the nub of what I want to get across in this book. There is no more important principle in practical writing. It governs everything from style and register, through vocabulary choice and decisions about "correctness," to line spacing and typography.

Day-to-day practical writing is not about making words look pretty on the page or showing stylistic sophistication or an impressive vocabulary. It's about connecting with the reader. As the American political pollster Frank Luntz likes to put it: "It's not what you say, it's what people hear."

The idea of putting yourself in the reader's shoes is not a new one. You find it in almost every style guide ever put on paper. But what does it mean, why is it important, and how can it be achieved?

Aristotle, the first person to think systematically about rhetoric, identified three different ways that people are persuaded. He called them "ethos," "pathos," and "logos." Pathos is the way in which we are swayed by emotion. Logos is the intellectual shape of an argument. But ethos is more important than both of these two. It comes first. It describes the bond a speaker or writer forges with his or her audience.

That bond has to do with whether an audience warms to you, trusts your authority, and believes that whatever you're selling will be in their interests. If an audience dislikes or mistrusts you, or is bored by you, you get nowhere. You won't sway their emotions with pathos, and even if they can't see the flaws in your argument, they will resist it nevertheless.

Ethos, overwhelmingly often, boils down to the question: Do they think of you as "one of us"? It has to do with how they see your identity in relation to their own. It's not quite true to call human beings herd creatures. But we incessantly construct meaning in terms of communal identity; we think in sets and groups.

My identity is constructed out of a whole collection of commonalities I share with others of my species: "white," "male," "middle-aged," "British"; "father," "husband," "member of the Leith family"; "keen baker of bread," "wearer of size-nine Doc Martens boots," "X-Men fan." These commonalities will affect not only how other people see me but how I see myself—and the two things are, of course, intimately linked.

That idea of bunching and grouping—what's sometimes derisively called "pigeonholing"—underpins the language itself. Nouns (with the exception of so-called "proper nouns," such as "Fred" or "Blenheim Palace") don't describe single things, they describe categories of things. Verbs don't describe single actions, they describe categories of action. Even conjunctions and prepositions—words that signal the relationships between phrases, clauses, and sentences—describe *types* of relationship: "under," "over," "after," "while," and so on.

"The man kicked the ball over the house." To understand that sentence you are marshaling not a particular image of a particular man kicking a particular ball over a particular house. You are marshaling a set of agreed ideas about what properties define "man," "ball," and "house"; what spatial relationship the word "over" denotes; what physical gesture qualifies as a "kick."

Your image and mine—if we are asked, say, to draw a picture—will not be identical. Is the man in your more or less hazy mental image black or white; short or tall; clothed or naked? Is the ball a football or a tennis ball or a beach ball? Is your house a North London semidetached or a bungalow in the Pasadena suburbs? Is the ball sailing high or skimming the roof? Is the man kicking the ball from his hands or from the ground or intercepting his six-year-old son's throw-in? The answers to those questions will be rooted in your experience and therefore, to an extent, in your identity.

But the chances are that to start with you aren't seeing the image with that sort of specificity—precisely because you know without really thinking about it consciously that those differences will exist. For the sentence to be meaningful, it relies on a common understanding of these definitions, and the awareness that until you hear different, it's safest to keep your interpretive options open. You're trying to tune in to the broad meaning of what the speaker is saying and not go beyond it. If you form a super-specific image right off the bat, and the next sentence makes clear that your image is wrong, you have to go back and unpick your assumptions and start from scratch. That involves cognitive work; it's a waste of energy.

Your communication will of course be more meaningful—more instantly precise—if the shared references are stronger. You have to work harder to communicate exactly if the connotations of the words are likely to be different for your audience or absent altogether—but, fortunately, the language supplies the tools where context does not. In mental energy terms, the closer you are to the audience in the first place, the easier your task will be; particle physicist speaks unto particle physicist more easily than particle physicist speaks unto six-year-old.

The point is that the successful communicator takes as much of the work of interpretation on him- or herself as possible. If your frame of reference is different from your audience's, you reach them faster by adopting theirs. You see people doing that all the time. When that particle physicist is speaking to that six-year-old, she's more likely to prosper if she uses an analogy from the six-year-old's world—explaining, say, the way that the universe is made up of little bits with reference to Lego bricks rather than plunging straight into the mathematics of subatomic particles.

These categories are not simply intellectual ones—they're not just a filing system. We think in sets and groups but we also *feel* in sets and groups. Think of the emotional content of a political rally, a foot-ball crowd, a friendship group, or membership of a family. We define ourselves in groups and against groups, and are in turn so defined.

Indeed, a whole category of language—so-called "phatic communication"*—is directed solely to establishing human, or tribal, commonality. This is the human, or at least the linguistic, equivalent of cattle rubbing flanks, monkeys picking fleas, or dogs sniffing each other's bums. "How do you do?" we ask, neither seek-ing nor overtly conveying information. "Hello!" we exclaim, neither in surprise nor in alarm. "How 'bout them Dodgers?" we wonder, not caring much about the Dodgers. We're not communicating, there, so much as establishing that the line's open. We're tapping the mic and rumbling, "One, two, three: testing."

In this case I'm using examples of set phrases. But there's a phatic, or tuning-in, element to all sorts of communication. Small talk is primarily phatic. And, conversely, a number of other ele-ments of language—from accent to dialect words to the formulaic exchange of courtesies—do what you could see as phatic work: They establish speech communities. When a native Midwest-erner finds her accent disappearing after a time living in Manhat-tan, and returning when she goes back to Iowa to visit her elderly mother (a phenomenon linguists call "accommodation"), she's not making some sort of social or linguistic mistake; she's adjusting her language to suit her context. We all do it, all the time. None of us speaks a single English.

In practical terms, how can you apply this knowledge in your writing?

Socially or emotionally, it means working to pass the ethos sniff test. It doesn't necessarily mean that you have to sound exactly like your audience. It means that you sound as if you're on their side, or as if

---

* The phrase was minted by an anthropologist named Bronisław Malinowski (1884–1942).

you're making an effort to see things from their point of view. You work on the common ground. The literary critic and theorist Kenneth Burke said: "You persuade a man only insofar as you can talk his language by speech, gesture, tonality, order, image, attitude, idea, *identifying* your ways with his."

Stylistically, it means trying to minimize ambiguity. It means being simple without being patronizing, and clear without being obvious. And it means above all remembering that—now more than at any time in human history—you are competing for attention in a world of distractions and interruptions. As I said, take the work on yourself. The less work the reader has to do to understand what you are saying, the more readily he or she will read on, and the more favorably he or she will be disposed to receive it.

Audience awareness also means knowing your genre. "Genre"— a term used by literary critics to describe a particular type of writing—is all about the expectations of your audience. If you take a sip from a mug containing tea, and you were expecting coffee, it'll taste disgusting. Genre is pigeonholing applied to literary form.

A sentence of prose isn't just a sentence of prose. It fits into a wider pattern. Later in this book I'll be talking about different literary forms, from business letters to social media posts. Each form has its own requirements or expectations, not only in terms of the style used but in terms of where the white space goes and how the text is broken up by design features or paragraphing.

A newspaper report will have headlines, subheads, photographs, and breakout boxes; company documents might have bullet points, infographics, and so on. Some forms of writing ask for continuous prose. Some are more in the direction of a collection of numbered paragraphs. Get your genre features right and you're on your way. Get them wrong and you're headed to an ABBA-themed fancy-dress party got up as Marilyn Manson.

Plain and Simple

Lots of style guides suggest using "plain English." There is even a Plain English Campaign in the UK that pressures official bodies to adopt a simpler style of communication, and has done so over the years with some success. In the US the Plain Writing Act of 2010 requires all federal agencies to express themselves in plain language.

But what do we mean by "plain English"?

As an analogy, think of the iPhone. If you read Walter Isaacson's biography of Steve Jobs, you'll be flabbergasted by the technical difficulties that had to be overcome—the toughness of the glass, the design of the interface, the cramming of all those doohickeys and gizmos into that pocket-sized device. The technical specifications for building an iPhone would run to thousands of pages.

But—which is what makes it the success story it is—here is a pocket computer that does everything, and yet which ships to the customer without a manual. It is designed to be so self-explanatory—so intuitive—that you can learn to use it simply by fiddling around with it.

Now compare the video recorder you had in the early 1990s (those of you who remember the early 1990s). The iPhone does much more than that video recorder ever did. But the video recorder came with a large, incomprehensible manual, and even then only your children could work out how to program it. Writing plain English is being the iPhone rather than the video recorder.

So the test of plain English is whether it works. There isn't a scientific test for the plain style—though, as I'll discuss later, there are some rules of thumb. In that sense it's a negative quality; you can say of plain English not that you know it when you see it, so much as that you notice like hell when it isn't there. It's the simplest language that the widest possible segment of your intended audience will understand.

Plain English, simply, makes the reader's life easy. It minimizes the cognitive work he or she has to put in. So as a writer aspiring to produce plain English, you need to put yourself constantly in the position of the reader.

And be aware that—as with building an iPhone—the contract isn't symmetrical. Something that's easy for the reader to consume isn't necessarily easy for the writer to produce. You may sweat. You may labor. And if you get it right, all the hard work you've done will barely be noticed by the person on whose behalf you've done it.

In that sense, it might seem self-explanatory that you'd want to write plain English. But it's not quite that simple. There are all sorts of circumstances in which plain English isn't appropriate. If all we had was the plain style, we'd have no rousing oratory, no poetry (or very little)—not much, in fact, to cause the heart to sing.

Take an example.

> *I caught this morning morning's minion, king-*
> *dom of daylight's dauphin, dapple-dawn-drawn Falcon,*
>   *in his riding*
> *Of the rolling level underneath him steady air, and striding*
> *High there, how he rung upon the rein of a wimpling wing*
> *In his ecstasy! then off, off forth on swing*

In plain English, the opening lines of Gerard Manley Hopkins's "The Windhover" could be rendered:

> *I got up early, went for a walk, and saw a bird.*

In other areas, sometimes a particular subject matter demands a particular language—not complexity for its own sake but because, say, scientists might need a specialist technical vocabulary to be exact. And that specialist language can, in effect, do for scientists what plain English does for the general reader: minimize the cognitive work. If you already know what Planck's constant is, those two words will get the idea across instantly.

Plain English aims to be understood, then, by the maximum number of readers in any given audience with the maximum ease. It will usually draw from common vocabulary—and common vocabulary, even when unambiguous, can be imprecise. So it's not as simple as choosing only short words, or only common words. It's about considering the simplest words that will do the job.

This has immense practical advantages.

One: Where writing is intended to be communication rather than performance, it needs to get through. And that means it needs to get through to the least linguistically able of its readers. According to the UK's National Literacy Trust, the average reading level among adults in Britain corresponds to the target level for thirteen-year-olds. US figures show an approximate equivalence. That's the *average*. From that it seems pretty clear to me that, even if most of your communications are in the white-collar world, you may need to pitch things a bit lower even than you'd expect.

Two: Unclear writing wastes time and money. If you're in the public sector, people's access to public services depends on them understanding how to navigate the system—which means that the instructions need to be clear. In the private sector, leave alone the misunderstandings, the confusions, the follow-up phone calls to clarify what the blithering hell that email was all about; if you aren't able to make what you are offering or accepting clear to a business partner, at the least you will lose goodwill, and at the worst you will trigger lawsuits.

Not long ago, when my three-year-old was suffering from a pink and gunky eye, I bought him a bottle of eye drops from the pharmacist. The side of the pack, under dosage, said: "Adults and children over two years of age—1 drop every 2 hours for the first 48 hours and 4 hourly thereafter." Does that mean four drops every hour thereafter? Or one drop every four hours? The grammar of the sentence leads me to the first conclusion. Common sense leads me to the second. But if I'm squirting this stuff into my toddler's eye, I'd really like to be sure.

Finally, clear, grammatical English helps your ethos appeal. People judge you on your language. When an employer gets a CV, a journalist a press release, or a colleague a memo that's obtuse, repetitive, misspelled, or grammatically muddled, he or she will always think less of the sender. Your reader is always, always looking for an excuse to move on. You don't stand to gain readers in the course of a given piece of writing, only to lose them—and making some of them struggle to understand you is a surefire way of doing it.

In this respect a piece of continuous prose follows the publishing model of collectible magazines published in a series. Part one of *Locomotives of the Golden Age of Steam*, say, would be offered at the bargain price of two dollars, and bundled with a free binder and a cover-mounted toy locomotive. Maybe it would sell ten thousand copies. Two weeks later, part two would appear in the newsstand for $3.50. Inspired by the free binder—collect them all!—those who liked part one would pick it up. Maybe you'd get seven thousand readers. A fortnight later, part three would come, and a fortnight later, part four, and so on. The best the publishers can hope for is a low attrition rate—but with each successive issue you lose readers to apathy, disorganization, or a sense that they are not getting value for money. By the time you get to part twelve, the hope is that a decent number of readers will still be with you— impressed by the quality of the product, the collector's desire for completeness, or the sense of by this stage being already invested in the series. The business model is one of retaining readers, not gaining them. You never sell more of the last issue than you do of the first. You will never get more people reading the second half of your article than read the first.

This has implications for structure. Crudely, it says that the first few sentences really matter: That's where you offer the free binder and the cover-mounted model engine. But it also makes the more basic point that for the writer, just as for the publisher of *Locomotives of the Golden Age of Steam,* you retain only as many readers as you keep engaged and offer—metaphorically—value for money. The writer who aims for the stupidest and least attentive person in his or her audience is not a stupid or inattentive writer.

There are a couple of rough tests, as I mentioned above, for the plain style. For many years, a number of mechanical "readability tests" have been in circulation. The best known is probably the Flesch-Kincaid score—which now comes bundled with many word-processing programs.* Readability tests make an estimate of a text's complexity based on the number of syllables per word and the number of words per sentence. The lower the score—given as a US school grade level—the easier the text is to read. A grade score of eight or nine indicates that an average teenager should be able to make sense of your work.

Politicians know instinctively that simple language reaches more people. In October 2015 the *Boston Globe* applied Flesch-Kincaid metrics to candidates in the US presidential elections.† The Republican candidates clustered around the middle of the seventh grade. Donald Trump—who, I feel sure, uses the trisyllable "president" only because he can't think of a way not to—had a Flesch-Kincaid score of 4.1; his speeches were pitched to be understood by nine-year-olds.

There's no harm in using readability metrics as a ready reckoner. If your average sentence is much longer than eighteen to twenty words, and your words are on average four or more syllables long, the chances are that your text will be trickier for a reader

---

* There's also a decent online aggregator of these tests at checktext.org.
† Matt Viser, "For Presidential Hopefuls, Simpler Language Resonates," *Boston Globe,* October 20, 2015, bostonglobe.com.

write to the point

to digest than one whose sentences are ten words long and made of one-, two-, or three-syllable words. But these tests are, by their nature, pretty unreliable. It's the familiarity of a given word, rather than its syllabic length, that makes the main difference to a reader. And when it comes to sentences, syntactic structure is far more important to readability than bare length.

In other words, don't treat these scores as anything more than a finger to the wind. Making something readable is work that needs to be done by the writer, sentence by sentence. It can't be reliably subcontracted to a syllable-counting machine. I'll go into this further in the chapters that follow.

Finally, I should mention the point that plain English can help the writer. We've all encountered writing where it's hard for the reader to understand what the author means. But what of writing where it's clear that the author doesn't know herself what she means? Muddled writing and muddled thought often go together. If you can write something clearly, it's almost always a sign that you are thinking it clearly.

Hitting the Right Note

That said, there is no single plain style. Good writing is also about capturing a tone of voice. That tone of voice needs to be appropriate to the audience and to the occasion. Even within the plain style, you'll want to make adjustments. Are you being mocking, celebratory, solemn, arch, austere, or pragmatic? Are you looking to amuse your readers, or to persuade them of the importance of what you're saying?

This is what in linguistics gets called "register," and in rhetoric gets called "decorum." It's how language changes according to the particular social circumstance of its use: when it's being used, who is hearing, who is overhearing, and in what context. It will affect vocabulary choice, diction, mode of address, and even typography.* Register is how you use style to position yourself with regard to your reader, and tell the reader about that positioning.

One sort of register is appropriate to a memo from manager to employee; another to an exchange of letters between friends; another to a letter of complaint written to a utility company. The degree of formality is the most obvious, but not the only, feature that marks out one register from another. An actual or implied power relationship often enters into it. That might affect how you cast sentences and whether you speak "I" to "you" about a "we," or whether you select an impersonal construction: "we think we should do X" as against "the circumstances mandate this course of action."

Violations of decorum or register are, in effect, ways of getting the relationship between writer and reader wrong. They tell your audience to regard you or themselves in a way they will feel is inappropriate. Pomposity is one obvious example; it tells your audience that you have an unduly high opinion of yourself (though a more confident audience might diagnose the opposite: that you're writing pompously because you're nervous). To be patronizing is to tell your audience that you have a low opinion of them. Other mistakes in register—overfamiliarity, say—don't necessarily imply a boast or an insult, but they will still put an audience off.

When David Brent in the UK's *The Office* tells his staff to think of him not just as a boss ("you'll never have another boss like me") but as a "chilled-out entertainer," you see a pantomimic version of such a violation. Here is someone apparently attempting friendliness— but in context he's underlining his role as boss and more or less commanding his staff to like him. The bossiness is up front—but so too is the pitiable need to be liked, and the failed attempt to set the terms of his relationship with his audience by dictation.

* As a teenager, I wrote a letter to a girl with whom I was in the process of breaking up. It didn't really matter very much, in the end, how carefully I expressed my feelings and thoughts. What really, really made her angry was that I composed it on a manual typewriter. A lesson learned.

For instance, my writing in this book is conversational. That is a deliberate strategy. I'm attempting to put across some practical and technical ideas about writing in a way that will be accessible and, I hope, entertaining. So I'm giving myself license to make silly jokes, to tell personal stories, to choose more or less playful examples—and to address you directly and pretty informally. That might not be how an otherwise very similar book would have been written twenty years ago.

This is a change you can see across the board. Particularly in the age of social media, the face that big companies present to their customers—often laddish, teasing, and avuncular—is quite different from the face that they showed half a century or even a decade ago. Your bank, nowadays, wants to sound like your friend—at least until it comes to the fine-print legal boilerplate with which it actually defines your relationship.

Within my own profession, journalism, you have always found quite different registers in different parts of the paper. News reports tend to be more impersonal than features. The unsigned editorial representing the opinions of the newspaper will tend to be more formal than the bylined opinion columns. And those columns themselves are changing.

In 2011 the *London Times* columnist Matthew Parris wrote about having been given the Columnist of the Year award at the Press Awards dinner. After making conventionally polite noises about the honor and those who better deserved it, he wrote:

> *I fell to thinking about the judges' citation, which I seem to remember being about elegantly crafted prose, or "classy" prose, or something like that.*
>
> *Crafted? Classy? Well, maybe (I thought) sometimes—on a good day. This is what I aim for. I can spend hours trying to get a paragraph right, swapping words around, searching for*

the right adjective, avoiding repetition, thinking of fresh or felicitous ways of expressing things.

He went on:

It's been lovely while it lasted, but all this "fine writing" stuff, all this palaver about the grand tradition of English essays, may be approaching some kind of a sunset. My generation of sonorous, careful-crafting newspaper columnist may be the last of our kind. I'm not sure if I regret it.

Parris noted that in an age in which comment is transmitted so quickly online, and so informally, a new style was emerging: one that showed its workings.

Where opinion, judgment and reflection are called for (and they always will be) the reader will increasingly feel he wants to be, as it were, with the columnist, alongside him, as he hums and hahs and feels his way to a response. His hesitations, his little internal jokes, his playfulness, his doubts, his half-hints and second thoughts—these will become part of the essay, deconstructed, exhibited, rather than part of its secret history.

Such writing will not—I stress this—be more superficial, more trashy or less intelligent than my kind of column; but it will have a lightness, directness and frankness, and, with all those things a sort of formlessness, a train-of-consciousness quality. We will write more as we think, or speak.

I think Mr. Parris is dead right.* And he mentioned the names of a handful of younger colleagues whom he saw as exemplars of this

---

* Also, sly. If you look at the register of that column, it much more closely exemplifies the talky, hesitant, train-of-consciousness style he looks forward to than the more formal one whose passing he laments.

new sort of writing. Newspaper columnists, even in broadsheets, might now (it's almost a cliché) begin a column: "So . . ." and might pepper it with the slangy expression of annoyance or outrage. "Yeah, right." "WTF?"

All this is part of a general tendency in the culture for written communication to become more personal and more conversational. That's in part because, as Mr. Parris observes, everything is happening faster. We drink our writers, like our wines, younger.

It's also in large part because the logic by which not only news but opinion and marketing travels is social. We get news through social media, and we decide what we think about it socially, and advertisers piggyback on all that and weave their tendrils through it. So when you get a much-shared list of "27 Amazing Facts About Angela Merkel That Will Make You Spit Your Cornflakes," are you reading reporting, or commentary, or a joke, or bait for the pop-up on the side of the page, or a mixture of all these things that doesn't mind much which it is?

The logic by which it reaches you is personal—it will have been "shared" by a friend, or algorithmically served to you because a large number of people have already shared or "liked" it. And a great deal in the way that these things proliferate is to do with their tone of voice.

The question of register—more, perhaps, than any other—is what will be the final arbiter of the issues I address in my discussion of "Perils and Pitfalls." Correctness, you could say, is a feature of the written dialect we call standard English. Decorum asks you to use that dialect in most formal and semiformal communications. If the mistake of the pedant is to mistake that dialect for the only dialect, it's a mistake of the naive anything-goes relativist to think that correctness doesn't matter at all. It may be something that varies over time, and that admits of gray areas—but if a majority of formal users stick to a convention, that convention is worth knowing.

In his idiosyncratic and entertainingly splenetic treatise on the language, *The King's English*, Kingsley Amis articulated in exact and vulgar terms a useful distinction. (He was writing mostly, here, about the spoken word, but with implications every bit as serious for the written.) The distinction is between berks and wankers.*

Berks are careless, coarse, crass, gross and of what anybody would agree is a lower social class than one's own.† They speak in a slipshod way with dropped Hs, intruded glottal stops and many mistakes in grammar. Left to them the English language would die of impurity, like late Latin.

Wankers, on the other hand,

are prissy, fussy, priggish, prim and of what they would probably misrepresent as a higher social class than one's own. They speak in an over-precise way with much pedantic insistence on letters not generally sounded, especially Hs. Left to them the language would die of purity, like medieval Latin.

The task of the good writer, you could say, is to find a position in the happy middle ground between the berks and the wankers.

Abstract Versus Concrete

The late novelist David Foster Wallace was once asked about "genteelisms" such as "prior to" and "subsequent to." He replied:

* For US readers, these might need glossing. Both, basically, are insults. The berk is a fool and the wanker is a fool with pretensions.

† Note how, in both definitions, Amis emphasizes (not without signaling some irony in "anybody would agree") the social and class issues that play so big a part in the arguments over correctness.

*Well, I have trouble parsing your question. "Genteelisms"
seems to me to be an overly charitable way to character-
ize them. To me they're like puff-words. They're like using
"utilize" instead of "use," which in ninety-nine cases out
of one hundred is just stupid. Or "individual" for "person."
Four syllables. It's just puffed up. Why say "prior to" rather
than "before"? Everybody knows what "before" means. It's
fewer words. And I think technically, given the Latin roots,
it should be "posterior to," if you're going to use "prior to."
So if you are saying "prior to" and "subsequent to," you are
in fact in a very high-level way messing up grammatically.
But would you ever want to say "posterior to"? [. . .] But you'll
notice this is the downside of starting to pay attention. You
start noticing all the people who say "at this time" rather
than "now." Why did they just take up one-third of a second of
my lifetime making me parse "at this time" rather than just
saying "now" to me? And you start being bugged. But you get
to be more careful and attentive in your own writing so you
become an agent of light and goodness rather than the evil
that's all around.*

I'm not sure he's right about the Latin roots of "prior to"—and in
invoking them, in any case, he falls into the fallacy that etymology
tells you what a word means now—but his basic premise is sound.

In some professional environments, however, you'll be expected
to use terms that to outsiders look like jargon. If you're a banker and
you start talking about "credit default swaps" or "shorting bonds" to
a civilian, there's a high chance the person will look baffled or intim-
idated; whereas if you start explaining the terms to a fellow banker,
your colleague will likely feel patronized. Within the trade those few
syllables get the meaning across with maximum economy.

Most people will be familiar with the advice to keep words short
and simple. A more interesting distinction than the one between

short and long words—a wrinkle, if you like, in the plain English discussion—is the one between abstract and concrete words.

Abstraction is not, mind you, a bad thing in itself—quite the opposite. The progress of human language, be it in the language development of children, the elaboration of a spoken language, or the history of writing, has always been toward greater abstraction. That is how we have gone as a species from crudely indicating the presence of something edible on the other side of that hill, to being able to describe the attributes of complex mathematical objects or theories of ethics and ontology.

Children learn to name objects—to point at a ball and say "ball"—before they learn to name ideas. But they soon pick up on the elaborate grammar and subtle system of tenses that allow us to talk not only about objects that are there but about objects that are not there, or have been there, or could never be there, and to articulate the relationships between these objects.

The earliest forms of writing were pictographic; they were pictures of what they denoted. These became more abstract as they became conventional. They became more abstract still as they started to stand in for sounds rather than objects; the development of alphabets severed a connection between the image on the page and a single thing it denoted.

So when I say abstraction makes the brain work harder, you could put it the other way around. You could say that as our brains get more powerful, we find it easier to handle abstraction. We have more capacity for it. And that capacity has brought huge benefits to us as a species. Consider it as a computing problem, then. It's not a question of avoiding abstraction altogether, it's a question of allocating resources sensibly. The drivers' training manual for a bus company once said, for example:

Ensure location factors and conditions in which maneuvers are to occur and are considered with regard to safety,

minimal disruption to other road users, residents, legal con-
straints, and regulatory requirements.

This was rightly amended to:

Look where you are going, check mirrors, etc.

Or take this beauty from David Wolfe, who chairs the UK's Press
Recognition Panel.

The organizations have raised a concern that the indicative
view on the interpretation of aspects of the charter which
we expressed earlier in the summer after our second call for
information might have prompted them or others to provide
us with additional information about the Impress applica-
tion had it been known at the time of our second call for infor-
mation.

To quote the late Auberon Waugh: "I thought I understood the
English language well enough, but just what the fucking, sodding,
shitting hell is this idiotic sentence trying to tell us?"

Where you can make things concrete, do. We'll get back to this,
but just bear in mind that all else being equal, the stronger the verb
and more concrete the nouns you use, the more impact and directness any given sentence will have.

3

Nuts and Bolts

The sections that follow are intended to introduce the basic workings of English prose, from the different parts of speech (or sorts of word) to the grammar and punctuation that organize them into sense-making sentences. It covers a lot of what you will already know—or, at least, a lot of what you will already do. But, just as having a rough sense of how a car engine works might help you when you break down on the side of a highway, having a basic technical vocabulary to talk about sentences will help you fix them.

This does not pretend to be exhaustive.* Rather, I follow William Strunk's view that it's better to give "three rules for the use of the comma, instead of a score or more," because those three will generally cover "nineteen sentences out of twenty."

But in talking about sentences, I'm getting ahead of myself. Let's start with nouns.

Nouns and Pronouns

Nouns, we're usefully told at elementary school, are words that stand in for things: commonly objects in the world ("cat"), people

---

* *The Cambridge Grammar of the English Language*, edited by Rodney Huddleston and Geoffrey K. Pullum (Cambridge University Press, 2002), is a professional shot at doing that. It runs to 1,842 closely printed pages, will considerably tax the brain of non-linguists, and for all its magnificence is a threat to the structural integrity of my bedside table.

("Donald"), concepts ("antidisestablishmentarianism"), feelings ("sadness"), and situations ("disaster").

They are a tiny bit more slippery than that, though. What really makes a noun is how it works in a sentence. A noun—as it has memorably but unhelpfully been expressed by Steven Pinker—is "simply a word that does nouny things," and he goes on to offer a couple of examples of nouny things—among them being able to come after an article* ("a cat"; "the Donald"), being the subject of a sentence ("the cat sat on the mat"; "the Donald won the election"), and so on.

Does the role of a noun in its sentence come before or after its quality as a repository of meaning about things? That may be one for the philosophers. But in terms of knowing how to decode a sentence, it's the structural aspect, oddly, that comes first. You'll know whether "face" is a noun or a verb from its role in the sentence, not the combination of letters in the word on the page.

There are two main types of noun.

PROPER NOUNS

These are nouns that, in context, denote one specific thing and one thing only—such as "Julio," "Scotch tape," "Madonna," or "the Taj Mahal."† Brand names, people's names, individual buildings, planets, makes of car, and so on all fall into the category of proper nouns. They're easy to spot because they take a capital letter.

Note my slightly weaselly use of the words "in context." Many proper nouns do denote more than one thing. There are lots of people called "Julio"; "Scotch tape" is a company or brand as well as what you've got stuck to your finger; "Madonna" is a pop singer as

---

* Words like "a," "an," or "the."

† You may object, here, that "the Taj Mahal" is two words (plus an article), or that—to simplify with an article-free example—"Julio Iglesias" is two words. Does that prevent them from being nouns and make them, instead, noun combinations or even noun phrases? Here, you're more or less splitting hairs. You can make a distinction, if you want to, between proper nouns (one word) and proper names (two or more words)—but the grammatical role (the nouniness) remains the same.

well as the mother of God; "the Taj Mahal" is a monument in Agra and any number of Indian restaurants. The thing is that in any given context they will only denote one of them.

COMMON NOUNS

These are nouns that denote, out of context, a whole category of things—such as "cat," "intelligence," "pop singer," or "sadness." They indicate something general.

Note, though, my slightly weaselly use of the words "out of context." Many common nouns do denote one specific thing. "This cat ate my hamster"; "his intelligence won him a scholarship"; "that pop singer duetted with Frank Zappa"; "sadness was the reason he called the help line." Common nouns are often modified by determiners—such as "this," "the," or "my"—which make them, in context, more specific. Adjectives, also, narrow things down. In fact, when positioned in a sentence, a common noun can be every bit as exact as a proper noun.

The distinction between common nouns and proper nouns, then, is not something absolute that inheres in them as words. "Silence," "nothing," and "mathematics" are common nouns—even though they mean one specific thing that is, at least in theory, the same everywhere. "Marxism" is a proper noun, even though it denotes a whole category of systems of political thought, and we pluralize it—as "Marxisms"—quite cheerfully and correctly.

So, to adapt Pinker, a common noun is a word that does common-nouny things (such as cozying up to attributive adjectives or indefinite articles [the *a* or *an* before an unspecified person or thing], and being allowed to be plural), and a proper noun is a word that does proper-nouny things (such as taking a capital letter or signing up to a golf club).

You will often hear people say that the most important thing in vocabulary choice is precision. They'll lament someone using "uninterested" to mean "disinterested," or using "shall" and "will" in free variation, since there is a useful difference of meaning between the one and the other. And, in many cases, there is.

But when you consider how many of our most useful nouns are, in isolation, as ambiguous as hell, it becomes clear that actually their *imprecision* is arguably more important. A world of absolute precision would be a world where all we had were proper nouns. It would render communication all but impossible; the language would be like a map of the world on a scale of 1:1.

Talking about words in isolation is like talking about Lego bricks in isolation; meaning doesn't inhere in the words themselves. It is constructed by a combination of all their possible connotations and denotations, and their role in a sentence, and the context in which that sentence is placed. And that's the work the reader's brain is doing, all but unconsciously, in fractions of a second.

When it comes to grammar, English nouns are as easy as pie. They account for at least half of the language's total vocabulary and—hurrah!—they don't inflect.* For most of them, you add an *s* or an *es* (if they already end in *s* or *z*) to form the plural, and an *'s* to form the possessive.† And that's it. But there are—aren't there always?—exceptions.

---

* That is, the form of the word doesn't change to reflect its grammatical role. A dog is a dog whether it's biting or being bitten. That work is done, in English, by word order and/or the use of prepositions: "the dog bit the man"; "the man bit the dog." It doesn't work like that in Latin, Russian, German, or Proto-Indo-European. This has advantages (no case system! yay!) and disadvantages (the work is done by word order and/or the use of prepositions, but the work *has to* be done by word order and/or the use of prepositions).

† I'm indebted to Harry Ritchie's *English for the Natives* for the delightful discovery that plural isn't a simple concept in itself: "English defines a plural as any number more than one—e.g., 1.00001 liters—whereas French, for example, takes plural to mean a minimum of two (1.00001 litre, deux litres). Both English and French have opted for the binary model of singular + plural, but there are others, most popularly the three-way singular + dual + plural." But let's leave it there for the minute.

ABSTRACT NOUNS

As MC Hammer would put it, you can't touch this. Abstract nouns denote things unavailable to the senses, such as "peace," "anger," "freedom," and—ironically enough—"materialism." Many of them don't pluralize or take an article—"the angers in the room were palpable"; "looking shifty, he took a handful of materialisms out of the trunk of his car."

But then again, we talk about "freedoms" or "a lasting peace." How to account for this? These are abstract nouns being used in a concrete sense, you could argue—just as you could make a distinction between "Toyota" (proper noun, referring to the company) and "a Toyota" (common noun, referring to a car made by the company).

I raise this neither to sow confusion nor to imply that anything goes. Rather, I do so to indicate that once again it's a relationship between the lexical meaning of the word and its syntactic behavior that determines its meaning in context. That means—at least to a certain extent—you can stop worrying. Your wonderful brain does an awful lot of this on autopilot.

PLURAL NOUNS AND INVARIANT NOUNS

Some nouns are always found in the plural form. You would find it about as easy to put one pant on as you would to incorporate it into a sensible sentence; likewise to cut with a scissor, to do well in a mathematic, and to turn the television on at nine o'clock to watch an evening new. Some of these nouns take a plural verb ("your pants are on fire") and some of them take a singular verb ("no news is good news"). I call shenanigan.

Invariant nouns are nouns that have the same form in the singular as in the plural. Sheep would be a good example. So as you count them in the hopes of going to sleep, you'll say: "One sheep, two sheep, three sheep, four sheep, five sheep . . ." and so on.* They behave quite normally with verbs and modifiers: one sheep jumps over the fence; five sheep jump over the fence.

COLLECTIVE NOUNS AND MASS NOUNS

These are nouns that denote not one thing but a whole bunch of things. A "murder," used of crows, is a collective noun.† Likewise "team," "government," "family," "assembly," "audience," "choir," "lynch mob," and so forth. There's some lively debate about whether collective nouns take a singular or a plural verb. "The lynch mob are advancing on the castle"? Or "The lynch mob is advancing on the castle"?

Here, a decent guideline is emphasis. If you're considering the group in question as a collection of individuals, you'll sometimes use a plural verb: "My family are all murderers and scoundrels." If you're considering it as a whole unit, the verb's going to be singular: "My family is the only thing that keeps me sane." The singular verb is usually the more formal option—you seldom go wrong with "the government is . . ."—and, in general, the safest bet.

But it's not incorrect to use a plural verb. Here is an instance of what gets called "notional agreement"‡ rather than "formal agreement": the pedant-confounding tendency of language to shape its grammar according to the meaning, rather than to treat the meaning as something to be inserted into a rigid and invariable grammatical structure. A plural verb can agree with the singular "family," as above, because the verb is responding to the *meaning* of its antecedent, not to its grammatical number.

---

* If you're counting juveniles, though, you'll count: "One lamb, two lambs, three lambs, four lambs, five lambs . . ." And if you're eating them—hey presto!—both the invariant word "sheep" and the regular-plural-forming "lamb" become (see above) mass nouns: either "mutton" or "lamb." Grammatically, at least, they dress the same.

† Unless you're murdering crows, and you probably aren't because the verb "murder" takes a human object, unless you're a hard-core animal rights enthusiast using it for rhetorical effect, or Morrissey.

‡ Also, if you want to be fancy about it, "synesis."

A distinction is made—at least in *The Chicago Manual of Style*—between US English and British English when it comes to names of companies and institutions. In US English even plural forms generally take a singular verb—"General Motors is moving its headquarters"—where in British English (when, per *Chicago*, they are "singular nouns that refer to individuals who work independently") you'll see a plural verb. As *Chicago* puts it: "Manchester United have won the FA cup." But, as ever, test the usage on your ear.

Mass nouns, or "non-count" nouns, are nouns denoting something that's an indivisible bulk: flour, wine, butter, plankton, and so on. These might be divided by quantity ("a pound of flour") but not by number ("two flours," "half a wine").* They contrast with "count nouns," which can be numbered rather than weighed, scooped, or poured: You can have twenty-five balls in your bucket, but that does not add up to a bucket of ball.

Just as some proper nouns also have a usage as common nouns, many words are used both as count and as mass nouns. "He spends all day dreaming of beer. In the evening he goes out and has sixteen beers in a row. Beers give him a hangover. Beer is his undoing."

If feelings run high about collective nouns, the debate about count nouns is positively murderous. Are they one thing or lots of things? Here is that ancient inflamer of self-styled grammarians everywhere: the "ten items or less" lane in the supermarket. The reasoning is that "less" (as an expression of quantity) goes with mass nouns and that "fewer" (as an expression of number) goes with count nouns.

This is, in standard English, usually a sound distinction to make. But it's a question of touch, rather than an absolute. The count noun/mass noun distinction is subject to the same fuzziness as the verb

---

* You can have "two flours" when you're using "flour" to stand in for a type of flour—plain, whole wheat, Canadian stone-ground, or what have you—but here it's being used in a different sense. Context, again, is the key.

agreement for collective nouns. So: "He woke up less than four hours later" is perfectly idiomatic—because you're talking about (countable) hours as a measure of (mass) time. You'd sound eccentric, at the very least, if you said, "He woke up fewer than four hours later."

There's an analogy with collective nouns: Are you thinking primarily of the amount, or of the individual units that go to make it up? "Less than one thousand people turned up to the demonstration" is fine. "Fewer than one thousand people turned up to the demonstration" is also fine. In the latter case you're emphasizing the individual people; in the former, the size of the demonstration.

This is testament to the plasticity of the language. Consider how words such as "agenda," "data," and "media"—which originate in Latin plurals, "agendum," "datum," and "medium" being in each instance the singular—have by and large come to take singular verbs. "Agenda," etymologically, means "the things that need to be done," but the Latin singular no longer has a common English meaning. Grammatically, "agenda" behaves in English as a singular count noun. "The meeting's agenda was ratified by the board." "Data" and "media" are slightly different cases. In both cases the singular still has a meaning in English: "Datum" has a slightly more technical usage in science; "medium" (when used to mean television or radio rather than some muttering old mountebank in a wandering caravan) has a pretty widespread common application.

But we use the plurals, most often, as mass nouns. When you talk about "the media" you mean to speak about the press and radio and TV as a whole, and when you talk about "big data" you mean a big collection of things rather than a collection of big things. Both behave most idiomatically when teamed up with singular verbs. Don't get me started on "referenda."

PRONOUNS

These are the words that stand in for nouns. We use them a lot—because they avoid repetition and increase the economy of the language. Once you've introduced a concept, however complicated it may be, you can use a pronoun of as little as two letters to stand in for it.

Take that last short paragraph. It uses eight pronouns in three sentences. Without pronouns it would read something like:

> *Pronouns are the words that stand in for nouns. People use pronouns a lot—because pronouns avoid repetition and increase the economy of the language. Once a writer has introduced a concept, however complicated the concept may be, the writer can use a two-letter pronoun to stand in for the concept.*

Pronouns come in different flavors.

Personal pronouns are so called because they apply to people: "I," "you," "he," "she," "we," "they." They stand straightforwardly in for a noun or a noun phrase. The pronoun "it" doesn't usually apply to humans but behaves in the same way.

Possessive pronouns: "Mine," "your," "yours," "our," "ours," "his," "hers," "their," "theirs."

Reflexive pronouns: "Myself," "yourself," and so on. These are used when the subject and object of the verb are the same, e.g., "I'm going to kill myself."

Intensive pronouns: Same set of words as reflexive pronouns, but used specifically for emphasis, e.g., "I myself killed the Jabberwock."

Demonstrative pronouns: "This," "that," "these," "those." These, you could say, single their antecedents out for special attention.

Relative pronouns: "What," "which," "whose," "whom," "that," etc. These introduce relative clauses that bring us news about their antecedents: "the little engine that could."

Interrogative pronouns: "What," "which," "whose," "whom." These introduce questions.

As you'll be able to see, these form family groups. The possessive and reflexive pronouns are variations on the basic personal pronouns. The interrogatives and relatives are closely related, too. You could say that one asks a question and the other frames the answer: "Who killed Cock Robin?" "The sparrow, who killed Cock Robin, confessed immediately." Likewise, the demonstratives shadow the same words when used as determiners. "He didn't wash his hands before baking that cake. I'm not going to eat that."

Other words and phrases sometimes behave as pronouns. "One another" and "each other" behave as pronouns in phrases such as "we love each other." "Much" and "enough" get used as pronouns in phrases such as "there wasn't much left in the bottle" or "you've had enough, sunshine." This is testament to the elasticity of the language. The good news is that you don't, as a native English speaker, need to be able to write out an exhaustive list of every pronoun in the language. You do this stuff (most of the time) naturally.

For all their usefulness, though, pronouns do cause problems. The main one is to do with agreement. Pronouns are one of the last surviving users of the system of inflecting by case in English. Most nouns don't vary in form with their role in the sentence. "Dog bites man"; "man bites dog." "Dog" and "man" remain the same in form, as I mentioned above, whether the dog is biting the man or the man is biting the dog. With pronouns it's different. "I bite him" and "he bites me."

So a pronoun needs to be in the right case for the sentence, which means agreeing with its *antecedent* (the word or phrase it is standing in for). A singular antecedent takes a singular pronoun. A plural antecedent requires a plural pronoun.

So:

Willy Wonka ascended in his *Great Glass Elevator.*

Charlie Bucket and Willy Wonka ascended in their *Great Glass Elevator.*

It gets trickier when you introduce certain qualifiers. "Each" and "every" are singular, so they muscle a plural antecedent into taking a singular pronoun. Likewise "neither . . . nor" and "either . . . or."

The fathers and sons went trick-or-treating in their *zombie costumes.*

Each father and son went trick-or-treating in his *zombie costume.*

Every father and son went trick-or-treating in his *zombie costume.*

Neither father nor son got the sweets he *was hoping for.*

The agreement of personal and relative pronouns is pedant heaven, so it's discussed at more length in "Perils and Pitfalls." All that remains to mention is that there's a long-running controversy about epicene, or gender-neutral, pronouns. What do you say when you don't want to specify a person's sex? For a long time, "he" was used as the universal pronoun without objection. A university administrator, meaning to indicate students of both sexes, might write:

Every student should bring his *textbook to class.*

Feminists, in recent years, have taken the reasonable view that using the masculine pronoun as the default universal inscribes patriarchy at the level of language itself.

Various solutions are proposed. One, which I adopt as much as possible in this book, is:

Every student should bring his or her *textbook to class.*

This has the advantage of neutrality (you might insist on using "her or his" half the time for added PC points, though that sounds to me unbearably clunky), but can make for tangled and unwieldy sentences. When writing over greater length, some simply alternate male and female pronouns with each chapter. In Steven Pinker's *The Sense of Style,* for instance, his notional reader is female one chapter, and male the next.

Another common solution is to use the plural form of the pronoun.

Every student should bring their *textbook to class.*

If the missed agreement between singular "student" and the plural pronoun sounds grating because they are so close to each other, you could try a compound sentence.

If a student turns up to class without a textbook, they *will be sent home.*

Or you can rewrite the sentence to pluralize it.

All students should bring their *textbooks to class.*

Or (in the sort of context we're dealing with) you might be able to shift into the second person.

If you're a student you should bring your textbook to class.

The bottom line, I'm afraid, is that it remains a problem. And like lots of problems in writing, it doesn't have a single ideal solution. Fiddle, fudge, test the results on your ear, consider your audience, and see what works best.

Adjectives and Adverbs

To return to our elementary school classrooms once again, these are the "describing words." As I wrote above, nouns—and especially the most common ones—tend to start out being rather vague. In isolation, "cat" could denote anything from a lion to a two-keeled boat. These "describing words" help the process of narrowing things down. Adjectives modify—a.k.a. describe—nouns and noun phrases; adverbs do the same for verbs, verb phrases, adjectives, and sometimes other adverbs.

So, the adjective "crazy" gives us a *crazy* cat and a *crazy* time in my life.

The adverb "crazily" gives us shouting *crazily*, *crazily* reckless driving, and someone shouting *crazily* loudly across the pedestrian crossing.

The terms describe grammatical roles rather than something intrinsic to a specific group of words. "Yellow" appears in the dictionary as an adjective. But in certain circumstances words generally used as nouns (such as "shower") serve in an adjectival role (as in "shower curtain")—where they're known as "noun adjuncts." Similarly, when something "hits home," "home" is here an adverb rather than (its usual role) a noun or (as it is for pigeons) a verb.

ADJECTIVES

Adjectives come in two main flavors depending on where they sit in a sentence. When they sit next to whatever they modify, they are said to be "attributive": "the yellow curtain"; "the greedy banker."* When they sit behind the noun, linked by a version of the verb "to be" or another verb involved with a state or change of state, they're "predicative": "I was sad"; "he got wet"; "she became intolerable."

Most adjectives can sit in either position, but a handful can be used only predicatively. Most of these seem to begin with *a*. So, for instance, you can say "my mother is awake," but you can't say "my awake mother."† You can say, too, "my mother is asleep," but not "my asleep mother."‡ There's an even smaller handful of attributive-only adjectives. You can say "a mere trifle" but not "this trifle is mere"; "my elder brother" but not "my brother, who is elder." In all of these cases, though, your own ear will be the best guide. To any native English speaker, using one of these words in the wrong position will sound clangingly wrong.

But wherever they sit, they sit tight; they don't inflect to agree with case or number.

The only way in which they vary is when they are comparative or superlative. These form either with the addition of "more" or "most," or by a simple and universal inflection: "he was a smart boy"; "he was smarter than his friends"; "he was the smartest boy in his class." That's also straightforward, with the exception of a handful of irregulars. All of these will be familiar, though.

> *good, better, best*
> *bad/ill, worse, worst*
> *little, less, least*
> *old, elder/older, eldest/oldest*

---

* You could think of words like "the" or "this," acting as "determiners," as stapling these simple adjectives to their nouns.

† Idiomatically, in US English, the adjective "woke" has come to mean "politically conscious," and can be used attributively, as in "my woke friends in the Black Lives Matter movement."

‡ Again, a quirk—you can say: "my half-asleep mother."

much/many, more, most
far, farther/further, farthest/furthest

Inasmuch as you do ever find yourself in trouble with adjectives, it's likely to be when it comes to comparatives. Some words refuse to form comparatives with *-er* or *-est*, particularly but not invariably ones of three or more syllables. One Jewish person can't be "Orthodoxer" than another.* The dialogue for the film version of *The Da Vinci Code* couldn't be "banaler" than the dialogue in the book.† Again, try these out on your ear. You'll hit the right answer. Just use "more" or "most" instead.

Then there's the prohibition on what is seen as a sort of tautology—i.e., combining inflectional comparatives with a "more" or "most" form: "I've got a more bigger tractor in the shed." There's plenty of precedent for idiomatic, jocular, and dialect usage—Spike Lee made a fine film called *Mo' Better Blues*—but it has no place in standard written English.

Can you use a superlative when you're comparing only two things? Sticklers say no. In non-idiomatic usage you're safer using a comparative. "Of my two languages, Russian and English, I speak English better." Something to keep an eye on.

And finally, there's the old complaint—a cousin of the row about using "less" with count nouns—that you can't compare an adjective that is itself an absolute. Simon Heffer, for instance, makes the reasonable point in his *Simply English* that "When two people are *dead*, one cannot be 'more dead' than the other, and if three are dead one cannot be 'the deadest.'"

Likewise, at least logically, someone can be "pregnant" but she can't be "more pregnant"; you either are pregnant or you aren't. But "she's very pregnant" is a perfectly idiomatic response to a colleague

---

* Adjective, comparative, superlative: observant, Orthodox, frum.
† Not even if it tried.

who waddles into the office looking as if she has a bus strapped to her tummy. The comparative form, when used with so-called "absolute adjectives" ("perfect," "infinite," "complete," and so on), works along those lines: not as a strict comparative but as a general-purpose intensifier. "A more perfect union," in the preamble to the US Constitution, is not a grammatical howler—it's a nicely cadenced idiom.

A curiosity of the English language is that there is in fact a sort-of rule about the order in which adjectives come. Like most of the actual rules of grammar, it's one that pedants seldom concern themselves with because native speakers never get it wrong. If you have more than one adjective applied to a given noun, they are ordered according to their meaning.

That list goes, though it isn't invariable: general opinion, specific opinion, age, size, shape, color, origin, material, purpose, as in:

> *Indiana Jones broke into the underground space and found a bizarre, slightly arousing, millennium-old forty-foot circular yellow Aztec marble pornographic diorama.*

I say it isn't invariable. Age, size, and shape, in particular, sometimes swap around in order depending on idiom and emphasis—"a large young man"; "a big old catfish"; "an ancient rectangular stone." As a native speaker, you should be able to trust your ear as a guide. Certainly, you'll never hear a crowd of elementary school children singing about a "red little caboose" behind the train, or, for that matter, a "red little behind caboose."

Most writing advice says you should use adjectives sparingly. If you pick them wisely, and pick your noun wisely, you'll do so anyway. There's a freight of meaning you're trying to get across in your noun phrase. The right noun should carry most of it, and the odd modifier will help with precision. But if it's taking four or five words to get that meaning, you're increasing the reader's cognitive load and clotting the rhythm of the sentence. There's probably a more direct way.

To take a parodic example, you could call something a "furry, bouncy, yellow-green, fist-sized sphere," but unless you're describing the scene from the point of view of a Martian, "tennis ball" will do. Because adjectives are essentially stative—they say what something *is*—they take some of the action out of a sentence.

A late British newspaper columnist named Lynda Lee-Potter liked to roll out great long sequences of adjectives. It was a hallmark of her style. In an old column of hers I just picked at random, I found her complaining that British troops "faced death not only from enemy attack but also because of shoddy equipment, parsimony and disastrous Government planning which we now realize was furtive, chaotic, rushed and dishonest." I'd say five adjectives to qualify "planning" is too many. "Furtive" and "dishonest" overlap enough to make each semi-redundant; "rushed" and "chaotic" likewise. "Disastrous"—good and forceful when we first meet it—has by the time we reach the end of the sentence been qualified out of any sort of necessity. And (though I suppose that's at some level the intention) the noun that holds this all together, "planning," has come to mean its opposite. There's no difficulty understanding what Lee-Potter's getting at, but she does make it complicated.

Above all, beware of adjectives that glom onto nouns automatically: Are you meaningfully qualifying your noun, or are you bolting together a set phrase? In journalism, for instance, fights are always "furious," U-turns "humiliating," revelations "explosive," lessons "salutary," and civil wars "bloody." You might as well think of these not as nouns modified by adjectives but as woolly compound nouns.

ADVERBS

The usual way in which adverbs are formed is by adding -*ly* to the end of an adjective.* That's not the only way, however. So-called "flat

---

* Not that -*ly* is the infallible sign of an adverb. Some adjectives have that ending: "a silly goose"; "a comely maiden."

adverbs"—where the adjective and adverb have the same form—are common in all sorts of dialects and informal usages. When Bob Dylan was heckled as "Judas" for playing an electric set in Manchester in 1966, he told his band: "Play it fucking loud." The boy done good.

Standard English also includes a large number of adverbs that don't end in -*ly*, among them "very" (when qualifying an adjective), "far," "fast," "straight," "first," and so on. Adverbs can be tricky beasts. Many of them actually change their meaning depending on whether they're "flat" or not, and where they come in the syntax of the sentence. There's a well-worn jocular distinction between "working hard" and "hardly working." Mr. Bojangles, in the old song, jumps "so high." Clearly he's a highly accomplished dancer; the singer thinks of him highly.

Most adverbs form their comparatives and superlatives with "more" and "most"—as in "she spoke to me more coldly after I said I had brought Donald to the pool party as my plus-one." But a few one- or two-syllable adverbs use -*er* or -*est* in the same way that adjectives do: "She escaped from Donald because she swam fastest."

One particularly Cromwellian school of writing advice has it that you should dispense with adverbs altogether. Stephen King is on record as thinking that "the road to hell is paved with adverbs." Elmore Leonard regards it as a "mortal sin" to use an adverb to modify the word "said"; indeed, he throws into a parenthesis that he thinks it's a mortal sin to use adverbs in "almost any way."

The thinking here is that adverbs clutter a sentence, and that they drain the energy from verbs. Just as with adjectives, there's truth in that. Thriller writers such as Leonard and King feel it particularly keenly; verbs are where the action is in any given sentence, and thriller writers are all about action. If your verbs always have to come with apologetic qualifiers, you may not be choosing your verbs right in the first place.

But, on the other hand, the good Lord would not have given us adverbs had he not meant us to use them now and again. They survive as a resource in the language because they have a use.

Auden's wonderful poem "The Fall of Rome" ends with the stanza:

Altogether elsewhere, vast
Herds of reindeer move across
Miles and miles of golden moss,
Silently and very fast.

You get nowhere by red-penciling the last line of that. And, for that matter, if you stripped out the other qualifiers too you'd have: "Elsewhere, herds of reindeer move across miles and miles of moss." That would do for David Attenborough, at a pinch, but not for W. H. Auden.

Just as you should be cautious with adjectives that attach to nouns too easily, try not to produce conga lines of empty adverbial intensifiers. If you're routinely presaging the arrival of an adjective with "really," "very,"* "absolutely," "quite," "extremely," and the like, you will be subject to the law of diminishing returns. Use the same caution with bet-hedging adverbs: "arguably," "possibly," "quite," "somewhat," and so on.

Verbs

Verbs, in the elementary school account of them, are "action words." If you want something to be running, jumping, shouting, hitting, or exploding, it's the verb department you need to consult. Verbs also cover such less exciting states of being as existing, enduring, reflecting, shutting up, and sitting absolutely still.

It's not only people or animate objects that can be the subjects of verbs; a car runs, a joint jumps, a headline shouts, an arrow hits, a grenade explodes, a subordinate clause exists, a rock endures, a

---

* We can forgive Auden "very fast," I think, because a) it does seem to have a particular force, and b) it scans.

mirror reflects, a door shuts, and a chair sits absolutely still. My old G.I. Joe toy (the UK equivalent was called "Action Man") was much better, now that I come to think of it, at existing, enduring, reflecting, shutting up, and sitting absolutely still than he was at any of the runny-jumpy-explodey stuff.

So there are verbs without action—they can denote a state of being* or an occurrence—but there's no action without verbs. The verb brings a clause or a sentence together. It helps to fix its parts in time and settle the relations of the nouns to each other. So verbs—even if they aren't action words—are where the action is.

Does every sentence need a main verb? No. Do most of them? Yes.

VOICE

"Voice" is the term linguists use to describe how a verb relates to its subject and/or object. In other words, is the subject of the verb doing, or being done to?

Active voice: "Everyone loves *America's Got Talent*."

Passive voice: *"America's Got Talent* is loved."

There's a neat trick—first suggested, as far as I can discover, by the American academic Rebecca Johnson—for identifying a passive construction in case of doubt. Try adding "by zombies" after the verb. If you can do so, you're looking at the passive voice.

"Everyone loves by zombies *America's Got Talent*" is recognizably not English. *"America's Got Talent* is loved by zombies" is not only a grammatical sentence, but probably true.

One of the oldest and most persistent writer's tips is that you should prefer the active to the passive voice; or, in its extreme form, that you should always avoid the passive.

---

* "Linking verbs," for instance, are verbs such as "be," "seem," or "become" that, rather than indicating an action, yoke a subject to a "subject complement" (either a noun or an adjective) that describes it. "The water was still"; "she's a private detective"; "he seems grouchy"; "that tastes foul."

That is just nonsense. If the passive voice had no value, it would not have survived in the language. In the first place, it is useful when the agent of an action is unknown, or when the emphasis needs to be firmly on the object. No decent newspaper reporter would write, "Someone stabbed a man outside a nightclub in Detroit yesterday" in preference to "A man was stabbed outside a nightclub in Detroit yesterday." Making the construction active actually increases the empty verbiage because you need to supply a subject and, not having one, are forced to put "someone" in.

One of the reasons that passive constructions can seem unwieldy, though, is that they add an extra layer of abstraction between subject and verb, particularly if an agent is involved. You always get an auxiliary verb (verbs used with other verbs to do things such as determine tense) and—where the agent is identified—the particle "by" (as in "by zombies") entering the construction.

"John F. Kennedy was shot": fine.

"Lee Harvey Oswald shot John F. Kennedy": fine.

"John F. Kennedy was shot by Lee Harvey Oswald": clunky. It conveys exactly the same information as the second example offers, but it adds two extra syllables and it articulates the event, as it were, backward.

So the principles of brevity and clarity—rather than a reflex disdain for the passive—should guide you. If an active construction is going to be clunkier, use the passive. Most often, though, it's the passive that will make the sentence knottier. Or, I could say, the sentence will be made knottier by the use of the passive.

Another problem with the passive is that because it makes it possible to dispense with an agent, it's a favorite of the mealy-mouthed. "Mistakes have been made," politicians will say, without wishing to dwell on who exactly might have made them. This goes along, as often as not, with a certain shuffling around with personal pronouns.

"I deeply regret the deficit in the pension fund"; "we deeply regret the deficit in the pension fund"; "the company deeply regrets the deficit in the pension fund"; "the deficit in the pension fund is deeply regretted." The perpetrator, in each version, inches a tiny bit further away from the scene of the crime.

Similarly, corporations and public bodies often use passive constructions to give an appearance of impersonal authority. "Patrons are kindly requested to return their glasses to the bar." "It is forbidden to walk on the grass."

Don't be afraid to say "I" or "we" and "you." A lot—probably most—of your communications will be personal. A lot of officialese—because we think that somehow if we take ourselves out of the scene it looks more professional—ends up in the third person or in abstract or passive terms.

> *The implementation of Boston metropolitan area's green space renewal project is expected to commence in three weeks.*

Here your subject is an abstract noun ("implementation") and your main verb is passive ("is expected"). Plus, the expectation is not what's important here; it's the commencing. And it's not the project but the green space. What it's trying to say is, roughly: "We will start building the new park in three weeks."

WHEN DID IT HAPPEN? DID IT HAPPEN OFTEN? SHOULD IT HAVE HAPPENED?

Questions such as these are addressed by what linguists call "tense," "aspect," and "mood." These are the ways in which a verb changes to indicate

1. when what it describes took place, relative to the speaker (tense);

2. the nature of the action—whether habitual or occasional, completed, or still going on (aspect); and

3. what you might call the attitude—is it a command, a wish, an obligation, a regret, and so on (mood).

English is a minimally inflected language. Most verbs have a simple present form ("blow"), a simple past form ("blew"), and a continuous form ("blowing")—and some irregular verbs, such as my example, also differ in the past participle ("blown"). The infinitive is formed by prefacing the simple present with the word "to." Most of the work, then, is done by auxiliary verbs: "to have" or "to be" for the past, "will" or "shall" for the future.

To start with, let's look at the various tense and aspect combinations: forms of the verb that tell us when something happened or will happen, and whether it happened once, several times, or is still going on. Let's use the example of a verb that works well in many tense-aspect combinations—and that might help you cope with them.

Present simple: "I drink"
This can indicate a single action, or a habitual action. Are you writing one of those terrible present-tense novels? "I walk into the cafe. Black waves of despair roll over me. I drink a shot of Mountain Dew." Or are you making a confession to your doctor? "Yes. I drink. So would you if you were writing a chapter about English verbs."

Present continuous: "I am drinking"
This is used to indicate an action that has started and is still going on, or that is happening right now: "I am drinking methylated spirits. Care to join me?" It is also, idiomatically, used to denote something that's happening in the future. "I'm drinking Jim Beam under the henhouse later. Let's make a night of it."

Past simple: "I drank"

Here's an action that either happened one time in the past, or that happened habitually for a period of time but has stopped. "I drank a glass of water." "I drank through my teens and early twenties until I let Jesus Christ into my life."

Past continuous: "I was drinking"

This denotes an action that started at some point in the past and went on for a period of time but has since stopped. It's often used in a scene-setting way, as if to tee up the action that interrupted it. "I was drinking gin and lemon when the vicar arrived."

Present perfect: "I have drunk"

This seems to English speakers a very intuitive tense, but as Harry Ritchie warns in his excellent *English for the Natives*, it "bewilders EFL students.* Each and every single one of them." It is tricky because it does several different things. It can denote actions that started in the past and continue into the present: "I have drunk Cointreau nonstop since I started going out with that French girl." Or it can describe a completed action located in a time scheme that is still going on—be that "today," "this week," or a lifetime: "For he on honey-dew hath fed, / And drunk the milk of Paradise."† Or it can be a completed action that stopped recently, and whose results or implications are still present. To adapt William Carlos Williams: "I have drunk / the Grey Goose / that was in / the icebox //

---

* English as a Foreign Language, i.e., students learning English who grew up speaking a different language.

† To make this clearer, consider a counter-example. If the time span in which the action happened is itself complete, you need the past simple. You could say "he has drunk fourteen pints today," but not "he has drunk fourteen pints yesterday." The same applies to the completion of a lifetime. You could say "I have drunk opium," but not "Samuel Taylor Coleridge has drunk opium." Dead men don't wear plaid, tell tales, or act as the subject in a clause whose verb is in the present perfect.

and which / you were probably / saving / for breakfast // Forgive me / it was delicious / so sweet / and so cold."

Present perfect continuous: "I have been drinking"
There's a certain amount of overlap with the present perfect but there's more emphasis on the continuing—"I have been drinking Wild Turkey since 7:00 AM"—or just-completed nature of the action: "Why are you making that noise? I have been drinking tequila."

Past perfect (or pluperfect): "I had drunk"
Here's a further wrinkle in the timeline. The past perfect signals that an action took place before something that is itself in the past. "I had drunk most of a bottle of claret before I started in on my host's scotch." Three points on the timeline: claret, then scotch, then the present tense in which the speaker is suffering the unspeakable consequences. That's a horrible example of an extremely useful and expressive construction. If we had no past perfect, we'd tie ourselves in knots trying to distinguish between more than one time frame in the past.

Past perfect continuous: "I had been drinking"
The same triple situation as the past perfect, but here—as with the present perfect continuous—the aspect indicates that the action is an ongoing or recently completed one. "I had been drinking for three hours by the time Curly joined me." "I had been drinking, but I nevertheless attempted to ride my moped home."

Future continuous: "I will be drinking" / "I'm going to be drinking"
There's a light neutrality to this tense and aspect combination; it indicates, as a gentle inevitability, that a state of something happening will obtain at a specific time. "I will be drinking in the Bald Faced Stag this evening."

Future perfect: "I will have drunk"
This involves a sort of mental time-travel. It describes—future tense, perfective aspect—a completed action as if viewed from the future. "By closing time, I will have drunk about a gallon of cider and will very much need a whiz."

Future perfect continuous: "I will have been drinking"
This effects the same frame shift as the future perfect, but with a continuous or progressive aspect. At the time from which you're viewing the action, the action is still going on, or is only just coming to an end: "I will have been drinking cider for a good few hours, and the landlord will want me to go home."

That's tense and aspect. Now let's add in mood. Mood describes, as I said above, something of the flavor of the verb. Is it expressing something that has definitely happened, that has definitely not happened, will not happen under certain circumstances, might be happening, or ought to happen?

When you hear people talking about the conditional, the subjunctive, the imperative, the interrogative, or the indicative, these are all grammatical moods. The indicative is the straightforward one; as per its name, it indicates something real. The imperative issues a command. Conditionals indicate something that might or might not happen according to a particular circumstance. The subjunctive (all but vanished in English) refers to imaginary situations or events, and expresses wishes or requests.

The two main sorts of modality are "epistemic" and "deontic." The first deals with the state of knowledge of the speaker. The second deals with possibility, permission, advice, desire, or obligation.

This is most easily demonstrated by example.

Epistemic modality: Do we know whether Joe Strummer fought the law or is planning to?

He fights *the law.*

He may *fight the law.*

He might *fight the law.*

He would *fight the law if it came to it.*

He must have *fought the law (i.e., from the sweat on his fore-head and those rocks he is breaking).*

Deontic modality: Can he or should he fight the law? Here's our attempt to persuade him.

If only he were to fight *the law!*

He can *fight the law.*

He may *fight the law.*

He could *fight the law.*

He should *fight the law.*

He ought to *fight the law.*

He must *fight the law.*

Fight *the law!*

And we know how that goes. Most of this stuff, happily, native English speakers do naturally. You thread your way expertly through the thickets of epistemic and deontic modality, quite unaware you're doing so. But it's worth taking special care with epistemic modality. In the wider sense, for instance, certain verbs come with a mood baked in. So "knew" has a different epistemic force than "thought" or "suspected." Some verbs of knowing, saying, or thinking commit you to a particular position. Anyone with a care to the laws of libel, or just good manners, will be careful with them. This is at the heart of the rebut/deny distinction I discuss in the chapter "Perils and Pitfalls."

CHOOSING VERBS

When you're choosing which verbs to use, a common piece of advice is to keep them concrete, to keep them active in voice, and to keep them indicative in mood. This is all right as far as it goes. And, indeed, you'll struggle to produce a long run of verbs in any voice other than the indicative. A marine drill instructor might manage a long run of imperatives, but an essayist or the writer of a winning memo to head office will not.

You should watch out for verb inflation, though. That's when you don't "head" something, you "head it up." You don't "start" something, you "roll it out." You don't "evaluate" something, you "conduct an evaluation." Less confident writers are often tempted to substitute orotund phrasal verbs for simpler alternatives, or to nominalize their verbs (i.e., put the action into a verbal noun; "take delivery of" for "receive").* They add, you might think, a certain grandeur and sophistication to the prose. Their cadence might be appealing. But they also cause problems of clarity.

Particularly for foreign language speakers, phrasal verbs can be very difficult to parse. This applies to the supposedly simple Anglo-Saxon constructions we're meant to prefer, as much as if not more than to complicated Latinate ones. That's because these simpler words have acquired a whole range of idiomatic phrasal uses. For

---

* See also: "Perils and Pitfalls," under "Nouning Verbs; Verbing Nouns."

instance, "put up," "put in," "put out," "put down," "put off," "put back," "put forward," and "put on" all have very different meanings, and there's seldom an intuitive relation between those meanings. You might "put in" for a job and "put out" in the back seat of a car. To "put forward" and to "put forth" are not quite the same thing—a plant might "put forth" foliage, and a person might "put forward" a proposal. Many phrasal verbs themselves change their meanings according to context: I might "put up" shelves badly; my wife, too cheap to hire a professional to correct my work, might resolve to "put up" with them.

The problem with nominalizations is that, effectively, simple main verbs are replaced by clusters of nouns and prepositions glued together with weak secondary or auxiliary verbs. After all, every verb you turn into a noun leaves you needing a fresh verb—and that "fresh" verb is likely to be far from fresh. If all the action in your sentence—the verb's change of meaning—has leached into the surrounding nouns, you can find yourself with long, bristling sentences anchored with a version of "to be" or "to have."

To take a caricatural business-speak example, "I have had sight of your letter of the twentieth" turns the verb "to see" into a noun, and makes the main verb "to have." "I saw": two words. "I have had sight of": five words. It's not hard to understand, sure, but it's windier, and it sounds pompous. "My thinking is that a consultation should be undertaken with the clients" can be more directly put as: "I think we should consult the clients." And so on.

None of this is to say that there's anything wrong with the verbs "to be" and "to have." "He is an idiot" is an invaluably forceful and simple construction. Likewise: "He has a gun!" is the quickest way to clear the hotel lobby. But using them as jacks-of-all-trade to give nouns a verbal force is a habit to avoid.

Building Sentences

Having taken a tour through the main parts of speech, let's look at how these things come together to make meaningful units of prose.

The basic unit of writing, most of us think instinctively, is the sentence. But how you define a sentence isn't always that easy. A simple way of doing it in the written language is to say that a sentence is something that begins with a capital letter and ends with a period or a related punctuation mark—question marks, exclamation points, and ellipses (dot-dot-dot) being, as it were, cousins of the period. The problem with that is, as I'll discuss in more detail later, spelling and punctuation are conventions for marshaling the grammar of the spoken language on the page.

A more satisfactory definition is that a sentence is a self-contained unit of meaning consisting of one or more clauses. A "clause" is the basic unit of meaning: It's a sentence-chunk with a subject and a predicate in it.

The "subject" is a noun ("a cat"), or a noun phrase ("the big ginger cat with ragged ears"), or something that stands in for one (a pronoun such as "it" or "she") and behaves like one. The "predicate" is, simply put, the bit of the clause that isn't the subject: It's the bit of the clause that gives us some news about the subject. It consists of a verb and, if appropriate, some other material that goes with the verb.

If a clause can stand alone and hold its meaning entire—if it could be a sentence on its own, in other words—it's called an "independent clause" or "main clause"; if it can't, it's called a "dependent clause" or "subordinate clause." A "phrase," by contrast, is a sentence-chunk that may have a subject in it and may have a verb in it but that doesn't have both; if it did, it would be a clause.

At the risk of boring veteran grammarians, let me roll through some examples in ascending order of complexity. In each case I'm putting the predicate in bold.

*The cat **slept**.*

The cat is the subject; it's the one doing the sleeping. The verb tells us what it's doing. This is a single-clause *simple sentence*.

*The cat **ate the mouse**.*

Still a single-clause simple sentence. The cat is again the subject. It's the one doing the eating. The wrinkle is that we're using a transitive verb (a verb that has not only a doer but a done-to). The mouse is the object: It's the thing being eaten.

*The mouse **gave the cat a tummy-ache**.*

The mouse is now the subject. In the predicate "gave the cat a tummy-ache," the tummy-ache is the grammatical object (it's the thing being given) and the cat is the indirect object (it's the thing to which the tummy-ache is being given). Again, it's a simple sentence—one subject, one predicate containing one main verb—but we've introduced the wrinkle of an indirect object.

*The cat **ate the mouse**, and the mouse **tasted horrid**.*

Yikes! Two subjects, two predicates, and two main verbs. This is what's known as a "compound sentence": a construction in which two or more independent clauses share sentence space. These can be linked by punctuation—"The cat ate the mouse; the mouse tasted horrid"—or by a class of words called "coordinating conjunctions." The mnemonic for these conjunctions, of which there are seven main ones in English, is FANBOYS: "for," "and," "nor," "but," "or," "yet," and "so."

Compound sentences can usually be split very easily into two (or more) separate sentences—though whether or how you do so is a stylistic decision. For reasons of rhythm, for instance, you might like to have a longer sentence. You might also want to emphasize the connection between the two independent clauses. Consider the shades of effect. "The cat ate the mouse, and the mouse tasted horrid." This is pretty neutral: a fait accompli—an unfortunate fact of life, delivered as a package. "The cat ate the mouse. The mouse tasted horrid." There's more of a sense, here, of an unpleasant discovery made in short order after a rash decision, the news delivered in a tone of pained neutrality. "The cat ate the mouse. And the mouse tasted horrid." To my ear there's a certain theatrical relish here: That period gives you a pause; the conjunction launches you into the second clause as a consequence of the first. Here's the whipping away, in a small way, of the magician's hankie from the cat's discovery.

The stricken cat, which was now suffering grievously, **crawled onto the sofa, hoping it would feel better after another nap***.*

Here, we are in the territory of the "complex sentence." The subject is modified by a subordinate clause. You can tell "which was now suffering grievously" is a subordinate clause because it can't stand alone. "Which was now suffering grievously" isn't a sentence in anyone's book. Complex sentences involve joining a main clause to a subordinate clause with a coordinator or a piece of punctuation that explains the relationship between the two things.

The cat, which had imagined its troubles were over for the day, **dozed off on the sofa, but was rudely woken up when its owner sat down to watch the NFL highlights without looking***.*

This is a "complex-compound sentence." It has two main verbs— "dozed" (an active verb: the cat is doing the dozing) and "was woken up" (a passive verb: the cat is being woken up). The subject of both of these is the cat. So here's a compound sentence. Stripped down, it says: "The cat dozed off but [the cat] was woken up."

The sentence also has a number of nested subordinate clauses. First, "which had imagined its troubles were over for the day." The cat is the subject of the first verb "had imagined," but that verb's object ("its troubles") is itself modified by "were over for the day." Then we have "when its owner sat down to watch the NFL highlights without looking": "When" introduces another subordinate clause, modifying the waking up, whose subject is the owner and whose verb is "sat down." And within that subordinate clause we have yet another: "Without looking" is a participle clause, behaving a bit like an adverb, and modifying the owner's sitting down. And so, merrily, you can go on.

The coordinators and the punctuation of that sentence help you through the thicket. The first subordinate clause is sandwiched between two commas and introduced by "which." The second half of the compound sentence is marked off with another comma and introduced with the conjunction "but." Further subclauses are flagged by "when" and "without."

I run through this stuff not because this book is intended as a guide to syntax—rather, because if you get a handle on the basics of how sentences work, you'll be better able to disentangle your own. And also, because you can see how quickly those basics can be slotted together and nested inside each other to make quite complicated constructions.

There are two encouraging things to remember.

The first is that, even if your head spins when trying to sort your coordinating conjunctions from your subordinate clauses, this is something you do very naturally in speech. You understand all of these sentences—which means that you understand their grammar even if you can't immediately label it. You both make and decipher complex-compound sentences without even thinking about it. You know more than you know you know. The grammarians aren't telling you how you do it; they're trying, with incomplete success, to describe systematically what you are doing.

The second encouraging thing is that the basic idea is the most important one. Beneath the curlicues of subject-predicate grammar are two very familiar things: nouns and verbs. All these complicated sentences are built on very simple ones. There's always, always a main clause in there somewhere, and it has a subject and a verb. Shunt two of them together and you get a compound sentence. Festoon one with subordinate clauses and you get a complex sentence. Do both and you get a complex-compound sentence.

But right at the bottom, under all the ornamentation, is the spine of your sentence: subject and verb. The successful sentence surgeon identifies it, reaches in, grabs it, and doesn't let the little rascal go. In the chapter "Sentence Surgery," later, I'll give some examples of how you can apply this understanding.

* * *

What makes a sentence easy to read, and what makes it go wrong? The most obvious thing to say is that, by and large, the longer the sentence, the harder it is for the reader. So you're looking to make sentences short. That doesn't mean they can't convey grown-up ideas.

As Hemingway is supposed to have said: "The only kind of writing is rewriting." So reread each sentence. How many words long is it? The average sentence should be between fifteen and twenty words. Sometimes they will be longer. But if you're regularly hitting forty, your writing is going to be much, much harder going. You don't have to confine one thought to one sentence. But the fewer thoughts per sentence you go for on average, the better. (Zero is too few.)

But, as I've said, keeping sentences short is only one part of it. You also need to consider their structure. A very good way to do this is to keep your eyes firmly on the main clause. What's the subject of the sentence? What's the main verb? Can the reader easily see the connection between the two? These are the spine of your sentence; lose sight of them, and you're lost.

At root, a tricky sentence is one that demands a lot of cognitive work from the reader—and we know, roughly, what this consists of. It has to do with the concept of "working memory." This is to your brain as the "clipboard" on your computer is to its hard drive; it acts as a sort of mental holding pen. As a sentence unfolds on the page or in the ear, you hold its elements in working memory as you wait for the clues that tell you how to interpret it. And the roadmap to a sentence is that subject-verb connection; the longer it takes to become clear, the harder the brain is working.

The problem is that working memory has limited space. Remember how Microsoft Word sometimes bleats: "You placed a large amount of text on the clipboard"? So does the brain. An influential 1956 essay by the psychologist George Miller made a stab at describing the limits of working memory. That essay was called "The Magical Number Seven, Plus or Minus Two," and it argued that the average person is capable of storing only between five and nine pieces of information in working memory.

What linguists call "right-branching sentences"—that is, sentences that give you the subject and verb up front—are therefore easier on the brain. Once you have subject and verb established, you know where you're going with the sentence. Sentences where you have to wait a very long time between subject and verb, or where you're having to fight through a thicket of modifying clauses before you even reach the subject, tax the working memory.

English has advantages in this department. Unlike so-called "verb-final languages," where you tend to put the verb at the end of the sentence, you can put subject and verb close to each other. Keep them there, if possible. And if you can manage subject-verb-object order—the default position in English—so much the better.

Crime writing is a good place to look for examples of right-branching sentences; its first job, after all, is to make it easy for readers to keep turning the pages. The mystery writer Harlan Coben, for instance, is no sort of literary stylist. But he's almost infallible in his kindness to the reader's working memory. Here's a paragraph more or less at random from his novel *The Woods.*

> *She* **parked** near her father's old car, a rusted-out yellow VW Beetle. *The Beetle* **was** always in the exact same spot. *She* **doubted** that it had moved from there in the past year. *Her father* **had** freedom here. *He* **could** leave anytime. *He* **could** check himself in and check out. But *the sad fact* **was,** he almost never left his room. *The leftist bumper stickers* that had adorned the vehicle **had** all faded away. *Lucy* **had** a copy of the VW key and every once in a while she started it up, just to keep the battery in operating order. *Doing that,* just sitting in the car, **brought** flashbacks. *She* **saw** Ira driving it, the full beard, the windows open, the smile, the wave and honk to everyone he passed.
>
> *She* never **had** the heart to take it out for a spin.

I've put the subjects in italics and the verbs in bold. Notice anything? Of those twelve sentences, fully three-quarters go directly from subject to verb. All are indicative in mood. All are in the active voice. The odd sentence is more complicated—an absolutely rigid commitment to slamming subject-verb into the first three or four words of a sentence would become monotonous—but not much more complicated. There's the sentence whose subject is a gerundial phrase*—"doing that"—where another gerund phrase in

---

* A "gerund" is the word given to a noun made out of a verb. It usually takes the same form as a present participle, i.e., it ends in *-ing.* A place "setting" at a table, a good "showing" in the football game, or a good "kicking" in a fight: All are nouns that come from verbs. Those are gerunds. In the case above the phrase containing the *-ing* word is working as a noun phrase. You could expand it to say (awkwardly) "the doing of that" or "her doing that," and it serves as the subject governing "brought flashbacks."

apposition,* "just sitting in the car," intervenes between subject and verb. And there's another sentence where an eight-syllable modifying clause, "that had adorned the vehicle," gets between the bumper stickers and their fading. None of these are much of a challenge to the reader's brain.

Lee Child, author of the Jack Reacher novels, is a thriller writer who does have some claim on being a stylist. Most of his sentences are brisk, businesslike, and right-branching, as per the Coben model. Here's a representative extract from *Worth Dying For* (my italics and bold as on page 75).

> *Sixty miles north* Dorothy Coe **took** *a pork chop from her refrigerator.* The chop **was** *part of a pig a friend had slaughtered a mile away, part of a loose cooperative designed to get people through tough times.* Dorothy **trimmed** *the fat, and put a little pepper on the meat, and a little mustard, and a little brown sugar.* She **put** *the chop in an open dish and put the dish in the oven.* She **set** *her table, one place, a knife, a fork, and a plate.* She **took** *a glass and filled it with water and put it next to the plate.* She **folded** *a square of paper towel for a napkin. Dinner, for one.*

> Reacher **was** *hungry.* He **had** *eaten no lunch.* He **called** *the desk and asked for room service and the guy who had booked him in told him there was no room service.* He **apologized** *for the lack.*

This is tough-guy prose. Child is idiomatic and informal—as witnessed in that curt, verbless sentence "Dinner, for one." There's

---

* "In apposition" means that two phrases are placed side by side as if in parallel. The second phrase is explaining the first: "Harlan Coben, the writer, is a favorite of mine."

a methodical and unfussy feel about it, too, artfully produced. There are structural parallelisms—"she put . . . she set . . . she took . . . she folded"; "he had . . . he called . . . he apologized."* There are repeated words and simple connectors: "and a little . . . and a little . . . and a little."

One of Child's stylistic quirks, though, is that he goes completely to town when his hero thumps somebody. Here's the equivalent of slo-mo, or "bullet time," and it can produce quite absurdly long sentences.

> *Then Reacher's blow landed.*
>
> *Two hundred and fifty pounds of moving mass, a huge fist, a huge impact, the zipper of the guy's coat driving backward into his breastbone, his breastbone driving backward into his chest cavity, the natural elasticity of his ribcage letting it yield whole inches, the resulting violent compression driving the air from his lungs, the hydrostatic shock driving blood back into his heart, his head snapping forward like a crash test dummy, his shoulders driving backward, his weight coming up off the ground, his head whipping backward again and hitting a plate-glass window behind him with a dull boom like a kettle drum, his arms and legs and torso all going down like a rag doll, his body falling, sprawling, the hard polycarbonate click and clatter of something black skittering away on the ground, Reacher tracking it all the way in the corner of his eye, not a wallet, not a phone, not a knife, but a Glock 17 semi-automatic pistol, all dark and boxy and wicked.*

That second sentence is 168 words long, contains no main verb, and is as easy to parse as any sentence you're likely to come across. Technically, it isn't a sentence at all—it's a set of modifiers for the four words "Then Reacher's blow landed." Period or no (you could as

* Different "he"; same structure.

easily recast it with a colon), here's an extreme right-branching construction. It's easy to follow because the logic of what it describes moves from clause to clause: This happened, then this happened, then this happened. The first couple of phrases are appositive (the "moving mass," the "fist," the "impact") and then we have a trail of consequential effects (moving, with loosely parallel constructions, from "zipper," to "breastbone," to "chest cavity," to "lungs," to "heart," to "head," to "shoulders," and so on). The knee bone's connected to the anklebone. Each gobbet of information is entire; the working memory isn't working all that hard.

Favoring right-branching sentences is not the whole story, though. Your choice of nouns and verbs will also have an effect on how easy your sentences are to digest. And for reasons of cadence or emphasis, you may well want to throw in some left-branchers here and there. Nobody, not even the simplest of thriller writers, writes exclusively in that sort of sentence. Nor should they. Variation in sentence structure (and length) is what prevents your prose from sounding robotic and repetitive or even babyish.

As ever, I want to make the point that you don't write well by following an absolute set of rules. You write well by developing an ear that will tell you when something isn't working—and you can use the analytical tools I'm offering here as a series of possible strategies for understanding how to put it right. Some more practical work on this appears in the chapter "Sentence Surgery."

Paragraphs, Sections, and Chapters

Words build into phrases and clauses; phrases and clauses build into sentences; sentences build into paragraphs; paragraphs build into sections and chapters. The hardest work is done at the level of a sentence, but organizing a longer document also requires application. It needs to be navigable. Paragraphs and chapters—along with other design features apt to the genre you're writing in (pie charts, block pagination, or whatever)—help make that possible.

If you're writing something very technical and exact—be it a company report, a legal document, or a scientific paper—paragraphs are a vital part of the logical structure of the piece. They may begin with so-called topic sentences and end with a sort of recap—a very narrow and precise form.

Not all forms of writing are that tight. The paragraph, as most of us think of it, is a unit of thought. It's also a unit of prose rhythm. It's also a design feature. Compare the staccato style of tabloid reportage with the more digressive movement of a literary essay. As Keith Waterhouse notes in his book *Daily Mirror Style:** "Fowler wrote that the purpose of paragraphing is to give the reader a rest. Had he been more of a student of the popular press he might have added that it is not the purpose of paragraphing to give the reader a jolt. That, however, is often the result." Nor, *pace* Waterhouse, are those jolts always a bad thing.

It's impossible to make absolute rules for paragraphing. One-word paragraphs look odd in serious continuous prose. One-sentence paragraphs are a tabloid mainstay, and present in some technical writing, but don't usually look good in an essay. But you need to gauge the context and develop a feel for what works.

In doing so just keep those two very nebulous ideas—giving the reader a break, and the paragraph as unit of thought—front and center. A paragraph is a prose mouthful. The breaks between paragraphs—lovely white space—give the reader a chance to swallow what has gone before. But what's in a paragraph needs to be in some sense homogeneous. You don't want to be presenting the reader with a forkful of roast beef and gooseberry crumble.

I'm afraid that here we are once again in the territory of know-it-when-you-see-it. Or, if you like, know-it-when-you-taste-it. A paragraph might well have more than one thing in it; those who dement themselves by obsessing on the one-thought-per-paragraph idea

---

* A style guide to a UK tabloid paper, published in 1981.

will produce some stiff and eccentric paragraphs. But the things in any given paragraph need to belong together. Hot dog, kraut, a handful of french fries, some pickle, ketchup, and a dab of mustard might make a delicious if challenging mouthful. Hot dog, kraut, a cinnamon roll, and Phish Food ice cream will likely be ejected onto the tablecloth.

This is meant to be encouraging. Remember: You don't need special training to spit out the ice-cream-and-sauerkraut mouthful. You've already had the training through a lifetime of lunches. You've read a lot of paragraphs in your life. You've had a lot of thoughts. Your sense of what belongs in a paragraph may be better than you think.

Sections and chapters are paragraphs writ large. They are units of thought and design and intellectual rhythm. They, too, are subject to the gooseberry crumble test.

In the later chapter "Out into the World," I discuss the ways you might structure a longer document in terms of style and argument.

4

Punctuation and Symbols

Almost nothing occasions more confusion in less confident writers, and more rage in proud pedants, than punctuation. Lynne Truss sold three million copies of her wittily irritable book on the subject, *Eats, Shoots & Leaves*. It's reasonable to see that as a reflection of how deep—though hitherto how little examined—our feelings about punctuation are.

People really mind. The so-called greengrocer's apostrophe—as in "Clementine's fifty cents each"—is a pet peeve of countless sticklers. Pages shouty with exclamation points, or where commas are scattered as if shot from a blunderbuss, vex many even quite free-and-easy language users. The perpetrator will be marked down in the reader's mind as either sloppy or semiliterate.

That means that the writer hoping to persuade needs to pay special attention to how he or she punctuates. There are rules. These rules may not be what some sticklers imagine them to be, and they have changed over the years and are continuing to change. But many punctuation usages, in standard written English in a formal context, are pretty firmly established.* You won't find a comma in the middle of a word, for instance. A sentence in continuous prose can't end in a slash. You can't open a parenthesis with a comma and close it with a bracket.

---

* As ever, in literary and informal contexts all bets are off.

It's worth starting by thinking about exactly what punctuation is for. It's one of the things, along with word order and morphology (the way words change their forms and endings), that help orient the words in a sentence. Punctuation marks are signposts through a sentence. Some of them inflect a sentence's tone or meaning: A question mark or an exclamation point change what you might think of as a sentence's tone of voice. Some of them denote a relationship between one part of a sentence and another: Brackets tell you that what's in them isn't part of the main flow of the sentence; a colon signals that what comes after it elaborates or depends on what goes before.

Originally, though, punctuation began as a device used by scribes to help people reading aloud know where to pause. The big four marks—the comma, the semicolon, the colon, and the period—were primarily understood to denote the length of a pause, with a period in some accounts of it four times as long as a comma. But those marks were taken up by printers and grammarians and repurposed as aids to semantic understanding. In effect—as with many other features of the language—prescriptive grammarians attempted to fold them into a logically consistent system. So punctuation now plays two parts: It both marks time for the reading voice *and* signposts grammatical relationships. Many of the arguments about punctuation arise from the overlap between its two functions. A comma can be there simply to mark a pause—but it can also have a role in marking a parenthesis or separating two clauses. As the linguist David Crystal writes in his book *Making a Point: The Pernickety Story of English Punctuation:* "This is where we see the origins of virtually all the arguments over punctuation that have continued down the centuries and which are still with us today."

Punctuation is also subject to fashion. We live in an age that favors light punctuation. We use fewer commas than our forebears. We omit periods at the ends of sentences in many circumstances— in the titles of books, on signposts, and in text messages or social media posts. We are more likely to do away with hyphens when writing compound words—preferring "semicolon" to "semi-colon," for instance.

But with relatively rare points of genuine dispute, it is possible to set out something like a set of rules for the standard use of punctuation marks in continuous prose.

Let's go through point by point.* First, the trio of what sometimes get called "sentence-final punctuation marks": the period, the question mark, and the exclamation point.

The Period

In formal writing a period's main job is to signal the end of a sentence. That is the straightforward part.

Not all sentences, or not all statements, need to end in a period. Question marks and exclamation points and ellipses can end a sentence, too—though they can be seen as special cases of the period. As mentioned, newspaper headlines, book titles, advertising slogans, or other forms of signwriting, and informal communications such as text messaging and social media status updates, often dispense with the period or use it differently.

The Question Mark

The question mark is another form of sentence-final punctuation. You could think of it as a period with a waving flag on top, that flag signaling that the sentence (or sentence fragment?) in question is a question—if that's not begging the question.†

---

* Groan.

† According to the actor Christopher Walken, in his foreword to the *KISS Guide to Cat Care* (2001), "I've heard that the symbol we use to signify a question (?) is, in origin, an Egyptian hieroglyph that represents a cat as seen from behind. I wonder if the Egyptians were expressing suspicion or an inquiring mind . . . or something else?" I wonder, too. There's no evidence I know of to support this, but since it's a) Christopher Walken, and b) Christopher Walken writing a foreword to some cat manual, and c) turns an ordinary punctuation mark into a cat's bottom . . . well, it's worth passing on.

The one big rule for using question marks correctly is: Use them for direct questions and direct questions only. This is, apparently, easier said than done. You now see them used—and it makes sticklers wince—in the case of indirect or implied questions as well.

1. "Hi, I hope you are well?" This seems to be the near-universal greeting from the public-relations professional attempting to give a mass email press release the personal touch.* The confusion arises, obviously, because this seems to be another way of asking whether you are well; there is an implied question as to your wellness. Doesn't matter. "I hope you are well" is, grammatically, a statement about your hope, not a question about my wellness. "Are you well?" is a question. "I hope I never hear from your insincere mail-merging ass ever again" is a statement.

2. "Surely you're not getting worked up about a friendly press release?" Again, wrong. "Surely"—a sentence adverb that seems to attract question marks like flies to a cowpat—does not ask a question; it offers a supposition. The presence of doubt in a sentence about the world—and we have a whole delicate grammatical apparatus for conveying degrees of epistemological certainty—does not in itself mandate a question mark. That is reserved for . . . direct questions.

3. "My friend heard what you were saying about question marks, and he wonders if you need to get out a bit more?" Again, no. This is what in grammar is called an indirect question. An indirect question is, you could say, a statement

---

* Sometimes the computer will even have inserted the recipient's first name. Sometimes the author—whom you will never have met—will ask every one of his or her several hundred victims how their weekend was.

about a question. The question is being reported, not asked. "He wonders if" is indicative in mood; it's a statement. And no matter how intensely that wondering is going on, it doesn't warrant a question mark.

Informally, question marks can appear mid-sentence—usually as part of a parenthesis, though they're unwieldy even then: "I first started getting pompous about the misuse of question marks twenty (or was it twenty-five?) years ago. . . ."

In dialogue, too, you can use them—usually mockingly—to signal the various forms of rising intonation that young people use: "He was like, and I was like, so he was like, and then I was just whatever, and then he asked me to the prom?"

And as ever, the system has wrinkles. Some sentences that are questions, grammatically speaking, can get away with taking a different punctuation mark because of their meaning. In *The Cambridge Grammar of the English Language,* for instance, Huddleston and Pullum note that you could write: "Aren't they lucky to have got away with it!" or "Who cares what I think about it, anyway!" Sticklers may demur. But if our concern is with the expressive range of the language, there's no question that a distinction between "Isn't she lovely?" and "Isn't she lovely!" adds to that resource.

Like exclamation points, these are best used singly—except, possibly, when expressing outrage and bafflement in the margins of someone else's work. Two handwritten question marks in a margin is an economical way of saying: "Are you absolutely sure about that? It sounds like you've gone right off your onion." But then, marginal doodles—like the proofreading signs that make marginal doodling a profession—are a little outside the province of this book.

The Exclamation Point

"Like laughing at your own joke," F. Scott Fitzgerald reportedly said of this most gaudy of punctuation marks. He had a point. Overusing exclamation points makes you sound hectoring and overexcited. That idea of laughing at your own joke—of paying yourself a compliment—has been there from the beginning. When they arrived in the language in the fourteenth century, David Crystal tells us, they were called the "point of admiration"—and later, the "admirative point" and the "wonderer." It's since Dr. Johnson that we've had "exclamation"—shifting the emphasis from admiration to the expression of strong feeling.

In any case, the exclamation point signals excitability. It may be a sense of this that led to a notably stupid edict from the UK's Department for Education in early 2016. Ministers told primary school teachers that sentences ending in an exclamation point could be marked correct only if they began with the words "how" or "what." As in:

How silly this advice is!

Or:

What asses those education ministers are!

That's plain wrong. There are many other sorts of sentences that either can or must take an exclamation point. Exclamations, obviously, ask for them—and sentences of the "how" or "what" variety are near the top of the list. *Fowler*, indeed, begins its discussion of exclamation points with "how" and "what" sentences. But it goes on to mention wishes, alarm calls, commands, calls for attention, and all-purpose shouting.

So:

If only I could swim! (wish)

Help! I'm drowning! (alarm call)

Pull me out of the water! (command)

Over here! (call for attention)

Glub glub! Aaargh! (all-purpose shouting)

It's hard to see how you could punctuate "Help! I'm drowning!" in any other way. "Help. I'm drowning." does not convey quite the same sense of urgency. But then again, if you're actually drowning you're unlikely to be writing your feelings on the subject down on a bit of paper—and there's a useful hint there. Many, if not most, legitimate uses of the exclamation point in prose are ways of punctuating speech.

The default position of the written word is one of calm consideration; even strong emotion is being reflected on and given shape. You are composing sentences, not blurting them. So you'll almost certainly need an exclamation point only if you're writing in an informal way designed to replicate the effects of speech. A talky newspaper column might warrant the odd one—but if they're popping up in your business letters, essays, reports, or presentations, they almost certainly shouldn't be. *The Economist Style Guide* is so mortified by the very idea of them that it makes no mention of their existence.

Fowler's position is the conventional one. Except for literary uses, in which all bets are as usual off,* it says that it should be used "sparingly": "Excessive use of exclamation marks in expository prose is a certain indication of an unpracticed writer or one who wishes to add a spurious dash of sensation to something unsensational." It's the mark that says: "Go home; you're drunk."

---

* Wordsworth, for instance, wrote: "She lived unknown, and few could know / When Lucy ceased to be; / But she is in her grave, and, oh, / The difference to me!" The opening of *Beowulf* is usually punctuated "*Hwæt!*" i.e., "Listen up!"

The use of double or even triple exclamation points in a formal context is a complete no-no. "OMG!!" is fine for a text message. Indeed, "OMG" with no punctuation, or with a period, will look positively sarcastic to some.

The Ellipsis

There are two main uses for the ellipsis—a.k.a. dot-dot-dot—in normal writing.

One is as a half-hearted cousin of the period used when a sentence just sort of trails off . . . It conveys hesitancy or tentativeness, something unspoken or something implied. In this role it effectively stands in for a sometimes pregnant pause in the spoken word.

> *"I was wondering if I could get one of those . . . you know . . . something for the . . ."*
>
> *"A packet of condoms, young man? Why, all you have to do is ask!"*

As in the above example, if the ellipsis is indicating broken speech in short chunks, you don't have to recapitalize after it as you would for a period. It behaves more like a comma or dash.

In a more technical context it can imply the continuation of a list: "1, 2, 3, 4, 5, 6 . . ."

The other use for the ellipsis is to indicate missing material in a quotation. It's fairly easy to see how this can be confused with its first role. If you're being punctilious, or quoting formally, it's almost always best to put that ellipsis in square brackets to make clear that you're indicating excised material rather than simply a pause.

> *He was, at least until he murdered my wife, my dearest friend.*

He was [...] my dearest friend.

No surprise that the abuse of the ellipsis is a particular favorite of the designers of posters for critically savaged films, or the harvesters of book reviews for paperback editions.

My note above that it's often a punctuation of the spoken language can be helpful when deciding whether to use it in writing. It's for that reason, I think, that it has acquired a whole new life in the more conversational communications we now have on email and social media. It can say "um" or "etc." or "to be continued." This is especially handy when a writer under pressure from the character count of Twitter, for instance, wants to make a point over the course of more than one tweet.

@periodlover I think the period is being seen less and less on social media because we...

@periodlover... like to keep things informal and conversational in those circumstances and sometimes...

@periodlover... we need to be able to indicate that we haven't stopped talking...

But it is also one of the alternatives that seems to be taking over, somewhat, from heavier sentence-final punctuation on the internet. I frequently find myself ending emails to book reviewers I commission with ellipses: "Let me know if the idea appeals..."

To return to Crystal's real point, the ellipsis—along with no sentence-final punctuation at all—is one of the period's replacements in these arenas.

The Comma

The comma is a very versatile piece of mid-sentence punctuation, used more than any other single punctuation mark. The rules governing its usage are a bit of a nightmare. This is not least because it retains more strongly than any other mark its use as a general-purpose pause signaler.

So, for instance:

When you're writing a mid-length sentence like this one you don't absolutely need a comma.

When you're writing a mid-length sentence like this one, you could on the other hand put a comma in.

When you're writing a mid-length sentence, like this one, you could use two commas to mark one phrase out as a parenthesis.

All three of those are perfectly grammatical. Version two is a little easier on the reader; it allows for a catching of the breath. Version three lets you catch your breath on either side of the parenthesis. But the decision is a stylistic one rather than an absolute rule.

Do keep in mind, though, that if you're using a comma as part of a parenthesis, or to mark out a dependent clause, it needs an opposite number. Parenthetical commas work just the same way as brackets: They hold a chunk out of the main text as if between tongs. So you wouldn't write:

When you're writing a mid-length sentence, like this one you could use two commas to mark one phrase out as a parenthesis.

As so often, reading a sentence aloud and making a point of pausing on the commas will help you to notice when there's one missing. The above sentence simply doesn't sound right if you have only one comma in it.

The importance of getting commas right is illustrated by an apocryphal story about a teacher who got on the wrong side of a school inspector. The inspector—an anything-goes type—complained that the teacher was paying too much attention to punctuation.

The teacher went to the blackboard. He wrote:

The inspector said the teacher was an idiot.

Then he added a couple of commas.

The inspector, said the teacher, was an idiot.

Commas can be hard to keep track of because—though they all look the same—they have more than one possible use. Lots of sentences have single commas (or odd numbers of commas), so it's harder to notice when you've failed to close a parenthesis. A single bracket sticks out. A single comma is camouflaged. It's especially prone to get lost if you need to use a comma within the parenthesis itself.

When Sam embarked on this sentence, whose lengthy parenthesis, he hoped, would make punctuation tricky, he didn't bank on having to rewrite it several times.

That one might work better if you used brackets or, as below, dashes.

When Sam embarked on this sentence—whose lengthy parenthesis, he hoped, would make punctuation tricky—he didn't bank on having to rewrite it several times.

The comma also often articulates between two linked clauses, particularly if the dependent clause comes first.

When he saw Snoopy wasn't at home, Charlie Brown slammed the kennel door.

If you put it the other way around you can usually dispense with the comma.

Charlie Brown slammed the kennel door when he saw Snoopy wasn't at home.

Another use of commas that causes confusion is, if you like, a special case of parenthesis: when they are used to mark out a relative clause.

The man who smelled of fish showed me the door.

Here we're indicating that of all the men in the room, it was the fishy-smelling one who saw the speaker out. The fishy smell is the defining quality of the subject. This is what's called a "restrictive" or a "defining relative clause." You don't need commas.

The man, who smelled of fish, showed me the door.

Here we're indicating that the man who showed the speaker the door happened to smell of fish. Perhaps the other men in the room smelled of fish, too, but perhaps not. It's a parenthetical observation—an optional extra. The commas mark it out as such. See also "That, Which, and Who" in "Perils and Pitfalls."

The comma also serves to separate adjectives or adverbs when you have a number of them affixed to the same referent. Light punctuation means that short runs of adjectives can be left comma-free, though.

I saw funny little green men trooping out of the spaceship.

The Oxford comma, or "serial comma," is something people like to argue over. This is the comma you see (or don't) between the second-to-last term of a list and the word "and." If you're using the Oxford comma, you'd write "parsley, sage, rosemary, and thyme"; if you're not using it, you'd write "parsley, sage, rosemary and thyme." This is a choice about style. The serial comma isn't a mistake—it's a long-attested usage that was in fact the dominant one in an era of heavier punctuation—though many people prefer not to use it. I use it here, in line with my publisher's stylebook, but in the UK edition of this book I do without it. Neither is wrong. That said, on some occasions you positively need to insert one to resolve an ambiguity.

> *The guests at the party included two prostitutes, my ex-wife and the guitarist from Pink Floyd.*

The attentive reader will notice that this is at best ungallant and at worst libelous: Without a serial comma the suggestion is that rather than being a list, the second half of that sentence is in apposition to the first. Much safer to write it as follows:

> *The guests at the party included two prostitutes, my ex-wife, and the guitarist from Pink Floyd.*

The Colon

Nice and robust, the colon. It doesn't mess about. If you have two clauses that need linking, the colon is your man. *Fowler*'s line on it—that its job is "delivering the goods that have been invoiced in the preceding words"—gets the sense of it pretty well. Whatever comes after a colon explicitly unpacks or develops on what comes before it. It stands in, as *Fowler* notes, for expressions like "viz.," "for example," "that is to say," "namely," and so on.

I had only one reason to stay sitting: I was shackled to the chair.

In the same vein, the colon introduces lists and examples.

He packed his usual gear for the beach: surfboard, trunks, binoculars, shark spray, and waterproof hammers.

In UK English the letter after a colon is lowercase. US usage will sometimes capitalize after colons if the text after the colon forms a complete sentence and lowercase if not, but guidelines vary.

The Semicolon

I know one shouldn't have favorite punctuation marks, but I have a particular fondness for the semicolon. It's supple in its use, precise, and—which is the best thing about it—unshowy. It can coordinate a compound sentence, mark out items in a complex or extended multi-clause list . . . and it does so with a very becoming modesty. If the comma is fire and the period is ice, to adapt *This Is Spinal Tap*, the semicolon is lukewarm water. Semicolons allow you to get away with much longer sentences, and help make those sentences decipherable to the reader. If you have a succession of related thoughts, the semicolon allows you to articulate the links between them much more easily and clearly than any other mark.

If those thoughts are separated by periods, any relationship of consequence, dependency, or subordination has to be inferred by the reader. You are presenting two things as if independently.

He sat on the chair. He was tired.

A colon staples the two things together. It insists on a relationship. But remember the colon gun is a one-shot weapon. You look very odd using more than one colon in a sentence.

He sat on the chair: He was tired.

But not:

He sat on the chair: He was tired: It had been a long night.

Where the colon insists, the semicolon suggests. Also—though not everyone would, as a stylistic decision—you can get away with using more than one semicolon as a coordinator.

He sat on the chair; he was tired; it had been a long night.

The two main uses of the semicolon are

1. to separate independent clauses in a compound sentence; and

2. to separate items in a list, particularly if the items are long and unwieldy enough that commas won't quite do it.

In *The Medusa and the Snail: More Notes of a Biology Watcher* (1979), the doctor Lewis Thomas wrote:

> *The things I like best in T. S. Eliot's poetry, especially in the* Four Quartets, *are the semicolons. You cannot hear them, but they are there, laying out the connections between the images and the ideas. Sometimes you get a glimpse of a semicolon coming, a few lines farther on, and it is like climbing a steep path through woods and seeing a wooden bench just at a bend in the road ahead, a place where you can expect to sit for a moment, catching your breath.*

It's a mark that divides writers like no other, though. "Do not use semicolons," wrote Kurt Vonnegut. "They are transvestite hermaphrodites representing absolutely nothing. All they do is show you've been to college." George Orwell—another enemy of pretentiousness—took so strongly against semicolons that he made a point of writing *Coming Up for Air* without using a single one. But then, a little poignantly, he wrote to his publisher to boast about it because—we can presume—he was worried that nobody would notice.

On the other hand the Czech writer Milan Kundera, whose side I take in this, wrote in 1988: "I once left a publisher for the sole reason that he tried to change my semicolons to periods."

The Dash

There are, for the ordinary user, two main sorts of dash:

1. The em bar or em dash (which was originally the width of the letter *M* on a printer's block): —

2. The en dash (which was the width of an *N*): –

The dash, as they used to say about absinthe, *rend fou*.* Depending on your word-processing package, your nationality, and the time of day, the rules about dashes will vary. The em dash and en dash are often in free variation.

A dash can do the work of a colon, a semicolon, or a comma— essentially, marking off a pause or introducing (with a bit more emphasis) the coordinator in a compound sentence.

Compare:

He went to the chemist, but they were out of pregnancy tests.

He went to the chemist—but they were out of pregnancy tests.

---

* Absinthe makes you mad.

write to the point

The latter, with that slightly more dramatic pause, makes the case seem a little bit more urgent.

Unlike commas or semicolons, however, they can't be used in a limitless series.* You'll find either one of them, or a pair, in any given sentence.

Paired dashes work to mark out parentheses or interpolations. I recognize in myself—because you end up noticing these things—an addiction to them. They seem to me to occupy a role somewhere between the comma and the bracket proper in this case: a little more swashbuckling than the bracket in terms of maintaining the conversational flow of the sentence; a little more emphatic (and, potentially, less confusing) than the comma. The material included between two dashes is slightly more likely to be important to the meaning of the sentence than material between brackets—an addition or qualification rather than an optional extra.

There are some qualifications to their use in this role: You can't use a pair of dashes to separate out part of a word or an entire sentence, as you can with brackets.

Book(s) may not be removed from the library.

He looked sheepish when he came in. (I didn't know that he'd removed some books from the library.)

Try punctuating either of those with paired dashes and see where you get.

Other punctuation marks don't always play nicely with dashes. If a stronger punctuation mark such as a period finds itself next to a dash, for instance, it will likely absorb the dash. So some single-dash sentences are in effect parentheses whose second dash has been gobbled up by a period.

---

* This wasn't true three hundred years ago. They were bastards for dashes in the eighteenth century. As I said: Punctuation style changes.

We should play some Pixies songs at band practice—"Wave of Mutilation," for example.

If that were in brackets, they would close:

We should play some Pixies songs at band practice ("Wave of Mutilation," for example).

Likewise, if the parenthetical phrase were brought forward it would earn a second dash.

We should play some Pixies songs—"Wave of Mutilation," for example—at band practice.

That's what I mean about hungry periods. Poor dash!
Dashes are also used to mark interrupted dialogue.*

"They couldn't hit an elephant from this dist—" was the last thing the general said as he surveyed the enemy guns.

The Hyphen

This cousin of the dash deserves separate treatment because where the dash has a function in the syntax of the sentence, the hyphen is involved with the guts of the words themselves. What *Fowler* calls the "stretchingly difficult subject of hyphenation" is stretchy for two reasons. One is that in the hyphen's main use—linking the elements in compound words—there's huge variation in practice, and it changes fast. The other is that the hyphen has two seemingly opposite jobs: It pushes things together, but it also separates them. (In this, if in nothing else, it is the Wonderbra of punctuation.)

---

* Dialogue that just trails off rather than being interrupted is usually indicated by an ellipsis.

In its most common use, the hyphen indicates that a word or a series of words (or word fragments such as prefixes) have been glued together to form a single expression. It's a favorite of cowboys. Hence:

You no-good, low-down, double-dealing, back-biting, flea-bitten, two-timing, double-crossing, two-bit, polecat-bothering, anti-feminist son-of-a-bitch.

Roughly speaking, the more common the compound's usage, the more likely it is that the hyphen will disappear altogether. You might very well see "backbiting" and "doublecrossing" written as one word; "polecatbothering," not so much. There's considerable variation transatlantically, too. The disappearance of the hyphen is especially common (for the same reason) when it's used to attach prefixes. "Anti-matter," "re-invigorate," and "de-regulate" are all now more likely to appear hyphen-free than otherwise. "Antidisestablishmentarianism," one word with two prefixes, has been proudly hyphen-free ever since, when I was a lad, it took its place in my collection of long words.

But—and here's where the separating function of the hyphen comes in—you should retain or even insert a hyphen when leaving it out makes a word tricky to parse or pronounce. So though "coterminous" is seldom seen with a hyphen, "co-op" is seldom seen without one—because the reader's brain naturally pounces on something to do with chickens. Likewise, a hyphen is useful when you want to "re-cover" your sofa rather than "recover" from a bout of the flu. If your compound word looks odd because it doubles up a vowel or a consonant, a hyphen can help, too. Hence: "anti-intellectual" rather than "antiintellectual," or "sword-dance" rather than "sworddance."

It's also worth keeping an eye out for the way in which a hyphen can resolve ambiguities. A "man-eating fish" is much more alarming than a "man eating fish." "Two-hundred-year-old books," "two hundred-year-old books," and "two hundred year-old books" will all fetch rather different prices at auction. "Twenty-two odd socks" and "twenty-two-odd socks" are different propositions: The first would embarrass a football team but keep their feet warm; the second might all match but could leave the star striker with nothing on one of his feet. After years of listening to the formulaic way in which nightly bulletins on the BBC World Service came to a close, Anthony Burgess wrote a novel called *The End of the World News*. Ghost hyphens.

A peculiarity of compounding hyphenation is that—particularly when you're dealing with phrasal adjectives—syntax makes a difference. If the phrase is being used attributively—i.e., before the noun—you are more likely to hyphenate; if it's being used predicatively, you are less so. This is often the case because the attributive version crunches a phrase containing different parts of speech into a single compound adjective.

So:

The storm was fast approaching

becomes

The fast-approaching storm.

In the first instance, "fast" is an adverb modifying the participle "approaching"; in the second, both of them have combined to become an adjective: "Fast-approaching" is, in effect, a single word.

I should offer a caution about the vexing question of adverb-participle combos. There's a widespread presumption against hyphenating this sort of phrase where the adverb ends in -*ly*.

So:

The widely admired society hostess

rather than

The widely-admired society hostess.

But the rule is not absolute, and you'll see it flouted—to the extent that I'd call it more of a tendency than a rule. For a start, it defies all reason that *-ly* words should have their own special category. Why should a "well-upholstered chair" have a hyphen but a "badly upholstered chair" not? You'd expect a lack of horsehair, not a lack of punctuation.

The one thing that most authorities do seem to agree on is that when you're using such a phrase predicatively, i.e., after the thing it qualifies, you definitely don't hyphenate. You might get away with "a clumsily-punctuated essay"; but "your essay was clumsily-punctuated" will strike most readers as, well, clumsy. Here, as above, the attributive version can be argued to make a one-thought adjective from a more straightforward verb phrase. If that doesn't feel entirely reassuring, I apologize—but better honestly to mark a minefield than to send your troops through it at the double in a straight line.

The so-called "suspended hyphen" is the one you use when you're linking two or more compounds that share a base word. It's easier instanced than described: "Nineteenth-century and twentieth-century oratory" becomes "nineteenth- and twentieth-century oratory." The suspended hyphen can introduce a precise distinction of meaning. My proofreader's pencil hovered, recently, over the phrase "drink-and-drug-addled Afrikaners." Did the author mean "drink- and drug-addled Afrikaners"? I decided not: He was describing not two groups with separate addlements but one group addled by both drink and drugs.

Quite aside from their compounding role, hyphens are also used to indicate when a word is broken over two lines of text.

Happily, arguments about where you should break the word (whether according to morphological structure or pronunciation), for ordinary users, are all but redundant; your word processor will do it for you.

If you're not sure whether to use a hyphen, Google can be your friend, not because it will give you a definitive answer but because it might give you a sense of whether one usage is prevalent over another. Hyphenation in this case is a matter of trying to get a sense of where the language is at the moment. If you're trying to write plainly you should go for the usage that is least likely to detain the reader by sticking out. That means finding the least controversial one.

The Apostrophe

An apostrophe does two main things.

1. It indicates possession.

- ◆ Singular possessives take 's: "the pope's nose"; "Jane's Addiction."

- ◆ Plural possessives ending in s take ': "the dogs' kennel" (if you have more than one dog); "the workers' canteen" (if you have more than one worker).

- ◆ Irregular plural possessives, where the plural doesn't end in s, also take 's: "the children's book"; "the Women's Equality Party."

- ◆ A school of thought has it that certain proper names ending in s can take a bare apostrophe for the possessive: "Jesus' teachings"; "Moses' law." Personally, I don't see the point: "Jesus's teachings" and "Moses's law" are perfectly well-formed and don't open the possibility (silly though it might be on the face of it) that we have a number of people called Jesu or Mose going about teaching or laying down the law.

♦ Pluralizing family names seems to cause people all sorts of trouble, too. Let us say, for the sake of argument, that you have two neighbors: Mr. and Mrs. Park on one side, and Mr. and Mrs. Parks on the other. Over the fence to one side is "the Parks' garden"; over the fence to the other is "the Parkses' garden." It's a useful distinction to have and I see no reason to ignore it.

♦ When possession is, as it were, shared by more than one noun, the apostrophe gloms onto the last in the series: "burger and fries' delicious aroma"; "Rod, Jane, and Freddy's unorthodox lifestyle choice."

♦ It's possible to construct instances that force you into a confoundingly awkward construction. If you are talking about the nave of St. Peter's Church, say, logic asks you to write "St. Peter's's nave." Common sense tells you to recast the sentence to avoid it.

♦ Possessive pronouns follow their own rules. The possessive of "it" is "its," of "her" "hers," of "him" "his," and of "us" "ours." None of them use apostrophes. Think of them as preformed units.

♦ Proper nouns and brand names follow no kind of rules at all. As David Crystal has pointed out, on the London Underground you can travel from Earl's Court to Barons Court in one stop—and Harrods, Selfridges, Lloyds, and Waterstones have all dropped their apostrophes over the years. You just have to treat them as proper nouns.

What the apostrophe, famously, does not do is indicate that something is in the plural. The so-called greengrocer's apostrophe, as mentioned previously, is the most notorious instance and is a great nourishment to the outrage of sticklers.

The sole exception I can think of is the (admittedly) ungainly use of the apostrophe when counting numbers of lowercase letters of the alphabet. "There are four *i*'s, four *s*'s, and two *p*'s in 'Mississippi'" is awkward, but the alternative—"There are four *i*s, four *s*s, and two *p*s in 'Mississippi'"—is even worse.

2. It indicates where a letter or letters are missing.

These are constructions such as "I'm" for "I am" or "you've" for "you have"; or, ubiquitously, *'s* for "is," as in "the game's afoot." This is very common in informal writing and less so in the more formal kind. So when deciding whether to use these contractions, keep in mind the register you're aiming at.

These contractions can indicate more than one thing. "He'd" can stand for "he would" or "he had"; "he's" can stand for "he is" or "he has." Context will establish which one is meant, and, indeed, govern whether the contraction is possible at all. As with hyphenation, the language adapts, and some contractions lose their apostrophes as they become established as words in their own right. We no longer—unless we want to sound particularly prissy—talk about "the 'cello" (originally contracted from "violoncello"). And there are regular irregulars such as "won't" for "will not."

A good few words and set phrases, though many slightly archaic, come with apostrophes built in. They follow the same logic of the apostrophe marking omission. "Ne'er-do-well" for one who "never does well," "fo'c'sle" for "forecastle," "fish 'n' chips" for "fish and chips."

Brackets and Their Friends

1. ROUND BRACKETS (PARENTHESES)

Round brackets, first of all, mark out parentheses.* That is their day job. They hunt in pairs and they isolate material from the rest of the text around them, usually adding information that is incidental to the main meaning of the sentence. A very simple instance is:

The cat (Henry) sat on the mat.

The material in parentheses can be as short as a word fragment, or as long as a self-contained sentence.

   i. They decided to (re)consider my proposal.

   ii. I took the essential equipment (curling tongs, rubber gloves, a length of rope, and a banjolele) for the job.

   iii. I had hoped that my lawyer would get me off on appeal (he was a graduate of a distinguished law school) but my hopes were disappointed.

   iv. There was nothing in the food cupboard when we got to the cottage. (The previous visitors must have cleaned it out.)

The material in brackets can share the grammar of the main sentence, but doesn't have to.

---

* NB: When they say "brackets" Brits usually mean round brackets, and Americans usually mean square brackets. Americans call round brackets "parentheses." Happily, what those marks actually do is the same on both sides of the Atlantic. In the present book I am aiming to reserve the terms "parenthesis" and "parentheses" not for any specific punctuation marks but for the held-apart-from-the-main-text material that goes into them.

Therefore:

*He threw the bathwater (and the baby in it) away. (the "baby"
in brackets is the object of "threw")*

Or:

*He threw the bathwater (there was still a baby in it) away.
(the bit in brackets is an independent clause)*

So the parenthetical material may or may not borrow grammatically from the sentence around it. The same freedom isn't available when you reverse things. Whatever the material in brackets may be, and whatever form it takes, the sentence around it *must* be fully grammatical and self-contained in meaning without it. "The cat (and the dog) are sitting on the mat" doesn't work because if you take out the material in brackets you're left with a singular subject and a plural verb. You can't write: "The cat are sitting on the mat."

According to the same logic, punctuation belonging to the main sentence remains outside the brackets. So:

*If Freddy had only turned up (he didn't), we would have had
enough people to play bridge.*

*The bouncers warned us that if we didn't leave the dance floor
we would be thrown out of the club (even though we'd done
nothing wrong).*

You can see, in *iii* on page 105, how an independent clause or sentence can be included in another sentence. In *iv*, you can see how a self-contained sentence can be placed in parenthesis within a paragraph. Note how in the latter case you punctuate the bit in brackets as a stand-alone sentence, with a capital letter at one end and a period at the other. In the former, though, it has neither a period nor a capital letter. If it's incorporated in another sentence, a parenthesis will never end in a period. So you would never write: "I had hoped that my lawyer would get me off on appeal (he was a graduate of a distinguished law school.) but my hopes were disappointed." Ellipsis dots, question marks, and exclamation points are acceptable, though. For example: "I had hoped that my lawyer would get me off on appeal (he was a graduate of a distinguished law school!) but my hopes were disappointed." Or: "I had hoped that my lawyer would get me off on appeal (wasn't he a graduate of a distinguished law school?) but my hopes were disappointed."

You'll seldom find more than one or two sentences at most inside parentheses. The limits on working memory, as discussed earlier, make a sentence with a long multi-clause sentence buried inside it very tricky to parse. Your brain notes the open bracket, and is then forced to hold its breath until it meets the closing bracket and it can get on with working out the meaning of the main sentence. So if you have a lot of material in brackets, it's always worth thinking about whether it can be better incorporated into the main text—either as a separate sentence or as two.

So to give one of my earlier examples a longer parenthesis:

> *I had hoped that my lawyer would get me off on appeal (he was a graduate of a distinguished law school, having been summa cum laude at Harvard Law School in a year that included many who went on to become appeals court judges) but my hopes were disappointed.*

That's just a mess. If your parenthesis is that long, you need to unpack it somehow.

> *I had hoped that my lawyer would get me off on appeal. After all, he did graduate summa cum laude from Harvard*

Law School in a year that included many who went on to be
appeals court judges. But my hopes were disappointed.

Or:

I had a good lawyer: He graduated summa cum laude from
Harvard Law School in a year that included many who went
on to be appeals court judges. So I had hoped he would get me
off on appeal. No such luck.

Brackets can nest inside other brackets.

Lycidas *was written by one of the greatest of the English*
poets (John Milton (1608–74), who also wrote Paradise Lost
(1667) and Paradise Regained *(1671)).*

That's usually fine if the brackets-within-brackets are something as simple as the odd date. It's generally regarded as bad style to do too much of that sort of thing, though. Your sentence will end up looking more like a mathematical formula than a chunk of English prose.

There are no fixed rules about how you present brackets-within-brackets. Not doing so is the best solution. If you absolutely have to—and you usually don't—square or even curly brackets can be used for the inner parentheses, to make the hierarchy of nesting clearer. But, as I seem to have said more than once, avoiding brackets-within-brackets is a service to your reader.

Round brackets also have a number of other conventional uses. They enclose dates of publication for books or birth and death for humans, as above. They add supplementary information in some formal contexts: "Bernie Sanders (D-Vermont)." They explain acronyms at first use: "FBI (Federal Bureau of Investigation)." And they can be used to indicate where a single word or phrase has been translated: "The *aficionado* (enthusiast) will go weekly to the *corrida* (bullfight)."

Singly, brackets can be used to tabulate numbered or lettered items in a list.

Well, it's

1) for the money

2) for the show

3) to get ready.

Now go, cat, go . . .

2. SQUARE BRACKETS

Except when they're being used, as mentioned above, in brackets-within-brackets, square brackets are used mostly for editorial interpolations. They indicate where a piece of quoted text has been amended or removed.

Here, for instance, is what Sir John Chilcot, a British civil servant, said in setting out the scope of his inquiry into the Iraq War.

Our terms of reference are very broad, but the essential points, as set out by the prime minister and agreed by the House of Commons, are that this is an inquiry by a committee of Privy Counsellors. It will consider the period from the summer of 2001 to the end of July 2009, embracing the run-up to the conflict in Iraq, including the way decisions were made and actions taken, to establish, as accurately as possible, what happened and to identify the lessons that can be learned. Those lessons will help ensure that, if we face similar situations in future, the government of the day is best

equipped to respond to those situations in the most effective
manner in the best interests of the country.

If you were quoting that in an essay or newspaper report, you would use square brackets with an ellipsis to indicate any material that doesn't belong to the speaker, or that has been cut in the course of quotation. So you might end up with something like the following:

Sir John said that "[his inquiry's] terms of reference are
very broad [. . .] It will consider the period from the summer
of 2001 to the end of July 2009." He added that "[t]hose les-
sons will help ensure [. . .] the government of the day is best
equipped to respond to those situations in the most effective
manner."

The first bracketed phrase is one that the person quoting has put in for clarity. It is not Sir John's. "Sir John said that 'our terms of reference are very broad'" would be awkward—his "our," integrated into the grammar of the journalist's sentence, implicitly includes the reporter in Sir John's first-person plural.

The second bracketed phrase—an ellipsis—indicates that between "broad" and "It" is some material that is not included in the quotation.

The third bracketed bit—perhaps more fastidious than ordinary journalism asks for; you'd probably simply put "those" outside the quote marks—is indicating that the uppercase T in "those" (it was originally the beginning of a sentence) has been made lowercase by the reporter to integrate it into his sentence, which is structured as a piece of indirect speech. (You wouldn't want to write: "He added that 'Those lessons will help . . .'")

The fourth bracketed bit marks another elision. The "[. . .]" stands for the chunk of text that reads: "that, if we face similar situations in future,." This square-brackets-ellipsis use is particularly important. Even if what's missing is a series of self-contained sentences, to be academically or journalistically scrupulous you need to indicate that text is missing.

Square brackets are also the best way of making clear that editorial commentary or information added to gloss a reference is separate from the text.

> *Frank Castle [the violent vigilante known as "The Punisher"] told the court that he considered it had been a "mistake" to leave [gangland boss] Ma Gnucci alive.*

If you're quoting somebody who has made a spelling mistake or used a word eccentrically, it's customary to write "[*sic*]" afterward to indicate that the usage isn't a transcription error. "*Sic*" gets italicized; the square brackets do not: "The Cranberries have a song on their second album called 'Yeat's [*sic*] Grave.'"

If you're kinder, you might simply use square brackets to amend it. You couldn't do that to the title of a song—the Cranberries are doomed, I'm afraid—but:

> *He wrote: "We're pouring [*sic*] over the report's proposals."*

could also be rendered as follows to avoid the suggestion of a sneer.

> *He wrote: "We're [poring] over the report's proposals."*

3. ANGLE BRACKETS (OR CHEVRONS) AND CURLY BRACKETS

Neither of these have any regular use in English prose. They have various specialized functions in mathematics, musical notation, manuscript scholarship, and computer programming. They need not detain us.

Quotation Marks

Quotation marks are, most simply, used to indicate direct speech or quoted material from written text. Here they are in P. G. Wodehouse's *My Man Jeeves*.

"What ho!" I said.

"What ho!" said Motty.

"What ho! What ho!"

"What ho! What ho! What ho!"

After that it seemed rather difficult to go on with the conversation.

In the UK whether you use single quotation marks ('What ho!') or double quotation marks ("What ho!") is a matter of house style or, in correspondence, personal preference. What matters above all is to be consistent. In US English, I gather from my wise editor, it's virtually always double quotes: " rather than '. But specialist usages vary so check your stylebook.

Like brackets, quotation marks move around in pairs. And as with brackets, it's possible to nest one set inside another—and, theoretically, to go on doing so. But unlike with brackets it is a rule rather than an option to use a different punctuation mark to indicate one quote nesting inside another. If you are generally using double quotes for speech, as is customary in American English, then you use single quotes for speech-inside-speech.

I asked Mary what had happened. "He threw the custard pie at me, and then he shouted, 'Take that, bandy-legs!'" she sobbed.

And vice versa.

> *I asked Mary what had happened. 'He threw the custard pie at me, and then he shouted, "Take that, bandy-legs!"' she sobbed.*

If you do end up with a quotation-within-a-quotation-within-a-quotation, or even a quotation-within-a-quotation-within-a-quotation-within-a-quotation, convention has it that you alternate single and double quotes with each layer of the onion. For the reader's ease and your own sanity, though, you don't want to go too far down that route.

One resource you have available, particularly if your main quotation is a long one, is block quotation. This is where you separate the quoted text from the introductory material not with quote marks but by indenting it. This at least allows you to get a quotation-within-a-quotation-within-a-quotation (a commoner situation than you might think) without the awkwardness of using more than one pair of single or double quotation marks each.

Block quotation, in fact, is an attractive option when you have a long passage to quote, even if you don't have difficulties with nested quotes within it. It sets the quoted passage clearly and easily out from the rest of the text, removes a layer of punctuation, and gives the reader a breathing space. That is why I've indented many of the examples I'm using here. Whether you italicize a block quote, whether you set it in a different typeface or type size, and the amount of space you leave around it are questions of house style or preference. Just be consistent about it.

As a rule, in anything approaching a formal context, you should be scrupulous in making sure that anything you place between quotation marks *exactly* reproduces the original quote. That means not just the right words in the right order and unexpurgated, but the same tense and parts of speech, the same capitalization, and the same implied reference to anything outside the quotes. News-papers, particularly in headlines, frequently bend this rule, to the annoyance of those they quote and to the confusion of the general public.

You have a choice between quoting as direct speech and quot-ing as reported, or indirect, speech. The distinction I'm making is a grammatical one to do with the sentences that frame the quoted material (the quoted material is always direct speech in and of itself).

Compare:

He said: "I'm tired." (direct speech)

He said he was "tired." (reported speech—his words are folded into your grammar)

The grammar of quoted material, where it's incorporated into the flow of a sentence as indirect speech, needs to accord with the sentence as a whole. Let's say you're quoting General Patton's speech to the Third Army as he prepared to roll up the Nazis at the end of the Second World War.

I don't want any messages saying, "I'm holding my position." We're not holding a goddamned thing. We're advancing con-stantly and we're not interested in holding anything except the enemy's balls. We're going to hold him by his balls and we're going to kick him in the ass; twist his balls and kick the living shit out of him all the time. Our plan of operation is to advance and keep on advancing. We're going to go through the enemy like shit through a tin horn.

You might write:

General Patton said his troops were "going to hold [the enemy] by his balls and [. . .] kick him in the ass."

The first set of square brackets, there, are to ensure that the quote's grammar fits in with the grammar of the sentence as a whole without falsifying it. Without them, you'd be left either altering the quote or producing something as awkward as this:

General Patton said his troops were "going to hold him by his balls and we're going to kick him in the ass."

The problem with that is that the reader doesn't know who "him" refers to, and that "we" puts the quote in the first person plural, which clashes with the third-person framing of it ("his troops" being the subject of the reported speech).

So if you wanted to avoid fussy square brackets, you could revert to direct speech.

General Patton said: "We're advancing constantly and we're not interested in holding anything except the enemy's balls. We're going to hold him by his balls and we're going to kick him in the ass."

Using a colon (or a comma) to introduce a quote and letting the quote stand on its own as direct speech does solve that tricky problem of integrating the grammar. But it also means that often you'll be forced to use a large and unwieldy chunk of text (so that it's grammatical on its own), and you'll have less chance to direct your reader to the important parts.

Very often you'll want to quote only one or two words from something. That almost always means using reported speech. If someone delivers a dull and rambling forty-six-word sentence at his wedding in which he describes it as "the best night ever," economy will often askyoutosaysomethinglike, "Hedescribeditas 'thebestnightever,'" ratherthanquotingthewholeshebangatlength. That'swhythegrammar-integration rule is important to understand.

As well as punctuating direct quotation, quote marks can be used to make clear you're introducing a new or unfamiliar term. For instance:

The fancy word for an invented word is "neologism."

You can also use quote marks to make clear that a particular usage or form of words (rather than, say, the specific words of a particular individual) is being used but not necessarily adopted by the author. It's a way, in other words, of preserving the author's neutrality.

Yesterday marked the opening day of "the greatest show on earth."

We're seeing the first legislative efforts to make "compassionate conservatism" a reality.

As an extension or distortion of that function, quote marks are sometimes used to indicate active skepticism, sarcasm, or a certain archness of tone. In that role they're sometimes called "scare quotes." These are the on-the-page equivalent of making rabbit ears in the air with your fingers when saying something you consider distasteful or absurd.

My nephew had me drive him to a "rave party." I had the misfortune before I left to see him start "dancing."

The homeopath I met at the party was very keen on "alternative medicine."

These should be used with great caution. Scare quotes—particularly applied to relatively well-established usages—more often than not make the author seem sneering or fuddy-duddy. They signal skepticism or distaste without arguing clearly and honestly for it, and they can make it look as if you're having your cake and eating it: simultaneously saying something and disowning it. That said, they can also be used by good writers for comic effect. The late Auberon Waugh, in the hopes of annoying socialists, always used to refer to "the 'working' classes."

Quotation marks are also sometimes used to add emphasis, particularly in amateur signwriting. This is, if you ask me, as close to downright erroneous as you are likely to get. Certainly, it's bad style in standard written English—and it annoys people enough that some of them have even set up a blog (unnecessaryquotes.com) on the subject. Recent instances include:

Check out our selection of "NEW" Vermont cheeses to enjoy with your wine.

"ESCAPE ROPE" "EMERGENCY USE" "ONLY."

We have plenty of ways to add emphasis as it is. Depending on context you could go for **bold**, *italics*, <u>underlining</u>, or even, if you must, BLOCK CAPITALS. Quotation marks do something different.

Something that I've (I hope) exemplified and certainly implied, but not yet discussed, is the other trickiness with quotation marks. That is: How do they get on with the nearby punctuation?

For the most part, the rules hold: Only material that belongs to the original quote goes between the quote marks, and that includes punctuation. For example:

"I'm ruined!" he wailed.

The exclamation point belongs to the direct speech, and so remains inside the quote marks.

An exception is that when punctuating speech—particularly when the sentence begins with a direct quote—it's conventional to use a comma inside the first closing set of punctuation marks.

"We're ready," he declared, "to take on every last one of them."

Logic seems to suggest that that should read:

"We're ready", he declared, "to take on every last one of them."

But in that format it does not. For what it's worth, my reading of this rule is that—since the "he declared" bit is, as it were, inserted into the middle of a complete sentence in quotes—it operates a bit like a parenthesis. It's in enemy territory: The main structure of the sentence belongs to the quoted material.

As often, there's no absolutely consistent rule that can be applied. If we're going to be strict about it, for instance, we could consider variations on the following phrase:

"Is he an idiot?" asked Dave.

"He's an idiot!" said Dave.

"He's an idiot," repeated Dave.

In the first two of Dave's expostulations, the punctuation is his own. In the third, Dave's sentence ended with a period; but it has been replaced with a comma. Yet nobody writes:

"He's an idiot." said Dave.

It gets worse. One of the major differences between US usage and UK usage is that in the UK, when a period or a comma (this does not apply to other punctuation marks, nor to the example of direct speech—"We're ready," he declared—mentioned above) finds itself next door to a quotation mark (i.e., a quotation ends a phrase or sentence), it remains outside. In the US, the rule is the other way around. So in the UK, you'd write:

> *In her book on what she calls 'guerrilla hairdressing', Leslie writes that it's 'perfectly possible to style an asymmetric bob with garden shears'.*

A US copy editor would change that to the following:

> *In her book on what she calls "guerrilla hairdressing," Leslie writes that it's "perfectly possible to style an asymmetric bob with garden shears."*

Even some American writers, such as Steven Pinker, and international organizations, such as Wikipedia, deplore the illogicality of this. Geoffrey Pullum has spoken wistfully of launching a Campaign for Typographical Freedom ("a huge rally will take place at the Lincoln Memorial in Washington D.C.").

But as far as things stand, Americans are stuck with this. And Brits have plenty of illogicalities to be going along with in any case.

The Slash

"What's O. J. Simpson's email address?" children used to joke in the early days of the internet. "Slash slash backslash escape." Not really very funny; nobody's email address looked like that even back then. That said, the backslash (\) does have a use in computer programming—and nowhere much else.

The common (or garden) slash, aside from its various technical applications, occurs in a number of set phrases in ordinary English. It usually stands in for "or" or "and" or "-*cum*-" or "per." Hence "he/she" or "and/or" in the first case; "Lowell/Berryman/Roethke generation" in the second; "kitchen/diner" or "live/workspace" in the third; and "$45/week" in the fourth.

It's also sometimes used to indicate the difference between a numerator and a denominator in a fraction ("5/6"), or to indicate a period spanning more than one year: "the 2015/16 tax year." It's handy, too, for punctuating line breaks in poetry or song if you're not setting them as block text, as in this Philip Larkin example, from "This Be the Verse": "They fuck you up, your mum and dad. / They may not mean to, but they do." Use a double slash for stanza breaks.

Outside these specific, usually abbreviative, functions, you won't find much call for it in continuous prose. And even in those uses, it has a slightly technical flavor; where you can unpack it into something more prosy, you're well advised to do so.

Bullet Points

These are less a punctuation mark than a layout convention. My discussion of "enumeratio" in "Using the Figures" should cover them.

The Hashtag

This is a form of punctuation that mostly belongs where it's most popular: on social media. On Twitter, Instagram, and other similar sites, you'll find it used either to mark a contribution to a particular debate or a common thread.

@KFC the Double Down kicks ass ##doubledown #newmenu

Or, as a development of this use, to mark a comment.

@KFC just had a Double Down #greasy #wheresthebread #wtaf

The Ampersand

This mark stands for "and" in various informal or iconographic situations. Its shape originates from a highly stylized cursive rendering of the Latin word *et,* and its name is a contraction of "and per se and" (which is how children in the nineteenth century, when it was the twenty-seventh letter of the alphabet, concluded the recitation of their ABCs: "*x, y, z,* and per se [by itself] and").

It's strictly a logogram (a character representing a word) rather than a punctuation mark. Business names may contain an ampersand, for instance: "Barnes & Noble" or "Marks & Spencer." They appear in certain compressed set phrases: "R&B" or "B&B." They are used by academics in citations for papers or books with more than one author, e.g., "quoted in Huddleston & Pullum (2002)."

Some poets are attached to them, too. John Berryman wrote: "Sick at 6 & sick again at 9 / was Henry's gloomy Monday morning oh." They are handy for keeping within the word limit in a tweet or fitting a newspaper headline into the available space. But ampersands don't have a role in day-to-day prose of a more or less formal kind.

The Smiley and Other Emoticons

Is a smiley even a punctuation mark? That is a matter for scholars. Emoticons and emoji don't have any function that I can make out in coordinating the grammar of a written sentence. However, they do offer a wonderfully subtle and various set of modal glosses (or, in less fancy terms, indications of tone) to the English words they accompany—which gives them at least a nodding relationship to marks such as the question mark or exclamation point. For instance, O_o seems to me to convey brilliantly that the preceding words are accompanied by the sort of hard stare pioneered by Paddington Bear.

They've been going for about thirty-five years—the original smiley being credited to Scott Fahlman, a computer scientist at Carnegie Mellon University, who suggested in 1982 that humorous posts on the departmental message board should be marked with a sideways smiley face :-) to indicate that they were jokes. It caught on.

Now, huge sets of premade emoticons (these premade cartoon sorts are the ones usually referred to as "emoji") are available to anybody with a smartphone. I have a soft spot for the old, homemade type, built from punctuation and other keyboard characters, however. Researching a piece on the subject a few years back, I came across d8= ("Your pet beaver is wearing goggles and a hard hat"), %\v ("Picasso"), and >-ii-< iiii ("Go fetch mother. A giant crab is attacking the penguins"). The existence on my phone's keyboard of a Walnut Whip–style cartoon dog poo with boggly eyes doesn't strike me as a great improvement on these, but heigh-ho. Emojipedia.org has a pretty good list of what's out there, along with "translations," for the curious.

The grammar of emoji, such as it is, seems to specify that more often than not they come after the message that they comment on or expand on. "It's my birthday!" is usually followed by the little row of thumbs-up signs, cakes, jugs of ale, and popping champagne corks rather than preceded by it. Likewise, "I've been dumped" is likely to come before the broken-heart icon, but need not always.

Nor, come to that, do they automatically need to gloss written text. Sometimes they can stand alone in reacting to it—which is more or less what Facebook formalized when in 2015 it augmented its "like" button with six emoji representing "love," "yay," "haha," "wow," "sad," and "angry." Many people find it fun—and intellectually testing, in a crossword-puzzle kind of way—to conduct entire conversations in emoji. In July 2016 a restaurant in West London published its menu in emoji form, which will, depending on your disposition, strike you as either a total riot or a hitherto unnoticed horseman of the apocalypse.

They are advisable only in informal communication: text messages, tweets, and occasionally email. They are likely to remain so, whatever the fears of those who imagine these things will soon be popping up in university essays. In part, they participate in the realm of what linguists call "phatic communication";* they tell you what sort of conversation you're having, i.e., the sort in which people use emoji. And those conversations remind us that our semiotic resources, of which standard English is just one, are gloriously bountiful, constantly enriched, and contribute to our gaiety as well as to our understanding of the world.

---

* See "Audience Awareness, or, Baiting the Hook" for a fuller discussion of this.

5

Sentence Surgery: The Writer as Editor

When I was learning to drive, some twenty-five-odd years ago, I had a driving instructor called Tony Agate. Mr. Agate—or "Old Agate," as he called himself—was a philosophical fellow. His small, diesel-powered Citroën smelled gently of the many cigarettes he smoked and of the powerful mints he sucked in the vain hopes of concealing his smoking from Mrs. Agate. Being an extremely slow pupil, I spent many hours in that car with Old Agate.

He had certain themes in his conversation—other than the predictable "Help!" and "Yikes!" and "We're both going to die!" One was the observation that there was "a lot of erraticism" in my driving. Was it something about the way I handled the gearshift? Anyway, I took it as a compliment.

The other was that even the best drivers have on days and off days. Sometimes, he'd say to me, shaking his head, "As I was driving over to your house this morning, I nearly hit another car. I thought: 'Agate: You should not be on the road this morning.' Anyway, mirror, signal, maneuver . . ."

What Agate said of driving is true of English prose. Everyone writes duff sentences or clumsy paragraphs. The main difference between a good writer and a bad one is that a good writer writes bad sentences less often. It's a matter of keeping your batting average up and your erraticism down.

In my day job as a literary journalist I'm occasionally asked to judge book prizes. In the judging meetings for such things, one of the easiest and cheapest ways to shoot down a book is to cherry-pick a handful of inept or cliché sentences, and read them out from your notes in a tone of scorn or, better, solicitous regret. There are few if any books of eighty thousand words that won't furnish a big enough handful to make this possible. Unless a very large-spirited defense is mounted by the other judges—who will by now be on the back foot, reluctant to look as if their ear for the language is defective—that will usually do the trick.

As with driving, the two things that make a difference are getting as much practice as possible, and paying proper attention to what you are doing. The first is a service to yourself; the second is a service to your readers. If you can avoid lighting a cigarette and/ or unwrapping a mint while overtaking on the approach to an off-ramp, so much the better.

I don't doubt that an attentive reader of this book will find many howlers, clunkers, and places in which I contradict my own advice. Filleting style guides for contradictions or mistakes is part of the fun. I mean this acknowledgment to serve as encouragement rather than otherwise: You'll never get it right all the time, and nor will anybody else.

One of the ways to keep your erraticism under control is to go back and edit yourself. Reading aloud, as I've said before, can help you identify awkward bits. Simple rules of thumb, too, can help. Are any of these sentences crazily long? Are the subject and verb clear—and, all other things being equal, are they close to each other and close to the start of the sentence?

There are two main ways in which sentences get out of hand.

Parataxis—*para* meaning "alongside" in Greek—is a way of forming sentences by adding extra bits on with conjunctions such as "and" or "but." A paratactic sentence is built like a string of sausages.

The cat, but not the pig and the duck or the chicken, came into the room and looked around to see what would be the best place to sit, then circled it three times, kneaded the mat in the middle with its paws, and sat down on the mat.

Parataxis makes a mouthful, but it's fairly easily dealt with: You just cut the sentence up into different sentences. In the above, for instance, the subject ("cat") has five verbs to get through—"came," "looked," "circled," "kneaded," and only then finally "sat."

The cat came into the room. The pig, duck, and chicken stayed outside. The cat looked for a good spot. It circled the mat three times, kneaded it with its paws, and sat down.

Hypotaxis is a hierarchical construction. Your main clause becomes the kernel of a sort of Russian doll, and the central meaning gets swamped by subordinate clauses.

The cat, which is to say an individual of the species— originally descended from Felis silvestris—Felis catus, in this case a blue-furred Persian four years of age whose eyes gleamed red gold in the light from the lamp in the corner, sat, being by this stage tired of standing up, on the mat which was in the middle of the floor of the room.

These can be trickier to unpack. You need to decide, when you split the sentence up, what comes first. So you could do it like this:

The cat sat on the mat in the middle of the room. Cats are of the species Felis catus. They are descended from Felis silvestris. This one was a four-year-old Persian with blue fur. Its eyes gleamed red gold in the light from the lamp in the corner.

Now, depending on what you want to emphasize you could parcel those thoughts up differently. Is the cat's position on the mat what you want up front? Or is it the individual cat's looks? Or are you introducing a lecture on feline genetics? You'll slice and dice it differently each time. But my original version has forty words between subject and verb; that's a huge problem for the reader.

You also want to keep an eye on parentheses—brackets or dashes and whatnot—because they interrupt the flow of a sentence. I had a teacher who insisted you should never use them at all. I think that's nonsense. But when you're rereading yourself and you find one, always at least run through the exercise of seeing if you can dispense with it or put it in another sentence.

In this section I want to look at some sentences or paragraphs that present problems to the reader, and talk through how as an editor I might go about tackling them. All of them are by people writing in a professional context, and most of them are by professional writers. Many of the edits I make are tentative: They are one possibility among many. But as I said in an earlier chapter, the plain style is what everything else builds on. You need to be able to strip even the most complex sentence down like a gun and lay its parts on the table—see what does what, and which parts need oil—before you reassemble it.

The discussions may look dauntingly long by comparison with the texts that prompt them. But that's exactly what I mean when I say that paying *attention*—close attention—is the way to get to the heart of how a bit of prose is working. And if my style seems informal, that's also a deliberate decision; I want this to be as close as possible to a seminar-room conversation. I'm trying to talk to you, to follow a process of thought. And the careful editor is, or should be, alive to the different possibilities any given sentence offers. You can be precise about your ambiguities.

Pomposo Furioso

The Plain English Campaign likes to give prizes each year to particularly hopeless pieces of gibberish. One of these coveted awards went, in 2012, to the following announcement from the UK's National Health Service Litigation Authority.

> *The Committee concluded, having regard to the totality of the factors considered above that choice could not be given significant weight and that there was not currently a gap on the spectrum of adequacy sufficient to conclude that the provision of pharmaceutical services is not currently secured to the standard of adequacy. Accordingly the Committee concluded: The application was neither necessary nor expedient to secure the adequate provision of services in the neighborhood, and therefore dismissed the appeal in this respect.*

In case it's not instantly clear, they were rejecting an application to open a pharmacy.

Let's look at the first sentence. There's a missing comma after "above," by the way—the phrase "having regard to the totality of the factors considered above" is in parenthesis. As ever, the first task is to identify the spine of the sentence. The subject and the main verb are right up front: "the committee" and "concluded." It's exemplary for those first three words—though "we decided" would have been more direct. What did the committee conclude? We have to wait until after that swamp of a parenthesis to find out.

The parenthesis is a mess in two respects. One is that it's full of cotton-wool officialese: "Having regard to" is a pompous way of saying "in light of" or "considering"; and "the totality of" is a pompous way of saying "all." The other is the *way* in which those phrases get so cotton-woolly. They add a level of abstraction. The first nominalizes the verb "regard"—forcing the phrase's emphasis onto the all-purpose auxiliary verb "having" rather than the operative word, "regarding." The second turns the nice straight-forward determiner "all" into an abstract noun. And by "the factors considered above," we can assume the writer meant the evidence that had been presented and discussed earlier in the same document. You could recast the first thirteen words of that sentence as follows:

In light of this evidence, we decided . . .

Or:

We looked at the evidence and decided . . .

Decided what? That "choice could not be given significant weight." That's a clumsy way of saying, or implying, that choice is one of the things that was considered in making the decision but that it did not carry the day. Again, here is the tug toward abstraction: a passive construction ("could not be given") coupled with another tricky expression ("given weight"), where the verb is weakly shoring up this abstract idea of weight. And do we care? If "choice" isn't "significant" we could, arguably, leave the whole phrase out.

So to the second half of the sentence. Here is, or rather isn't, another missing comma—this time after "weight." Inserting a comma here—though not a grammatical necessity—would be a kindness to the reader. As originally published we have a fifty-two-word sentence with a single punctuation mark to navigate by. And God knows you need a rest before tackling what comes next.

and that there was not currently a gap on the spectrum of adequacy sufficient to conclude that the provision of phar-maceutical services is not currently secured to the standard of adequacy.

By the time we hit that period we've had "conclude," "adequacy," and "currently" twice each in a single sentence, swirled in with a double negative: "not . . . not." Every chance to turn out an abstract noun phrase, or tack one onto a verb, is taken—"a gap on the spectrum of adequacy"; "the provision of pharmaceutical services"; "is [. . .] secured to the standard of adequacy" . . . All this acts on the poor reader like chaff on a radar operator.

If you puzzle it out, it's saying—I paraphrase as clearly as I can, but even in paraphrase it's a mess—that *there's not enough of a lack of pharmacies in the area to conclude that there aren't enough pharmacies in the area.*

Hold that thought. Now look at the second sentence.

Accordingly the Committee concluded: The application was neither necessary nor expedient to secure the adequate provision of services in the neighborhood, and therefore dismissed the appeal in this respect.

Both ends of that are redundant. "Accordingly" and "in this respect" are pure verbal throat clearing; you could substitute "so" or "therefore" for "accordingly" if you wanted, but there's no special need. Again, we've heard twice what the committee concluded, or didn't. The whole *idea* of the document is to tell us what the committee concluded. So that can be taken as read. And—give us strength— here come "adequate," "provision," and "services" yet again, bolted together in a fresh and equally brain-frying combination—along with the innovation of the grand-sounding syntheton* "neither necessary nor expedient." Boiled down, it says: "There's no need for another pharmacy in the area. They have hemorrhoid cream, Epsom salts, and adult diapers coming out of their damn ears. Couldn't you just open an IHOP instead?"

* Fancy term for using a pair of words together for effect.

So you could recast those eighty-one words, without great loss, to say something like:

> *We looked at the evidence and decided that the neighborhood has enough pharmacies. We rejected the appeal.*

That isn't to say that this is the only way of doing it. You could cast it in the third person—"The committee concluded"—if that's the style. But if you can get hold of what you actually mean in the simplest terms possible, and keep hold of it, you're much less likely to get lost in the woods.

The Academic Repeater

Not long ago, I was sent to review a biography of a well-known novelist by a literary academic, and one bit struck me. It ran as follows:

> *Experimental writing, by its nature, always needed an established cultural behemoth against which to pit itself and this obsession with reaction and reinvention has enabled modernists to obfuscate embarrassing inconveniences such as the essential quality of a prose passage. If the emphasis is upon the dynamic remaking of literary models then the notion of good or bad writing can be dismissed as contingent and relative. Pure modernism is among other things an escape route for the stylistically untalented or aesthetically apathetic. If you are concerned exclusively with eschewing conventional writing then the pure demonstration of radicalism sidelines any attendance upon questions of whether a sentence or paragraph is elegantly crafted.*

Leaving aside its slightly rococo phrasing—does one pit oneself against a behemoth?—that first sentence isn't too hard to understand. Modernists are pitting themselves against the establishment, and the obsession with reinvention means they can ignore "the essential quality" of their prose.* Roughly, it's saying that experimental writers get so hell-bent on writing *differently*, that they stop paying attention to whether they're writing *well*.

The second sentence, too, isn't that hard to understand: If the emphasis is on the "remaking of literary models," says our author, "the notion of good or bad writing can be dismissed." In other words, experimental writers get so hell-bent on writing *differently*, that they stop paying attention to whether they're writing *well*.

The third sentence says that "pure modernism"—i.e., an experimental interest in disrupting established forms—is a get-out for the "stylistically untalented." Or, as you could put it: Experimental writers get so hell-bent on writing *differently*, that they stop paying attention to whether they're writing *well*.

The fourth sentence argues that if you are "concerned exclusively with eschewing conventional writing"—pitting yourself against a behemoth, you might say—you don't have to worry too much whether "a sentence or paragraph is elegantly crafted." Which is as much as to say . . . but I see you're ahead of me here.

As the Talking Heads put it: "Say something once, why say it again?" When you're rereading your work, keep an eye out for this. It can afflict even well-regarded professional writers. If two or more consecutive sentences express *exactly* the same thought, you're publishing a draft rather than a finished piece. You need to turn them into one sentence that will express in a crystalline manner what you're getting at. And the clearer those sentences are in the first place—no behemoth-pitting, if you please—the easier it will be to notice that they're dancing around the same maypole.

---

* This is the highbrow version, perhaps, of the 1970s idea that if you were punk enough, it didn't matter whether you actually knew how to sing or play your instruments.

The Confuser

Here's a sentence—from an otherwise respectable and interesting recent literary biography—that I had to read three or four times before I even began to understand it. See how you get on.

> *And because portraying the disappointment of expectations required him to draw on his own experience to imagine how those expectations would feel to those who held them, the shuttling back and forth between expectation and disappointment, between belief and its betrayal, or simply between different points of view in turn animated the characters he created, pulling them into relief by virtue of the difference between their views and those of their counterparts.*

As ever: Where's the subject? In this case it is a noun cleverly camouflaged as a verb: "the shuttling." This is a gerund—a noun made of a verb in its present participle form. In this case it is embedded in a colossal appositive fugue: "the shuttling back and forth between expectation and disappointment, between belief and its betrayal, or simply between different points of view." What did that "shuttling back and forth," etc. do? It "animated." "Animated" is the main verb. And "the characters" is the object. Main clause, stripped bare:

> *The shuttling animated the characters.*

Before we even get that main clause, though, we have to fight through the long subordinate clause that sets it up: "Because portraying the disappointment of expectations required him to draw on his own experience to imagine how those expectations would feel to those who held them." The moment we hear "because" we're hanging in the air: Because all this . . . then what? That could be simplified and made into a main clause. For example:

He had to draw on his own experience to understand how
others would feel about their disappointments.

That could be a sentence in itself, or—to maintain the linkage the
original sets up with "because"—the first part of a compound sentence. Instead of "because" dangling at the front, you could put ", so . . ."

He had to draw on his own experience to understand how oth-
ers would feel about their disappointments, so the shuttling
back and forth between expectation and disappointment,
between belief and its betrayal, or simply between different
points of view in turn animated the characters he created.

But that's still unwieldy; you still have the problem of that huge
chunk of material between the shuttling and the animating. In
effect, the subject of the verb "animated" is that whole section.

Here is a good example of where the passive voice might actually make life easier. By using the passive, you can make the second
part of the sentence right-branching.

He had to draw on his own experience to understand how
others would feel about their disappointments, so the charac-
ters he created were animated by the shuttling back and forth
between expectation and disappointment, between belief
and its betrayal, or simply between different points of view . . .

It's not perfect—it's still what a teenager might call a fugly, fugly
piece of writing—but it's much better.

Still, we have the loose caboose to address. The original sentence ends:

, pulling them into relief by virtue of the difference between
their views and those of their counterparts.

In flipping "characters" forward in the sentence, I've solved one problem and created another: Where does this bit now fit in? You could keep it in place, and make it passive—"and were pulled into relief"—but the reader will still be struggling. So why not make it a new sentence? "They were pulled into relief by virtue of the difference between their views and those of their counterparts."

So the whole thing would read:

> *He had to draw on his own experience to understand how others would feel about their disappointments, so the characters he created were animated by the shuttling back and forth between expectation and disappointment, between belief and its betrayal, or simply between different points of view. They were pulled into relief by virtue of the difference between their views and those of their counterparts.*

That is a pretty rough cut. But grammatically it is much easier for the reader to parse. It keeps the subjects and verbs in each main clause up front and in natural order to help guide the reader through the sentence. "He had to draw . . . the characters were animated . . . they were pulled."

You might object that the sense is still a little obscure. Does it follow that the involvement of the author's own experience creates this shuttling? Are we talking about a shuttling between the points of view of different characters, or between the expectations and disappointments within each character? Does it follow from this shuttling that the characters' counterparts—i.e., other characters—are what pull the characters into relief, or is it their own multiplicity of perspectives?

I suspect that the author of the passage is himself a little confused. Here, then, is the point famously made by George Orwell: Clear writing is a fantastic solvent for muddied thought. It's not just that if you can't think clearly you can't write clearly: It's that if you can't write clearly you won't even know if you're thinking clearly.

The Monster

Now here's a sentence that is actually not bad—or not accidentally bad. But, being about two-thirds as long as the Gettysburg Address, it's certainly a candidate for the editor's pencil. I owe this one to its author's son, my old newspaper friend Tom Utley.

When Tom was a child, his twelve-year-old sister had been told for her homework to write a very long sentence. She asked their father, the blind journalist T. E. Utley. In Tom's account of it, T. E. "took a deep pull on his cigarette, thought for about three seconds, and began to dictate. The sentence that he uttered was so sensationally long—and so gloriously unfit for passing off as a twelve-year-old's homework—that my siblings and I set ourselves the challenge of committing it to memory. It has stayed in my head ever since."

Here it is:

> *The factors that bind a society together, whether that society be large or small, whether it be a nation or a school, are multifarious and complex, not easily to be defined, nor succinctly to be expressed in any code of conduct or profession of faith, but exerting their cohesive force in subtle and silent ways; yet, strong as these factors may be, which make for the spontaneous coordination of will and effort—which is in some measure the mark of all societies, but which is in particular the glorious mark of a free society—they can never be so strong as to dispense with those penal sanctions against the vandal, the thief, the sworn enemy of society itself, which are part of the normal apparatus of civil government and the absence of which signifies not a lofty regard for freedom, as is commonly supposed by "progressives," but a*

contemptible indifference to the conditions and limitations
that alone make freedom possible.

How on earth is one to break that down? As ever, start with the spine of the sentence: the main clause. The subject presents itself straight away: "The factors." There follows a good deal of mellifluous modifying material—"that bind a society together, whether that society be large or small, whether it be a nation or a school"—before we meet the verb "are" and its predicate "multifarious and complex."

The material that comes after is essentially polystyrene packing expanding on the other qualities of these factors. It's the reader's choice as to whether difficulty of definition, succinct expression, etc. are qualities *in addition to* (making it part of a list) or *constitutive of* that multifariousness and complexity, i.e., presented in apposition to it. The semicolon after "ways" marks off the first half of this compound sentence from the second. We'll cross that semicolon when we come to it.

If we wanted to simplify the sentence, we now have the means to do so. We know what the core of the statement is: "The factors that bind a society . . . are multifarious and complex." As it stands, that's more abstract than necessary: "Are" as the main verb is weaker than "bind"; "multifarious and complex" has a certain airy grandeur. There's less magniloquence—but not much less precision—in writing:

Many different factors bind a society.

Can you prune any of the various qualifying clauses? You could probably red-pencil "whether that society be large or small" altogether; it swells the cadence but adds nothing to the meaning. Unless the author is planning to tell us that medium-sized societies work completely differently, he doesn't really need to reassure us that what he says applies to both large and small societies; "a society" stands as a general statement until we hear otherwise.

The red pencil hovers over "whether it be a nation or a school," too. If it's considered essential in context to make clear that you're using "society" in a broader sense than tribe or nation-state, though, it has a role in the sentence.

Many different factors bind a society, be it a nation or a school.

The clauses piled on the back end of that thought ("not easily to be defined, nor succinctly to be expressed in any code of conduct or profession of faith, but exerting their cohesive force in subtle and silent ways") can pretty easily be relegated to a separate sentence or two themselves. And why not make those sentences indicative?

They are not easy to define or simple to express in a creed or code of conduct. They work subtly and silently.

Now—deep breath—let's tiptoe past the semicolon into the even more bloviating second half of that sentence. Where's the main clause? If you strip off all the dependent clauses before and after, it's this:

They [these factors again] can never be so strong as to dispense with those penal sanctions...

The basic meaning of the whole sentence, in paraphrase, is: "More things cause societies to hang together than can be summed up on the back of an envelope, but however strong these things are you still need laws."

But between the dread semicolon and the subject of the main clause, we have a parenthesis, nested in a parenthesis, nested in a parenthesis, nested in a parenthesis. Hypotaxis gone bananas. To make it (a bit) clearer, I've put each parenthesis on a new line.

yet,
strong as these factors may be
which make for the spontaneous coordination of will and
> *effort*
which is in some measure the mark of all societies
but which is in particular the glorious mark of a free society
they can never . . .

Stylistically this sentence flows rather marvelously. Utley had a fine ear for cadence. Considering its pretty exacting grammar, it's much easier to parse than The Confuser. But it's still tricky. So strip the gun.

The straightforward thing to do would, again, be to break it into smaller sentences. Remember: This whole monster sentence is governed by its subject, "the factors." So you could say, without stripping the thought down too far:

They make for the spontaneous coordination of will and effort that is the mark of all societies, and in particular the glorious mark of a free society.

Then you're back in business—at least temporarily. But parenthesis ahoy.

Yet,
strong as these factors may be, they can never be so strong
as to dispense with those penal sanctions against the vandal,
> *the thief, the sworn enemy of society itself,*
which are part of the normal apparatus of civil government
and the absence of which signifies not a lofty regard for
> *freedom,*
as is commonly supposed by "progressives,"

but a contemptible indifference to the conditions and limitations that alone make freedom possible.

Again, each line takes us further into a nested subclause. So let's apply the same un-nesting process, break the thoughts into smaller sentences, and put the main idea up front.

Yet strong as these factors may be, they can never be so strong as to dispense with penal sanctions against the vandal, the thief, the sworn enemy of society itself. These sanctions are part of the normal apparatus of civil government. "Progressives" think their absence signifies a lofty regard for freedom; in fact, it shows a contemptible indifference to the conditions and limitations that make freedom possible.

That's a light edit. I'm trying to preserve Utley's own idioms. You could go further into the plain style.

However strong these factors are, they can never be strong enough for a society to do without laws. Punishments for criminals are a normal part of civil government. "Progressives" think not having them shows regard for freedom; actually, it shows contempt for the rules that make freedom possible.

But, as ever, the editor's task is to think about tone of voice and decorum. Utley's orotundity is deliberately fitted to the grandeur of his subject.* It's possible to oversimplify a piece of writing. We've all had the experience of walking away from a haircut wishing we hadn't been quite so blithely categorical in asking for something "much shorter." So I prefer a middle path—one that preserves some

---

* Also, the need for his daughter to have a ludicrously long sentence for her homework; and, in the same context, a good joke.

of Utley's rhetorical flourishes and most of his language, while making his meaning more digestible.

Many different factors bind a society, be it a nation or a school. They are not easy to define or simple to express in a creed or code of conduct. They work subtly and silently. These factors make for the spontaneous coordination of will and effort that is the mark of all societies, and in particular the glorious mark of a free society. Yet strong as they may be, they can never be so strong as to dispense with penal sanctions against the vandal, the thief, the sworn enemy of society itself. These sanctions are part of the normal apparatus of civil government. "Progressives" think their absence signifies a lofty regard for freedom; in fact, it shows a contemptible indifference to the conditions and limitations that make freedom possible.

The Interrupter

I've warned often in these pages about the difficulty of parsing a sentence where subject and verb—or, sometimes, verb and object—get separated. This can be a problem—but is not always the only concern. You need to consider the sentence's relationship to those on either side of it, the emphasis given to different parts of the sentence itself, and its rhythm. So these calls are often marginal. The way to get them right is, if you have time, to tinker about and see what works. Here's one I stumbled over while proofreading a book review.

Whether Wilson's thesis—that the 1850s marked the advent of modernity—entirely stands up is debatable.

There's a bit of a clunk, there. Here you have a fifteen-syllable parenthesis—"that the 1850s marked the advent of modernity"—interrupting a sixteen-syllable main clause. The problem is that this huge parenthesis, though manageable, is spliced into the middle of the subject of the sentence, which is the conditional clause "Whether Wilson's thesis entirely stands up."

You might think—and your reading brain probably does think—that the main verb of the sentence is "stands up." It isn't. The main verb is "is," but the houselights are coming up on the sentence before your brain cottons on to that.

One way of doing it would be to give the sentence a more natural word order.

It's debatable whether Wilson's thesis—that the 1850s marked the advent of modernity—entirely stands up.

Here at least you get subject and verb in the first syllable. But you still have that great parenthesis stuffed into the middle. And the problem is that you can't put it anywhere else in a single-sentence version; it *has* to be next to the word ("thesis") that it explains.

So it might be kinder to the reader to lop the parenthesis out altogether and splice it into two different sentences. Thus, a light edit might be:

Wilson's thesis is that the 1850s marked the advent of modernity. Whether it entirely stands up is debatable.

Perhaps you object to the author's weakness for nouny circumlocutions and impersonal constructions ("Wilson's thesis is"; "the advent of"; "it is debatable that"). So a heavier edit might be:

Wilson argues that modernity began in the 1850s. I don't think he's right.

But here we are altering not only the author's style but the emphasis of what he is saying. In the original he's not actually saying the thesis is wrong, but that it's debatable—mealymouthed, admittedly, but a different thing. He isn't interpolating himself into it—which may be an evasion, but it's the author's own evasion. And even in my lightly edited version, which is more or less in the author's own words, we've changed the emphasis. In the original sentence the main point was the debatability, not the substance of the thesis.

In the end? I let the sentence go to print as was. Was that the right decision? You tell me. When you're editing you have a duty not only to make life easy for the reader, but to honor the author's precise meaning and the author's own voice (both of which are duties to the reader as well as to the author). All of these, I repeat, are stylistic judgment calls—and you make them when editing yourself as much as you do when editing the work of others.

6

Bells and Whistles: Bringing Things to Life

In 1897, Joseph Conrad wrote: "My task which I am trying to achieve is, by the power of the written word, to make you hear, to make you feel—it is, before all, to make you *see*."

This is something to aim for in all sorts of writing. What distinguishes Conrad's three goals is that they seek to bring writing as close as possible to the world it describes. Here, laid plain, is the root of the familiar style-guide injunctions to prefer the concrete to the abstract.

As I've discussed, even when you read silently you are activating parts of your brain associated with sound and vision. Language reaches deftly into the abstract—but it does so from concrete, embodied roots in sounds and images. It also, as any number of business communications manuals testify, does so most compellingly when it's rooted in a narrative. People respond to images and stories. They respond to things that give a human face to abstract ideas or large movements.

When politicians talk about the structural reform of large bureaucracies, for instance, or the virtues of state versus private provision of services—they invariably do so through case studies. In his first speech to a joint session of Congress, President Trump drew his audience's attention to the presence among them of Megan Crowley, a young woman who had survived a potentially fatal disease. President Trump sketched in the story of her father's fight to get her the medical care she needed, and used her example to introduce his desire to deregulate the Food and Drug Administration: "Our slow and burdensome approval process [...] keeps too many advances, like the one that saved Megan's life, from reaching those in need."

In writing, you are often seeking a Megan Crowley. The case might not always be so emotive. But something general will almost always be most effectively expressed if it's rooted in the particular, in what's sometimes called "lived experience."

STORYTELLING

Steve Jobs's 2005 commencement address at Stanford University has had a viral afterlife on the internet. He began it this way:

> *Today I want to tell you three stories from my life. That's it. No big deal. Just three stories.*

"I want to tell you a story." Instantly, our ears prick up. Why is storytelling so effective? In the first place, it offers a purchase for human sympathy or identification. When we hear of a little girl waiting for an operation, or of a frog kissed by a princess, we insert ourselves into the story. We imagine what it's like to be that little girl, or her parents; we are that frog, or that princess. Identification is the heart of persuasion.

Also, simply, we want to know what happens next. A story is an attention-getting strategy. If we see a rifle hanging on the wall in chapter one, as Chekhov said, "in the second or third chapter it absolutely must go off." The moment you introduce that glimpse of the rifle, you have your audience. If you describe someone in peril, or on the horns of a dilemma, the audience wants to know how the situation will resolve itself. How does the damsel escape from the railway tracks? Which suitor will the princess choose?

There's a larger point, too. Stories are a way of giving shape to experience. They imply order and causation. In life, things often happen at random. In stories, they tend to happen for a reason. A reader can be confident that if Harry Potter dies, it'll be as part of a dramatically satisfying face-off with Lord Voldemort rather than because he trips over a loose paving stone a quarter of the way through book four, tumbles into a well, and breaks his stupid neck. The closing scene of *Easy Rider*—in which some random pickup drivers we've never seen before simply blow the protagonists away and drive off—is a deliberately shocking challenge to our expectations of narrative.

Nicola Barker's novel *The Yips* puts it well. One character asks another what her philosophy is. "No philosophy," she replies. "No guidance. No structure. No pay-off. No real consequences. Just stuff and then more stuff."

"Stuff?" the first character asks.

"Yeah, stuff. Like, here's some stuff, here's some other stuff, here's some more stuff. Just stuff—more and more stuff, different kinds of stuff which is really only the same stuff but in different colors and with different names; stuff stacked up on top of itself in these huge, messy piles . . ."

Those huge messy piles are real life. Stories are a way of ordering them. And in a persuasive situation, a well-told story can borrow the promise of order implicit in the very idea of narrative. If the man who opened the tomb of Tutankhamen dies six months later of blood poisoning, the instinct is to find a connection between the two things. Narrative logic asks us to do so—rather, say, than to draw the soberer conclusion that archaeological success and septicemia are unrelated issues.

Literary theorists may bicker over the distinction between an anecdote and a parable, or between realism and allegory. But readers tend to have a muzzier sense of it. If someone tells us a story we'll naturally look for ways in which the shape of that story is archetypal, reflecting a pattern of experience or a larger meaning. As Dale Carnegie put it, "The great truths of the world have often been couched in fascinating stories."

Jobs's three stories—one of them about "connecting the dots," one about "love and loss," and one about "death"—were all expressly archetypal; he presented the stories about himself as stories about all of us.* So, again, stories are a way of establishing ethos: a common identity. The American scholar Brené Brown has called stories "data with a soul."

PAINTING PICTURES

The ancients used the term *enargia* to describe the way in which a speaker or writer builds a visual or sensual image out of words. Here is a close—sometimes a kissing—cousin of the storytelling instinct. Your readers will invest in the story you tell, or the scene you describe, if the details seem to make it tangible. Those details will be sensory—not only the look of something but the taste, the feel, the smell of a scene.

One example should suffice. In his address to a Democratic rally in Durham, New Hampshire, on the eve of the 2016 presidential election, Barack Obama told a story about his own presidential run in 2008. The story told how in the hopes of securing an endorsement, he had promised to visit the small town of Greenwood, South Carolina. He had been campaigning all over the country. He arrived in South Carolina at midnight and reached the hotel at around one in the morning. He was exhausted. But just as he went to bed an aide tapped him on the shoulder and reminded him—he'd forgotten—that he had to be up at six in the morning to drive to Greenwood.

---

* Practically every TED talk these days begins with some version of Jobs's formula. "Let me tell you a story . . ." In *Talk Like TED* (2014), Carmine Gallo estimates that the civil rights lawyer Bryan Stevenson, who won the longest standing ovation in TED's history, spent 65 percent of his talk telling stories.

Obama described waking up the next morning.

I feel terrible. I'm exhausted. Think I'm coming down with a cold. I open up the curtains. It's pouring down rain outside. Pouring down rain. Horrible day. I make myself some coffee and I get the newspaper outside my door and open it up. There's a bad story about me in The New York Times. *I get dressed, shave, walk out, just kinda still groggy, still staggering. My umbrella blows open—that ever happen to you?—as I'm walking out. I get soaked. Soaked! I'm just—soaked...*

Of course, this is a spoken rather than a written enargia. Many of its features—the present-tense narration, the repetitions, the hand gestures and facial expressions—are peculiar to its effect as speech. But the principle holds. The audience doesn't, on a logical level, need to know about his coffee, his shave, the newspaper. They don't need to know he had a cold eight years ago, or that the weather that day was bad. But they are drawn in—"that ever happen to you?" makes it explicit. The story feels real. It's available to inhabit. You know what that scene is like, and—the vital bit—you identify with the speaker. You're going with him to Greenwood that day—and when you get there you will be more invested in the story he went on to tell about an inspiring campaign volunteer whose energy helped to get a weary Obama back in the game.

METAPHOR, SIMILE, AND ANALOGY

Putting one thing in another's place—a word for a thing—is the very essence of language. So metaphor, which does that at the level of the image or idea, is something we respond to naturally.

An analogy can add something other than vividness, though. It can render unfamiliar arguments in familiar terms, and abstract ones in concrete terms. The late Douglas Adams, author of *The Hitchhiker's Guide to the Galaxy*, came up with a good example.

As a firm atheist, he wanted to argue against the apparently commonsensical arguments of believers in "intelligent design." Their case is that human beings are so perfectly adapted to their environment, and the world around us so complex and interdependent, that it must have been designed that way. He offered the following analogy:

> *This is rather as if you imagine a puddle waking up one morning and thinking, "This is an interesting world I find myself in—an interesting hole I find myself in—fits me rather neatly, doesn't it? In fact it fits me staggeringly well. It must have been made to have me in it!"*

Here's something that, in the first place, is funny. Making your audience laugh is a way of hot-wiring their goodwill. But also it takes a complicated and rather airy argument about intentionality and gives it an absurdist twist. Adams not only mocks the pride implicit in the intelligent design argument—offering the attractively humble notion that humans should be considered as no more special than a puddle of water—but he implies that there's topsy-turvy thinking behind it. Why should we assume, because we're well fitted to our surroundings, that the surroundings have been arranged to suit us rather than vice versa?

The abstractions of high finance are likewise susceptible. The veteran investor Warren Buffett, talking about the ebullience of markets in unproven tech stocks and complex artificial financial instruments, supposedly offered the excellently aphoristic: "Only when the tide goes out do you discover who's been swimming naked."

Metaphor and analogy are particularly useful—indeed, when it comes to the abstractions of advanced physics or mathematics, essential—to science writers. As Carlo Rovelli writes: "Science begins with a vision. Scientific thought is fed by the capacity to 'see' things differently." Very few of us can master the equations that underpin the general theory of relativity—but we can apprehend the curvature of space-time when we transpose four dimensions into three. A heavy ball sits on a trampoline; roll a Ping-Pong ball past it and the curvature of the trampoline's surface will affect the path the lighter ball takes. There's gravity for you.

And there have been few more crisp evocations of chaos theory, time's arrow, and the second law of thermodynamics than Tom Stoppard's in *Arcadia*.

When you stir your rice pudding, Septimus, the spoonful of jam spreads itself round making red trails like the picture of a meteor in my astronomical atlas. But if you stir backward, the jam will not come together again. Indeed, the pudding does not notice and continues to turn pink just as before. Do you think this is odd?

Metaphor and analogy are powerful juju. But they should be used with caution, too. Godwin's law—that the longer an online discussion grows, the closer to certain it becomes that a comparison involving Nazism or Hitler will be made—provides only the most obvious instance of why. When you're comparing one thing with another, bear in mind that you bring into the comparison all of the penumbral associations of your comparator. That may not be a problem when your comparator is rice pudding. It will be more inflammatory when there's an ethical or personal dimension.

Saying that a government proposing a large program of public works to kick-start the economy has something in common with Hitler's Germany might be technically correct, but it will cause immediate offense. Hitler comes loaded with a whole wagon train of baggage—and it's hard to separate his sort-of Keynesianism from his immediate associations with megalomania, mass murder, open-air shouting, and stupid moustaches.

The problem with an analogy or a metaphor is that it is, necessarily, a falsification. When politicians talk about macroeconomics in terms of household budgets—as, for instance, Margaret Thatcher liked to—they present an attractive and easily comprehensible analogy. But, as proper economists explain, it doesn't work like that at all. The same goes for the case study or illustrative example. As science-minded people sometimes like to say, "The plural of anecdote is not data."*

So you'll want to pick your battles. But there's no question that the humanizing example, the memorable analogy, or the resonant story can do a lot of heavy lifting. In his poem "A Meditation on John Constable," Charles Tomlinson wrote: "The artist lies / For the improvement of truth. Believe him."

Cadence

Rhythm. A play of syllables and even sounds. I hear sounds in a sort of indescribable way as I write. —Don DeLillo

Even silent reading, both neuroscience and experience tell us, is an auditory experience. When we talk about cadence in prose we're talking about the equivalent of meter in poetry: the sounds of the words. When we say something is "well written," a very large part of that will be to do with how it sounds. Cadence is prose rhythm. And it's a hugely important aspect of writing, but it's also one of the hardest ones to discuss in a formal way.

Prose doesn't scan in the metronomic way that traditional verse does. The basic iambic beat of English verse is *de dum de dum*

---

* Actually, this saying bears closer scrutiny. In the strict sense, the plural of anecdote actually *is* data. A medical trial, essentially, aggregates tens of thousands of anecdotes about the health of individuals into (hopefully) a predictively accurate data set. Which is, oddly, what the author of the phrase originally said. The political scientist Ray Wolfinger said, "The plural of anecdote is data," and has been misquoted by smart-asses ever since. The singular of anecdote, however, is *certainly* not data.

de dum de dum de dum, and if you wrote like that in prose it would sound ridiculous. But prose does have its pauses and its rushes and its arpeggios. Punctuation, as I discussed in my chapter on the subject earlier, has its origins as a means of marking pauses in reading out loud—and that remains part of what it does.

So where you put the commas, where you break sentences, whether you use polysyllables or short words . . . all will have an effect on the ease and fluency of reading. A good writer doesn't just have a brain; he or she has an ear. The more you read and the more you write, the better that ear will get. A sentence will come to *feel* right.

But—as cannot be said too often—that ear needs training. Experienced composers can read music and "hear" the sounds in their heads. Experienced writers, likewise. But many, many very experienced writers still use a simple technique for, as it were, double-checking: They read what they have written out loud. If you have time to do so once you've completed a draft, you have nothing to lose and everything to gain.

An awkward separation of subject and verb, for instance, becomes particularly stark when read aloud; you'll find your voice holding off as your brain waits for the second shoe to drop. You may even find—if there are enough subordinate clauses getting in the way of the main event; if, as in this sentence, there's a great long digression separating the word "find" from the question of what it is that you're eventually going to find—that you run out of breath trying to get through the wretched thing.

Peggy Noonan, who wrote speeches for Ronald Reagan, has said: "Once you've finished a first draft of your speech . . . stand up and read it aloud. Where you falter, alter." That applies especially to speeches, of course: In that case you're trying to produce something that's hard to stumble over when spoken aloud. Tongue twisters such as "red lorry, yellow lorry" are easier on the page than in the mouth. But it is also good advice to the prose writer.

There is a developmental connection between reading aloud and reading silently—and there is a neurological one, too.

The way you shape sentences can slow things down or speed them up. Right-branching sentences, particularly short ones, make it easier—as we've noted—for the reader to skip through from one to another. But you can also, sometimes, use a subclause or a parenthesis as a way of holding off the end of a sentence—giving it an extra sense of authority and satisfaction when the final words come in to land.

Cadence is the main reason that many of the standard pieces of writers' advice will lead you astray if you follow them with mechanical uniformity. Yes, a right-branching sentence with the subject and verb up front is easier to parse. But if every sentence in your work is syntactically identical, the reader's brain hears it as monotonous—and switches off. There's no bounce, no elasticity, no sense of sentences flowing one to the other. Yes, you should aim to remove unnecessary words. But sometimes a word may have a rhythmic rather than a semantic value. Syntheton, where, again, you place two words or phrases alongside each other—"strength and fortitude"; "men and women"—adds to the gravity of a sentence or clause and often does not add much to its meaning. And yes, short sentences are easier to digest than long ones. But if all your sentences are short you will sound like a grade school reading primer.

Just as in the case of poetic rhythm and music, where the reading brain starts to get excited is in that sweet spot between predictability and variation. Order without variation is monotony; variation without order—without a pattern to test it against—is white noise. This makes sense: We are, by evolution, pattern-seeking animals. We are wired to derive general rules from the world around us, and then to see how our predictions hold up in particular circumstances.

So varying sentence structure and sentence length—not wildly, but enough to keep the reader's attention—is important. Sentences don't stand alone; like their author and their readers, they have a relationship with their neighbors. A piece of text should not be a list of independent assertions made in sequence. Prose aims to capture the movement of thought—and when we think, we hesitate, qualify, assert, digress, reemphasize. Using transitions from sentence to sentence—which may mean beginning a sentence with a conjunction; knock yourself out—helps to give pattern to your work. A perfectly constructed simple sentence of the subject-verb-object form might be ideal in one spot, or in isolation. But if it comes at the end of a run of six sentences taking the exact same form, it can kill the flow stone-dead.

Let's look, to see a really well-managed cadence, at one of the most celebrated sentences in the language. Here's the last line of George Eliot's novel *Middlemarch*, which describes the life of anonymous goodness that Eliot's heroine Dorothea would go on to lead after the reader leaves her.

> *But the effect of her being on those around her was incalculably diffusive: for the growing good of the world is partly dependent on unhistoric acts; and that things are not so ill with you and me as they might have been, is half owing to the number who lived faithfully a hidden life, and rest in unvisited tombs.*

It's a bit of a sentence to fight through. ("Her being," for instance, is a gerund, a verbal noun, meaning "her existence": That could cause a hiccup if you read "her being on those around her" as a participial phrase meaning "her having been on those around her," as if she were somehow riding her neighbors like horses.) Few people would risk such a long complex-compound sentence now, and on the read-aloud test it might flummox all but a circular breather. Yet it sends you away with a poignant sense of human interconnectedness and how a little life can fit in to the whole scope of history.

There's a lot going on there. It uses a time-shift—so, suddenly, we're leaving the thick of the novel's action and looking back on it as an event in history. The living Dorothea we met, and whose daily struggles we followed, is now a figure from the distant past—a tiny thread in the historical tapestry. There's that intimate and moving shift in register—from the ornate and even pompous-seeming "incalculably diffusive"* to the almost childlike "things are not so ill with you and me as they might have been."

But the real payoff is in large part a rhythmic effect: It's precisely because you battle through the bulk of the sentence that the dying fall of the last clause is so effective. It's a release. "And rest in unvisited tombs" is an unstressed syllable, followed by two dactyls, followed by a single stressed syllable with a long open vowel. "And REST in unVISited TOMBS": di DUM-diddy DUM-diddy DUM. That's almost identical in scansion—though it's a world apart in effect—to the last line of a limerick.† If I seem to be making too subtle a point, try rereading that sentence aloud, substituting "and who rest in tombs nobody visits" for the last clause. It means exactly the same thing. And it does not fricking work.

There are some obvious points to make. One of them is about register. Sometimes, particularly if you are writing a memo rather than the last line of one of the greatest novels in the language, you will want not to cultivate but to avoid the sort of cadence with which George Eliot ends *Middlemarch*. You don't always want to sound musical. You may look for a simple declarative tone and prose rhythms that march rather than dance. But whether poetic or more prosy, the rhythm is there—and it's worth attending to.

---

* Though, rhythmically, the feminine ending—stressed then unstressed—of "diffusive" opens that tightly knotted little phrase up.

† Limerick form can be pretty loose—but the *Middlemarch* rhythm is one of the commonest, cf. "That SIlly young MAN from BraZIL . . ." If the silly young man is from Kentucky, you'll find an extra unstressed syllable bolted onto the end.

To go from the sublime to the ridiculous, let's consider a more recent example. A review of mine of a biography of the bad-tempered academic A. L. Rowse ended with this sentence:

> *This clear-sighted book emerges as the portrait of a deeply unhappy man: an erratic if sometimes brilliant scholar; a gifted memoirist; an indifferent poet and a first-class prick.*

If that works, it's not because of the justness or otherwise of the judgments on Rowse's character. It's because of the cadence: It ends strong. After winding wordily and perhaps a little pompously through the catalog of his achievements, making careful distinctions in polysyllabic terms, it bangs home three stressed syllables in a row*—as well as leaving the register of quasi-academic evaluation for one of open insult.

Stressed syllables, especially in the closing words of a piece, matter to writers. In 2008, the *London Times* journalist Giles Coren lost his shizzle completely after one of his restaurant reviews was edited in a way he didn't like.† The angry email he sent to the copy editors he suspected of being responsible, unfortunately for him, leaked onto the open internet and made everybody laugh a lot.

The thing he was really cross about was an edit made to what journalists call the payoff: "It was the final sentence. Final sentences are very, very important. A piece builds to them, they are the little jingle that the reader takes with him into the weekend."‡

What Coren wrote was:

---

* That's technically called a "molossus."

† Losing his shizzle completely is one of the things that Coren is famous for.

‡ The comma splice in this sentence—see "Perils and Pitfalls"—may be passed over on the grounds that it appears in informal email communication—and that the author is so crazy with anger he's not thinking hard about his grammar.

I can't think of a nicer place to sit this spring over a glass of rosé and watch the boys and girls in the street outside smiling gaily to each other, and wondering where to go for a nosh.

What appeared in the magazine was:

I can't think of a nicer place to sit this spring over a glass of rosé and watch the boys and girls in the street outside smiling gaily to each other, and wondering where to go for nosh.

Spot the difference? Of course you did. They removed the word "a" in his last sentence. One thing that annoyed Coren was that it blew a very subtle dirty joke: "A nosh" has the secondary meaning of a blowjob, which "nosh" (as a bare noun) doesn't.

But the main thing that annoyed him was entirely to do with cadence. To quote his email:

And worst of all. Dumbest, deafest, shittest of all, you have removed the unstressed "a" so that the stress that should have fallen on "nosh" is lost, and my piece ends on an unstressed syllable. When you're winding up a piece of prose, meter is crucial. Can't you hear? Can't you hear that it is wrong? It's not fucking rocket science. It's fucking pre-GCSE* scansion. I have written 350 restaurant reviews for The Times *and I have never ended on an unstressed syllable. Fuck. fuck, fuck, fuck.*

There's plenty you can learn about cadence from even that little paragraph of (Coren's words) "anger, real steaming fucking anger." Look, for instance, at the punctuation of all those "fucks." He should have capitalized the antepenultimate "fuck," admittedly—again,

---

* Something like an SAT in the UK.

written in haste—but had he separated all four with commas the effect would have been quite different.

As it is we get one, stark, "Fuck." We get a beat pause from that period. Then—as if an illustration or development of the thought—we get a little fugal trio of "fucks." A tricolon of "fucks." The inner ear hears them rising in pitch and emphasis—either building back up to or surpassing the pitch of the first one. "Fuck. Fuck. Fuck. Fuck." wouldn't have worked at all: too regular and flat. Nor would the pedestrian "Fuck, fuck, fuck, fuck." That's like a shopping list of "fucks." Instead what we have is an almost perfect enactment in informal prose of Joe Pesci venting his rage with a baseball bat. He swings it once. Pauses. Then goes into a little frenzy: three strikes of increasing savagery as the floodgates of his anger open.

There is one teeny-weeny point that bears raising. It's that Coren is wrong, in this case, about unstressed syllables. "Nosh" is going to be a stressed syllable whether or not it is preceded by "a." Both versions of his sentence end in a stressed syllable; try pronouncing the second one without a stress on "nosh" and see where you get.*

But he's also right in two ways. The cadence of the sentence *is* altered, subtly, by the removal of that article. "Where to go for a nosh" lands the stress with a xylophonic exactness on "nosh"—"where to go for a NOSH": diddy-dum diddy-DUM. That's two anapests. "Where to go for nosh" is hardly barbaric—"diddy-dum di-dum"; an anapest and an iamb—but it's weaker. It is different. Not so different as, perhaps, to merit the savagery of his complaint. But different nonetheless.

* And as for never having ended on an unstressed syllable, well—the first restaurant review that came up when I searched his byline on the *Times*'s website just now ended with this sentence: "Although I dare say there is a pompous restaurant critic somewhere in central China at this very moment, chewing on a pissy mouthful of the stuff and picking up his pen to write the Chinese for 'correct' in his little notebook." If you can pronounce "notebook" with the stress on the second syllable rather than the first, I doff my cap to you.

And the second way he's right is that, yes, what he informally calls "meter"—formally, cadence—does matter. The difference between a sentence that really comes off and one that doesn't may be just below the level of consciousness—but that's where some of the profoundest work of prose is done.

Look again at George Eliot. Let us say that, as a copy editor, I decided to follow through on my experiment on page 155 and alter the last line of *Middlemarch* so it ended:

> *and that things are not so ill with you and me as they might have been is half owing to the number who lived faithfully a hidden life, and rest in tombs nobody visits.*

Not only do I very much doubt that it would have made its way into the *Oxford Dictionary of Quotations*, I would also be quite unsurprised (her having been dead for nearly 140 years aside) to receive a letter from George Eliot: "It's not fucking rocket science. It's fucking pre-GCSE scansion. I have written seven novels and I have never ended on an unstressed syllable.* Fuck. fuck, fuck, fuck."

If all this seems excessively finicky—if making a fuss about something that most readers won't notice consciously seems like a waste of your time—let's look at another example.

In the run-up to a 2014 UK referendum on Scottish independence, the UK's then shadow foreign secretary Douglas Alexander wrote a newspaper article making the case against Scotland's leaving the UK. Keen to make clear, as part of his ethos appeal, that he was not some high-handed English imperialist, he wrote:

> *I am Scottish by birth, by choice, and by aspiration.*

---

* Actually, the last lines of Eliot's novels are about half and half—stressed and unstressed. But she did have a belting way with a payoff.

That sounds good, doesn't it? But it means absolutely nothing at all. If you're Scottish by birth, by definition you have no choice about being Scottish. If you then say you're Scottish by choice, you contradict yourself: You can't be both. And then to say you're Scottish by aspiration—since you aspire to be something that you are not—is to say that you're not Scottish at all.

So this ringing phrase tells us at once that Mr. Alexander had no choice about being Scottish, that he chose to be Scottish, and that he is not Scottish but wishes that he were. And yet a grown-up politician wrote this rubbish and sent it to a newspaper, and a grown-up newspaper editor put it in the paper, and grown-up newspaper readers nodded their way through it without turning a hair. Why? Because it actually works fine; it works fine because it sounds good. In that sentence sound is doing the work of sense.

It's an example of the "tricolon crescens," or rising tricolon. Here are three terms in a row.* The "rising" part of that phrase describes a metrical effect: The third term ("by aspiration") has two more syllables in it than the previous terms ("by birth" and "by choice"). "Aspiration"—dum-di-DUM-dum—has a pleasing cadence that gives the sentence a feel of coming to a natural and dignified conclusion.†

They are placed syntactically and semantically in parallel—something reinforced by the redundant use of "by" in each case, which also serves to swell the sentence, making it sound that bit grander. So though they contradict each other logically, they fall on the reader's ear as if they are reinforcing each other.

---

* See "Using the Figures," opposite.

† If not quite a "rule," it's at least a strong guideline for successful rhythm that you should put the shortest term in any list first, and the longest last. This is the principle of "climax" underscoring the rising tricolon. "I am Scottish by aspiration, birth, and choice" has nothing of the drumroll about it. "I will be fishing for cod, bluefin tuna, the inedible but mighty basking shark, and the many-tentacled deep-sea octopus" just, somehow, tends to sound better than "I will be fishing for the many-tentacled deep-sea octopus, bluefin tuna, the inedible but mighty basking shark, and cod."

In effect, Douglas Alexander is simply congratulating himself three times over on being Scottish. The message—even if the words are saying the opposite—is that he's Scottish by good fortune, that he chooses to be Scottish, and that even if the first two things were not true he would still want to be Scottish.

So that's why cadence matters. It can do more than just reinforce the sense of a sentence; it can create an impression of sense where none actually exists. I'm not suggesting you seek to use cadence as a substitute for sense yourself, only that you don't underestimate how effective something subliminal can be.

Using the Figures

The phrase "a figure of speech" comes, originally, from the formal study of rhetoric. "Figure" is the name given to all the decorative twists of language and argument that help make a piece of text memorable or persuasive. When you talk about a person's "figure," you're describing that person's shape; and it's the same when you talk about figures in a text. Figures are ways of identifying structure in a piece of writing.

Over the centuries in which rhetoric was formally studied—and during which it was really the only tool kit we had for analyzing language*—hundreds and hundreds of figures were identified. Sometimes called the "flowers of rhetoric," these cover everything from the wider flow of an argument to the relationship between individual words in a sentence. They were, rather like flowers, given a number of Latin and Greek names—some overlapping—that sound abstruse to the modern ear.

I don't suggest that you need to commit dozens of them to memory. If you take a stamp collector's interest in the difference between "aposiopesis" and "anacoluthon," you do so with my entire

* This is before we had literary criticism in an academic sense, still less linguistics or anything much in the way of formal discussion of grammar.

approval—but the reason I want to discuss them here is to show how, whatever name you give them, the figures pervade even informal writing. If grammar structures your sentences for basic meaning, figuration puts an extra persuasive twist on them.

The figures can make the difference between something flat and structureless, and something tight and dynamic. Rather than asking your reader to make his or her own way across the muddy field of your prose, you can instead offer stepping-stones, signposts, memorable landmarks, and pleasantly maintained picnic areas. Thinking about structure doesn't end, in other words, once you've been through the basics of sentence surgery. Now comes the physiotherapy.

There follows a run-through of a handful of the basic figures. I'll give their proper Greek or Latin names, but these are far less important for the purposes of this book than seeing how they work.

BALANCING ACTS

A number of different figures concern ways of using the number two. They deal with how you place two objects, two ideas, two clauses, or two words in a relationship with each other. That relationship will sometimes involve logical opposition, sometimes rhythmic balance, and sometimes complementarity—and sometimes more than one of those things at once.

"Parallelism," say, is when you place two (or more) clauses side by side and give them a similar structure. "Lolita, light of my life, fire of my loins." "Apposition" is when two clauses are in grammatical balance together: "My girlfriend, the light of my life, dropped the toaster in my bath one morning after she found her birth certificate in my bottom drawer."

"Antithesis," or contrast, is one of the basic moves for structuring either a sentence or a whole piece of work: on the one hand, and on the other. You'll find it—giving a satisfying sense of balance—in a single sentence, but in certain types of writing it will govern the relationships between paragraphs or the basic seesawing motion of the entire argument. Take these two verses of the hymn "All Things Bright and Beautiful."

> *The rich man in his castle,*
> *The poor man at his gate,*
> *God made them, high or lowly,*
> *And ordered their estate. [. . .]*
> *The cold wind in the winter,*
> *The pleasant summer sun,*
> *The ripe fruits in the garden,*
> *He made them every one.*

The first two lines of each verse are offered as opposites; but in the literary and theological scheme of the hymn, they are also in parallel. We're being offered not either/or but both/and. The divine order of nature reconciles opposites—so that the social estates of man give both of the first pair a place, and the fruits in the garden give both of the second pair a purpose. The phrases in which they appear are structurally similar.

So terms in antithesis, in its broadest use, don't necessarily need to be mutually exclusive opposites—as in "give me liberty or give me death." What we're interested in here is the sense of balance, and that balance is as often to do with rhythm and syntactic structure as it is to do with the logic of what the phrases signify.

When he rejected the draft to fight in Vietnam, Muhammad Ali said:

> *Why should they ask me to put on a uniform and go ten thou-*
> *sand miles from home and drop bombs and bullets on brown*
> *people in Vietnam while so-called Negro people in Louis-*
> *ville are treated like dogs and denied simple human rights?*
> *[. . .] I will not disgrace my religion, my people, or myself by*

becoming a tool to enslave those who are fighting for their own justice, freedom, and equality.

The central antithesis in the first sentence is the contrast between "brown people in Vietnam" and "so-called Negro people in Louisville"—but in the framework of the argument they are parallels rather than opposites. The Vietnamese peasant is, in Ali's imaginative scheme, an ally to the black soldier sent to kill him; they share a common enemy.

It's all about the effect on the ear. That second sentence contrasts "my religion, my people, or myself" with "those . . . fighting for their own justice, freedom, and equality." The contrast is made in the interests of emphasizing not difference but kinship—and the syntactic parallel, those groups of three emotive terms, does that work in the rhythm and shape of the sentence.

It should be fairly easy to see how antithesis can be ramped up so that a binary structure at sentence level can become the principle for a whole essay or argument. In its most stark form this will be to reject one thing and endorse another—and to do so all the way through an argument. But more subtly it can follow the pattern that we see microscopically reproduced in "All Things Bright and Beautiful": on the one hand A, on the other B, but in combination or in resolution C. Or, if you like: thesis, antithesis, synthesis—the basic movement of Hegelian dialectic.

You may not think of your letter disputing a parking ticket you picked up when parked in front of a fire hydrant as being an instance of the Hegelian dialectic in action—but in its small way it might well be.

TRICOLONS

Grouping things in three has an almost magical effect on the rhythmic authority of a given sentence or passage of writing. There's a reason that political speeches are so frequently peppered with such groupings. The tricolon, to give it its technical name, can make even nonsense sound compelling, as I discussed in the section on cadence.

I mentioned Douglas Alexander's "I am Scottish by birth, by choice, and by aspiration." What was important about that phrase was not what it said but the impression it gave. Tricolons work on the ear, not on the brain. They are a cadence effect. A good one will also cohere in its meaning—the three things will reinforce rather than contradict each other—but the extra work a tricolon is doing is all on the reader's inner ear.

That's a recommendation but also a warning. As with any special effect, overdoing tricolons will diminish the force of any single one. But used in a position to give them maximum effect—on the important bits: the end of a paragraph or a chapter—they are an extraordinarily valuable resource.

REPETITION

Repeating words or phrases has a strong effect on what a reader takes away from a given piece of language. This is especially marked, and especially necessary, in the spoken language—where readers can't flick back—but it has a place in written prose, too. "Anaphora"—or repeating words or phrases at the beginnings of sentences—is the commonest sort. It can give a sense of sentences yoked together and pulling in the same direction. "Epistrophe"—repeating something at the end of successive sentences—can also give an elegant coherence to a passage of work, often near its conclusion.

But these are set-piece figures. More informally, repetition allows you to control emphasis. "We have a problem; a problem that no single one of us can solve; but a problem easily overcome if we work together." That embeds "problem" that bit more firmly in the reader's mind—and the beat pause in the semicolon allows the first use to hang in the air for emphasis . . . before flowing smoothly on as if between the problem and its solution there's nothing more troubling than a couple of deftly negotiated semicolons.

ASKING A QUESTION

Most if not all of the pieces of writing we'll undertake ask and/or answer a question. It might be a simple question, such as "How come we ran out of avocado toast during the breakfast service?" or it might be a complicated one, such as "Does existence precede essence?"

Often that question, though, is left ill-defined or implicit. And if it's fuzzy in the head of the author, there may be trouble ahead. If you're able to articulate the questions you're answering to your audience, you can be confident that you have them clear in your own head. And if you're able to articulate them to your audience, why wouldn't you do so?

The so-called rhetorical question, asked in no expectation of an answer, is called "erotema." In practical communication you won't see it that often. (Why would you?) But its cousin "hypophora"—which is where you ask yourself a question aloud and then answer it—is very useful indeed. Still, in a sense, all questions in prose are rhetorical. The audience is not there with you to jump in with an answer.

In day-to-day communication the question works in three ways.

First, it's a framing device for an argument. It makes explicit to your audience what the passage of writing that comes afterward is trying to address. It can also be a way of breaking up a larger argument into smaller units and giving clarity to what those units are.

Why should the board consider my funding application for a new outreach center? For two reasons: A and B. Does A contradict B? Well, let me get into that . . .

Second, it's an attention-getter. Most sentences are indicative. Asking a direct question—switching to the interrogative mood—registers sharply on the reader's concentration. It marks a break, and a rolling-up of sleeves. The reader at once knows, or feels he or she knows, where he or she is.

Third, it makes a connection with the audience. It more or less expressly says: I'm seeing things from your point of view. It anticipates—and, to an extent, shapes—the issue of what the audience wants from you. It makes a monologue feel like a conversation.

When I'm writing a book review, for instance, I know that among the questions I'm hoping to answer are: What is this book trying to do, and why? How far does it succeed in doing it, and how? And (since I'm not reviewing for academic or scientific journals) does it do so in a way that gives pleasure and that makes it worth its cover price to a general reader?

Questions will make it not only clear to your audience, but clear to you, what you're setting out to achieve.

MAKING LISTS

"Enumeratio" is the fancy name for making a numbered list. It's something writers and speakers have been doing since the dawn of time. Political pledges, deadly sins, billy goats gruff, horsemen of the apocalypse, lords a-leaping, and commandments have all had the treatment. It remains a very effective way of organizing important points to make them both authoritative and—in particular—memorable.

As a written device, it descends from the trick in spoken oratory of numbering off points on your fingers. You could think of it as a more explicit and formal extension of the tricolon. It makes the core of an argument, or a section of an argument, memorable because it effectively highlights the key points. It also implies a fixed number of them—which has the effect of making an argument seem complete. It implies a certain command, and a certain analytical rigor, in the speaker. That's why you look like such a booby when you either promise four points and can only remember three, or promise three and go on limply to add a fourth as an afterthought.

This was how the former US presidential candidate Rick Perry so painfully crashed and burned in a 2011 TV debate. As part of his election platform, he had pledged to abolish three federal agencies. "It's three agencies of government when I get there that are gone," he said in a tone of can-do determination, "commerce, education, and the uh . . . what's the third one, there?" He looked awkward. "Let's see . . . I can't. The third one." Later: "Oops." Well worth seeking out the clip on YouTube. If you're telling the audience there are three vital points, and you can't remember one of them, they'll be unimpressed.*

Happily, it's not so easy to "forget" one or more of your points if you're writing them down—at least not so spectacularly. But you'd be surprised—it does happen on the page, and it will make the attentive reader wince. Instantly, you out yourself as someone who can't count, won't bother to proofread, and/or doesn't really have a grasp on his own argument.

Enumeratio can work as signposting in a paragraphed essay structure. "I will identify three key areas of contention in the Israel/Palestine debate and address them in turn," you might write in your introduction: "The status of the Temple Mount, the legitimacy of settlements in the West Bank, and the 'right of return.'" Then you would spend a paragraph or a cluster of them on each one. You might begin these subsequent sections: "First . . ." "second . . ." "third . . ." Instantly, your reader has a map of your argument to follow.

In business and official documents it can also be very effective in combination with a typographical scheme. There's a good reason that Microsoft Word has a button in the toolbar that will do it for you automatically. A bullet-pointed or numbered list—whether in a breakout box or indented as a block of text—will break up the flow, draw the eye, and give the reader a place to focus. It will say to the

---

* The opposite problem is exploited for comic effect in Monty Python's "Spanish Inquisition" sketch. "Nobody expects the Spanish Inquisition!" is Cardinal Ximénez's opener as he bursts into the room. "Our chief weapon is surprise. Surprise and fear . . . fear and surprise. Our two weapons are fear and surprise . . . and ruthless efficiency." He frowns. "Our three weapons are fear and surprise and ruthless efficiency . . . and an almost fanatical devotion to the pope. Our four . . . no . . . amongst our weapons . . . amongst our weaponry . . . are such elements as fear, surprise . . . I'll come in again."

reader skimming quickly: Here's the important bit. The "air"—or white space—around it frames it and gives the reader, figuratively, breathing space.

Enumeratio doesn't just help readers navigate a text; it also has an ethos effect. Enumeratio, as I say, makes an argument seem brisk and targeted and ruthlessly thought through. For this reason it has an almost limitless usefulness in business and official communications. If you're aiming at a more yielding and conversational tone of voice, though, use it with caution. In the first flushes of romance it might find a whimsical use. "How do I love thee?" asked Elizabeth Barrett Browning. "Let me count the ways." But a letter dumping your boyfriend won't seem sympathetic if it contains a numbered list of his shortcomings auto-formatted by Microsoft.

The other point to be made about this technique is that if you're using it for signposting and memory, you can't make a list too long. "There are five key points" is, as it were, a selling proposition—there's every expectation that the reader will retain those five in memory. Here I refer you back to the rule of the "magical number seven," that guideline for the working memory.

If you set out ten key points you're pushing it; they might work as a thumb-in-page reference, but they're unlikely to sit in the reader's head unless he or she is specifically enjoined to remember them. Rather, the reader will remember the fact of there being ten points rather than the points themselves. Eleven looks inelegant. Many more than that starts to look rambling and disorganized—it will tend to undermine rather than reinforce that impression of clarity and intellectual discipline. Can all of 17 key points be equally important? Won't some contradict others? Why 17 and not 18, or 19, or 129? We respond well to round numbers, arbitrary though that impression of roundness might be.*

---

* That we count in base ten is a cultural accident, presumably not unrelated to how many fingers we have.

The success of the "listicle" in the social media age taps into the attractions of enumeratio—but there's a twist that bears brief investigation. Cheap round-number magazine formats (*Rolling Stone*'s "100 Greatest Guitarists") gave way to cheap round-number television formats (Channel 4's "The 50 Greatest Comedy Characters"), which in turn gave way to something odder. The viral media site BuzzFeed, and its many copycats, took to producing listicles that positively shun round numbers*—and whose organizing principle is gleefully trivial.

In 2014, for instance, BuzzFeed published what may represent the pinnacle of the form: "44 Medieval Beasts That Cannot Even Handle It Right Now." It was a collection of illustrations of fantastical beasts from medieval illuminated manuscripts, with captions. So at number four, for example, you got some medieval monk's rendering of a reptile with what looks to the modern eye like a comically pained expression: "This crocodile just wants it all to STOP." Very funny it was, too. And it had more than three-quarters of a million page views at the time of writing.

What about working memory? What about the magic number seven? The comic effect of the quirky-numbered listicle, I think, relates exactly to the way that we usually use enumeratio to suggest something orderly, and that we usually use it to signpost importance. The fact that it's so specific—forty-four pained-looking monsters, not forty-three or forty-five—in the context of such arbitrary subject matter is the joke; it plays off our usual expectations. And yet BuzzFeed has its cake and eats it; the specificity of the number does its usual work of implying something thought about or at least curated—it promises a limit. "Some Medieval Beasts That Cannot Even Handle It Right Now" isn't nearly so clickable. Here is enumeratio in a playful postmodern incarnation.

---

* Indeed, by not using round numbers they give the implicit impression that none of the entries is filler.

7

Perils and Pitfalls

As I hope will by now be clear, this book is intended as an aid to the practical writer rather than as a cavalry charge across the battlefield of the language wars. I'm not primarily interested in exploding the prejudices of pedants, nor in ridiculing the "relativism" of descriptive linguists.

Nevertheless, there are a lot of rules for grammar, rules for spelling, and rules for writing in general—and rightly or wrongly many people take those rules very seriously. If some of those people are among your readers—and they will be—it is worth for purely practical reasons knowing what they're likely to balk at.

Forewarned is forearmed. Below I outline some of the fiercest areas of dispute—not as a plan of attack so much as a map of the minefield. If it makes you feel better to put "correct" in skeptical quote marks, feel free.

Contested Usages

SPLIT INFINITIVES

The notion that it's wrong to interpose—to blithely interpose, you could say—a word (usually an adverb) between the word "to" and its verb in the infinitive form is the king of zombie grammar rules. Not only is it wrong, it's actually famous for being wrong. There's a whole set of folklore about its wrongness (including the idea that the rule came about by analogy with Latin, where infinitives are one word and therefore unsplittable), and a lively mini-industry in tracking down the origins of the "rule" in long-forgotten nineteenth-century style guides. That said, some people still think it a bad habit.

I tend not to split them, all other things being equal. In the first place they occasion a microscopic upping of the cognitive load; the interruption of one or more adverbs means the reader has "to" in a mental holding pattern pending the arrival of the verb. It also produces, to my ear, a tiny hiccup in the sentence. Then again, the prissily unsplit infinitive can sound stiff and pompous. The most famous instance in history—*Star Trek*'s "To boldly go . . ."—is perfectly idiomatic. The cadence places the stress on the key word—"boldly." "Boldly to go" sounds stiff. "To go boldly" shifts the emphasis, to my ear, from the boldness to the going.

And sometimes—especially when your infinitive is near another verb that might want to steal its adverb—you need to split to avoid ambiguity. Recently I found myself writing: "Margaret Thatcher claimed only to need four hours' sleep a night." Did she *only claim* to need four hours' sleep? Did she claim to *only need* four hours' sleep? Or did she claim to need *only four hours'* sleep? Each has a subtly different shade of meaning, and by ruling out splitting the infinitive on principle you deprive yourself of the availability of one of them.

COMMA SPLICES

There's a special place at the end of the devil's toasting fork, if you ask me, for the perpetrator of the comma splice, or run-on sentence. Here's an example from the menu at a well-known British chain restaurant.

> *At Little Chef we care about food, all of our burgers are made from British Beef and they are all fully certified and prepared by our own butcher.*

No, no, no, and thrice again no. That—at least in standard written English—is just wrong. Not wrong because of the eccentric capitalization of "beef." Not wrong because of the very questionable truth of the first clause, and the expansive vagueness of the second. It's wrong because what you have there is two sentences, not one. The two subjects ("we" and "burgers") and two main verbs ("care" and "are made") are the giveaway.

So:

At Little Chef we care about food. All of our burgers are made from British Beef and they are all fully certified and prepared by our own butcher.

If you want to link two main clauses to emphasize their connection, you can use a colon, a dash, or a semicolon.

So:

At Little Chef we care about food: All of our burgers are made from British Beef and they are all fully certified and prepared by our own butcher.

Or, more informal:

At Little Chef we care about food—all of our burgers are made from British Beef and they are all fully certified and prepared by our own butcher.

Or, if you're going for a classier look:

At Little Chef we care about food; all of our burgers are made from British Beef and they are all fully certified and prepared by our own butcher.

You can also use a coordinating conjunction of some sort, as, in fact, Little Chef has done in the back end of that sentence, where "and" helpfully and correctly links the matter of their being certified to the matter of their being made from British beef.

It would be ugly but just about grammatical to write:

> *At Little Chef we care about food and all of our burgers are made from British Beef and they are all fully certified and prepared by our own butcher.*

Conversely, if you replaced the second "and" with a comma, you'd have a double comma splice of considerable horribleness.

> *At Little Chef we care about food, all of our burgers are made from British Beef, they are all fully certified and prepared by our own butcher.*

But, aha! Do you notice something going on there? Why yes: The version with the double comma splice is starting to look like something else. It's starting to look like a list. And here is where it gets a little complicated. As much as the comma splice is a crime that cries to heaven for vengeance, it's also a crime that—like so much else in language—isn't always an open-and-shut case. A list is another way of linking independent main clauses, and lists use commas. So you could write, and just about get away with:

> *Little Chef cares about food, all its burgers are made from British Beef, and its own butcher certifies and prepares them.*

But that works only because I've recast the clauses to put them into a similar form. And it only just about works; cast as a list the grammar is signaling that these three clauses—caring about food, the burgers being made of beef, and the butcher's shenanigans—carry roughly equal weight; in fact, the second two are offered as corroborative evidence for the first. If you were to write a grammatically identical sentence with the terms in a different order it would sound very odd indeed.

All Little Chef's burgers are made from British Beef, its own butcher certifies and prepares them, and it cares about food.

The point I'm making is that this sentence, because of its *meaning*, doesn't really want to be a list.

To complicate matters further, the comma splice is widely accepted in very short sentences, particularly if the different clauses share a subject or they're placed in opposition. "It's not beef, it's horsemeat." "I came, I saw, I conquered." And you're allowed to use it if you're Charles Dickens, Samuel Beckett, or Virginia Woolf; in literary style, all bets are off.

It does, on the face of it, seem arbitrary and a little eccentric that semicolons, colons, dashes, and periods are all acceptable ways of joining two main clauses, and that the comma isn't. Likewise, that FANBOYS—the coordinating conjunctions "for," "and," "nor," "but," "or," "yet," and "so"—can join them (usually but not always in a double act with a comma) but that conjunctive adverbs such as "nevertheless" or "however" can't. "The Little Chef burger was horrible, but he ate it." "The Little Chef burger was horrible but he ate it." Both grammatically okay, slight difference in emphasis and pace. "The Little Chef Burger was horrible, nevertheless he ate it." Wrong. "The Little Chef burger was horrible nevertheless he ate it." Even wronger (conjunctive adverbs tend to like a bit of punctuation). "The Little Chef burger was horrible, however he ate it." Wrong. "The Little Chef burger was horrible however he ate it." Correct, but because "however" without a comma isn't acting as a coordinator but as a qualifier; it was horrible regardless of whether he slathered it in ketchup, held his nose, or washed it down with Mountain Dew. Language: slippery thing.*

So comma splices are horribly wrong, except on the few occasions that they aren't. Got it? If in doubt, avoid them. Even the acceptable ones can be unspliced without much trouble—"It's not beef; it's horsemeat"; "I came. I saw. I conquered."—and you're more likely to mess up by splicing than not.

DANGLING MODIFIERS

"A fearless ironist, his mischief worked in curious ways." Here's the excellent writer Frances Wilson in her 2016 biography of Thomas De Quincey. Had she, grammatical sticklers would wonder, been at the opium? Curious as its workings might have been, De Quincey's mischief wasn't a fearless ironist.

Or try this one, from the introduction to a recent edition of Radio 4's *The Life Scientific*: "Spluttering molten rock, extraordinary heat, and intense pressure, my guest today has journeyed closer to the center of the earth than anyone I know." This makes an in-person interview with the vulcanologist Hazel Rymer sound like a dangerous proposition.

A "dangler" is the name given to a modifying clause—often a participle—whose implied subject is different from that of the main clause. A slightly careless travel writer might announce, for instance: "Walking around the corner, the Taj Mahal showed itself

---

* The writer Jonathan Franzen is particularly exercised by a special case of the comma splice. In his short essay "Comma-Then," collected in *Farther Away: Essays* (2012), he fulminates against people who "use the word *then* as a conjunction without a subject following it," as in (his example) "She lit a Camel Light, then dragged deeply." He thinks the "comma-then," here, should be replaced with the words "and she" to make a compound sentence. "Comma-then," he says, is an "irritating, lazy mannerism, unlike the brave semicolon or the venerable participial phrase." I can't see his objection at all. I read Franzen's short essay, then sat back in my chair quite baffled.

resplendent in the bright Agra sunlight." The Taj Mahal wasn't walking around the corner, obviously.

These are worth trying to avoid, not because they are a crime against the language—Oliver Kamm points out a humdinger from old *Hamlet* ("'Tis given out that, sleeping in my orchard / A serpent stung me")—but because they are a small stylistic clumsiness. The number of instances in which they can lead to actual confusion of meaning is small: Only a horse's ass (technical term) will have the slightest trouble making sense of either Frances Wilson or my imaginary travel writer. But, particularly in longer sentences, they can cause the reader to stumble.

NOUNING VERBS; VERBING NOUNS

"Can we *action* that report? I'd like you to *cascade* it to your team. We *brainstormed* it yesterday and there are some key *learnings* in it." These may seem to you, as they do to me, grotesque—but they are no sort of error. What linguists call "function shift"—a word taking on a new syntactic role—is one of the great engines of linguistic innovation. Verbs incessantly become nouns and nouns incessantly become verbs and verbs and nouns incessantly become adjectives.

Function shift is built into the language, in fact. We have the linguistic equivalent of a keyboard shortcut for making most regular verbs into nouns by adding -*ing* for the gerund form: "There is nothing either good or bad but *thinking* makes it so." "Nothing in his life became him like the *leaving* it." Nouns can become adjectives with the addition of -*y*: "There's a *farty* smell in here. Is that you or is it the dog?" Adjectives can become adverbs with the suffix -*ly*: "*Frankly*, Mr. Shankly, since you ask / you are a flatulent pain in the ass."

Nevertheless, people often feel very strongly about the subject so it's worth pausing before you make a particularly bold and innovative sally in this department. Is it apt to the register you're trying to strike? How established a usage is it? Does it draw attention to itself; and, if so, is that an effect you're trying to achieve?

Sometimes, even an established usage can strike certain readers as awkward. Not long ago I was editing a review, by the poet A. E. Stallings, of a new translation of *The Iliad*. Stallings noted that the translator was "the first woman to have Englished the poem." I liked the usage—feeling it had a slightly quaint old-fashioned vibe. A couple of my colleagues red-penciled it furiously, thinking it an "ugly Americanism." Stallings pointed me to the 1628 volume *Virgils Georgicks Englished*.

Curious, I tried my first Twitter poll.

"English" (vb, transitive): To translate into English.

Was this, I asked:

a) an abomination of a usage, or

b) quaint and elegant?

Long history or not, most people—or at least most of my Twitter followers—were against it: 82 percent voted a) and only 18 percent voted b). But along the way a medievalist friend directed me to a generous handful of well-attested usages from the fifteenth and early sixteenth centuries, while a scholar of the Renaissance noted that Milton "Englisht" Martin Bucer in 1644 and added that it was "one of [the] commonest verbs to describe translation to/between vernacular(s) in m'period." Another mentioned "Wycliffe, Caxton, Shakespeare . . . Browning, Wells, Graves, Vidal, Rushdie." And the novelist Philip Hensher went off on a tangent wondering whether "French" (verb, transitive) only means to snog someone. (Answer: Historically it could mean to translate into French; nowadays the snogging is primary.) It was an interesting rabbit hole to go down. We digested all that scholarship, basked in the richness of the language—and amended the review to read "translated the poem into English."

Businesspeople, as in those "cascaded" "learnings" above, seem to be addicted to function shift. I assume they feel it makes them seem dynamic and—in Sarah Palin's function-shifting phrase— "hopey-changey." Purely as a stylistic preference, business jargon function shift makes me hatey-vomity.

ENDING SENTENCES WITH PREPOSITIONS; BEGINNING THEM WITH CONJUNCTIONS

There's an elderly superstition against both these usages. It says that you can't write a sentence such as:

Frank had a lot to be annoyed about.

Or:

And then we came to the end.

Like the idea that splitting infinitives is wrong, these have become almost joke examples of rules not to take seriously. Hence the hoary witticism, usually attributed to Churchill, that ending a sentence with a preposition "is something up with which I will not put." Lots of phrasal verbs, passives, infinitive constructions, and other forms positively demand a stranded preposition.

There are a couple of points worth thinking about when it comes to the question of beginning a sentence with a conjunction. One is the imperfect overlap between the spoken and the written language. In speech, the neat division of one sentence from the next with a period isn't so clear. Sentences are often run together with "and" and "but" or "so," and neither speaker nor listener will be making a fine distinction between a compound sentence linked with a coordinating conjunction, and two separate sentences.

That means, to some extent, the usage becomes a marker of informality. So when you're aiming to write formally—i.e., taking your written language some distance from casual speech—it might make your prose sound too talky if you start a large number of sentences with conjunctions. And, like any tic, it can start to irritate. But there is no good reason to avoid it on principle.

It's funny that militant grammarians don't bother to have a prohibition against *ending* a sentence with a conjunction, i.e., "We were heading to the seaside and." The "rules" wouldn't be any fun if they were directed against things that are clearly wrong because nobody actually does them.

THAT, WHICH, AND WHO

In its pronominal use, "that" is pretty straightforward. "That's the badger!" "Is that really what you intended to achieve?" "To be, or not to be—that is the question." Likewise, it presents no great trouble in its role as a demonstrative adjective—a specially emphatic and finger-pointing alternative to "the": "That man stole my budgie." "I got that scar fighting the Nazis." Philip Larkin's short poem "Home is so Sad" ends with the desolating two-word sentence: "That vase."*

As a conjunction, too, it presents no special problem. It introduces indirect statements: "He told me that his wife had once played keyboards in ELO. I'm not sure that he was telling the truth." And it's often optional—"He told me his wife had once played keyboards in ELO. I'm not sure he was telling the truth."

Sometimes, though, it helps minimize ambiguity. The riddling phrase "dogs dogs dog dog dogs" works partly because of an elided "that"; to unpack it you could say "dogs [that] dogs dog [, in turn] dog [other] dogs," i.e., dogs pestered by some dogs go on to pester others. Dog hands on incaninity to dog . . .

---

* To put it in context, the last two lines run: "Look at the pictures and the cutlery. / The music in the piano stool. That vase." There's a world of nuance in the shift from the run of neutral "thes" to "that"—it seems to me to open out to an almost accusatory tone of exhausted familiarity.

Where it gets frisky is when "that" is used to introduce a relative clause. There are all sorts of bear traps here, primarily because "that" all of a sudden finds itself in competition with "which" and "who."

The first question is whether the subject being modified is animate (i.e., human, unless you're particularly tender toward animals). It's as close to an iron rule as you get that you never use "who" with an inanimate antecedent: "The brush that she used to sweep the floor," not "the brush who she used to sweep the floor."* In most cases, the opposite also applies. You use "who" rather than "that" or "which" with a human antecedent: "The man who answered the door."

The rule's not absolute, there, however. There are shades of meaning as to whether you're representing the human in question as an individual or a type, and, indeed, whether you're talking about an aggregate. "The sort of child that thinks peanut butter is a form of hair product" seems to me perfectly acceptable. "The crowd that gathered at the Trump rally" likewise passes muster.

Once you're in a "that"/"which" situation—i.e., the subject's inanimate—you run up against another sticking point. A large body of received opinion has it that, though many of us use "that" and "which" interchangeably in relative clauses, we shouldn't.

This school of thought says "that" should be used for restrictive relative clauses, and "which" for the nonrestrictive kind.†

So, as Dylan Thomas wrote:

The hand that signed the paper felled a city.

---

* This can trip up foreign language speakers, who don't always have the distinction in their native languages.

† An explanation of this is to be found in the section on commas in the earlier chapter on punctuation.

But:

The hand, which signed the paper, felled a city.

In the first instance the clause is restrictive or defining; sign-ing the paper is the defining characteristic of the hand in question. In the second (note, too, the commas), the fact of its signing is pre-sented as a bonus piece of information; the main thing we know about the hand is that it felled a city.

This is, again, a guideline rather than an absolute rule, though. In an odd asymmetry you can get away with using "which" instead of "that" in a restrictive clause, but you can't get away with using "that" instead of "which" in a nonrestrictive clause.

The hand which signed the paper felled a city.

The hand, that signed the paper, felled a city.

The first of these two is fine. The second sounds wretchedly odd. Also, "which" can take a pronoun but "that" can't. "The principle for which I would gladly lay down my life" is English; "the principle for that I would gladly lay down my life" is not.

Something I don't get tired of repeating is that having a formal knowledge of the "rules" is very useful, but developing an ear for what sounds right, which means giving yourself access to the grammatical knowledge that you have internalized through years of speaking and reading, is even better. You know more than you know you know—and paying attention, trying out alternatives, testing constructions on the ear, is at least as likely to steer you through areas of contested usage as clinging to one authority or another.

WHO AND WHOM

"Whom," a rare survival of our inflectional system, is the accusative case of the relative pronoun "who"; that is, you use it when "who" is the direct or indirect object of a verb.

That's the pedant whom I dislike, and at whom I flipped the bird.

It's a distinction that is going the way of the rest of the inflectional system—in many cases, "who" does service perfectly well—but it has not gone the whole way yet. There's a continuum. In the sentence above, for instance, "the pedant who I dislike" sounds more natural than "at who I flipped the bird."

To be absolutely sure you're getting it right, you can try recasting the sentence with "he"/"him" or "she"/"her" (that pedant: I dislike *him* . . . I flipped the bird at *him*). But though that's a good way of establishing whether the word is in the accusative case, it doesn't solve the stylistic choice between "who" and "whom." Since they are in variation, "whom" has become a marker of formality and, sometimes, of a certain stiffness.

"The bloke whom I met in the pub" sounds wrong because the precision of "whom" jars against the slanginess of "bloke." It's worth getting it "wrong" sometimes for stylistic reasons, in other words, and your ear will be the best guide.

Just don't get it actually wrong. You occasionally hear people so frightened of using "who" wrongly, or so convinced that "whom" is simply a posher version, that they use "whom" in the nominative as a hypercorrection. "The man whom laid our patio" is, if you ask me, even worse than "the pedant at who I flipped the bird." The "he"/"him" test, applied properly, would smartly dispatch that temptation.

Incidentally, Lenin's famous phrase "Who whom?" absolutely relies in that form on the inflection.* If Lenin had said "Who who?" he would have sounded like an owl.

BETWEEN YOU AND ME

The question of whether a personal pronoun should be in the subject case or the object case is one that causes considerable vexation. We're good at getting it right when there's only one involved; nobody except for Tarzan says things like "Me love Jane."† But the vapors rise when we find them yoked together in a more complicated way.

"Between you and I" is widely considered wrong because "between" is a preposition and pronouns tend to take the accusative or object case with prepositions—as in "behind us" or "after him."

Those who have been brought up to understand that "My wife and me love *Game of Thrones*" is an unpardonable vulgarism will always say, rightly, "My wife and I love *Game of Thrones*." The problem is that the first version is widespread in idiomatic use, and if you reverse the order it becomes practically compulsory. "Me and my wife love *Game of Thrones*" will sound to most ears more like an English sentence than "I and my wife love *Game of Thrones*." There seems to be a rule—though it's not one of logic—that if you're going to use a noun phrase like "my wife and I" in the subject case, you have to put the speaker last in sequence.

"Between you and I" is most likely an extension of this muddle: You think you know it's not "proper English" to say "my wife and me," because those are the subject of the sentence, and by

---

* From the Russian *kto kovo*: It has the force of asking "who [holds the whip hand over] whom?" or as Aretha Franklin put it (uninflectedly), "Who's zoomin' who?" It's a forcefully compressed statement of the basic issue of political power.

† The Incredible Hulk sidesteps the issue cunningly by referring to himself in the third person. "Hulk smash puny grammar pedant!" He's still shaky on verb morphology and the correct use of determiners, though.

(mistaken) analogy you assume that the phrase "between you and I" has the same grammar.

An awkward hypercorrection is also sometimes applied to pronouns with comparatives and linking verbs. Do you say "taller than me" or "taller than I" (or, indeed, "taller than myself")? "It's me" or "It is I"? The first, in each case, sounds more natural, though some sticklers, in thrall either to sketchy Latin analogies or to eighteenth-century prescriptive grammarians, will insist on the second. Neither is wrong. And, as so often, the showily "correct" version will affect your register. In the sitcom *'Allo 'Allo!* there was one character who always introduced himself: "It is I, Leclerc!" His usage was intended to sound ridiculous.

A cousin of this anxiety is the misuse of reflexive pronouns. You'll sometimes hear this pompous/anxious usage: "My wife and myself love *Game of Thrones.*" Sometimes you'll even find it in isolation: "Please don't hesitate to contact myself . . ." In both cases the reflexive pronoun seems to have been mistaken for a more formal version of the accusative "me." It isn't. There are arguments that it's an established usage, but I'd counsel establishing it no further by steering clear. It still grates on many ears.

DOUBLE NEGATIVES

As Roger Miller sings in "King of the Road": "Trailer for sale or rent: Rooms to let, fifty cents. / No phone, no pool, no pets. I ain't got no cigarettes." Here's one of the battlegrounds on which the logical brigade fight their defense of correct English. If you *ain't* got *no* cigarettes, you must have some cigarettes, right?

Double negatives may be illogical, but they are also idiomatic. And in an English governed purely by the laws of logic, "flammable" and "inflammable" would be antonyms rather than synonyms. Double negatives are frequently used, as above, for emphasis. They can also introduce a subtlety of meaning. To say somebody is "not unattractive" is to say something slightly more complimentary than that they are unattractive, but slightly more qualified than that they are attractive. The rhetorical name for this is "litotes."

To the extent that double and, especially, triple negatives can cause the reader to stumble, and because they annoy pedants, be cautious with them. "Ain't got no" isn't a standard written construction. And the "not unattractive" formula needs to be used precisely, rather than because it lends an impression of judiciousness to a phrase. The former prime minister John Major was much mocked for his use of the phrase "not inconsiderable"—a litotes that relies on negating a word nobody uses anyway.[*]

DUE TO AND BECAUSE OF

These two phrases are very often used interchangeably. There does exist a traditional distinction, though, and it's worth knowing. "Due to" is used adjectivally—i.e., it modifies a noun or pronoun. "Because of" modifies a verb.

The lateness of the train was due to the leaves on the line.

The train was delayed because of the leaves on the line.

In the first case "due to" refers to a noun: "the lateness." In the second, "because of" refers to a verb: "was delayed."

That distinction seems to be breaking down due to—sorry, because of—the pressure of usage. But understanding it will at least help you get a sense, if a sentence you've formed with either phrase sounds odd, of why that might be and of how to fix it.

NONE IS / NONE ARE

There's a school of thought that "none" is a contraction of "not one"

---

[*] I can't find any evidence of him ever using it, but it was a staple of *Private Eye*'s spoof *Secret Diary of John Major*.

and therefore can't take a plural verb. So: "None of us is innocent," not "none of us are innocent." A great pile of usage data shows that people have used "none" with plural verbs for centuries. So it's not an error—but it's something that will set sticklers bristling. And, actually, the distinction allows you to introduce a subtlety of meaning. "None of us is innocent," in a theological context, might make the point that no individual is without sin before God; "none of us are innocent," in the context of a mass trial for war crimes, tips the scales toward an implication of collective guilt (in which the individual guilt is subsumed). See what sounds most natural, and, with sticklers in mind, prefer the singular version if both sound fine.

THE ROYAL "ONE"

English lacks an impersonal pronoun such as *"on"* in French. So if you're speaking about an indefinite human subject you can use "one"—though it will sound rather affectedly aristocratic. "One can't get proper caviar at Whole Foods these days," i.e., nobody can get proper caviar there, is perfectly grammatical, though most people would say (and write): "You can't get proper caviar at Whole Foods these days." It's wrong, however, to say: "One popped into Whole Foods this afternoon and one wasn't able to find any caviar." In this instance you're talking about a specific rather than a notional caviar seeker, so you should say "I" or, if you're the queen, "we."

Red Rag Words

One of the great engines of linguistic change is error. If enough people get something wrong often enough, it becomes right. In language as in war, the victors write the history. But in language, as in war, the first people to go over the top get the worst of it from the enemy machine guns.

This is particularly noticeable when it comes to the meanings and spelling of words. Some of them I'm calling "red rag" words after the (apocryphal) effect on an angry bull. It might on the face of it seem odd that so many of the words that really exercise the language police—"decimate" being a good example—are arcane ones.* But to qualify for red-rag status, it seems reasonable to suppose, a word must be used frequently enough to attract the attention of the professionally outraged, yet infrequently enough that its meaning hasn't yet shifted wholesale.

A lot of the time a Latin or Greek root helps with red-rag status. To return to the social psychology of pedantry, there's a certain pride in knowing the root meaning of a word—and it's therefore attractive to think of that knowledge as being of some importance. But it isn't. Etymology may help tell you part of the story of how a word came to take the form it has today, but it does not tell you what it means now. For a while, for instance, sticklers objected to the word "television" on the grounds that it was a barbaric mish-mash of Latin and Greek roots.

The class anxiety underpinning this sort of prescriptivism is made pretty clear in one of Fowler's most delightfully absurd out-bursts.†

> *Word-making, like other manufactures, should be done by those who know how to do it; others should neither attempt it for themselves, nor assist the deplorable activities of amateurs by giving currency to fresh coinages before there has been time to test them.*

If we were to compile an exhaustive list of usages that incense sticklers we could be here some time. And it's often the case that

---

* The main reason we collectively forgot how to use the word "decimate" in its "proper" sense—meaning to punish a Roman legion by killing one man in ten—is that we stopped doing that. Good.

† Here I'm referring to Henry Watson Fowler (1858–1933), author of the original *Modern English Usage* (1926). Where I talk about *Fowler* elsewhere in this book, I'm referring to the 1996 third edition of his book, which was substantially revised and updated by Robert Burchfield.

the "wrong" usage has a longer pedigree than the "right" one—that some supposedly barbaric modern mistake is neither modern nor a mistake.* A little knowledge is a dangerous thing. And as ever, the very fact that the sticklers are objecting is a sure indicator that the word's "wrong" meaning is clear from the context in which it's used.

However, a few of the most common are as follows. As ever, we can argue the toss about whether such and such a usage is acceptable—most modern dictionaries will acknowledge both variants. In standard written English, though, the following are booby traps. Here are the pedant-friendly versions as an aid to the cautious.

affect; effect. These are different words. When used as a noun, "affect" means "emotion" and "effect" means the consequence or result of something. As verbs, to "affect" something is to have an impact on it (or, in the less common sense of "he affected a purple fur coat," to adopt a mannerism or image pretentiously); to "effect" something is to cause it to happen. "The Brexit vote *affects* all of us: It will *effect* the UK's departure from the European Union."

ageing; aging. By analogy with "rage"/"raging" or "stage"/"staging" you might think that "aging" would be the standard or only way of forming the participle. Actually both are standard usage, with "aging" preferred (though not mandatory) in American English.

alright. A much deplored variant spelling of "all right." I would always spell it as two words, not least because it drives sticklers

---

* An instance of the knots in which prescriptivists can tie themselves is offered by the Académie Française, which has traditionally waged war on the barbaric English loanwords it sees as polluting the true French language. It prefers, for instance, *ordinateur* to *computer* as a word for the thing on your desk. "Computer," mind you, originally comes—as its form makes pretty clear—from a French root (the *OED*'s etymology says: "Compare middle French *computeur*: person who makes calculations (1578)". And, in fact, "computer" was what the French called it first. "Ordinateur" didn't show up until 1956.

nuts when they see it spelled as one. But linguistically speaking there's no reason to accept "always" and "altogether" and reject "alright" as an abomination.

anticipate; expect. You can expect fusspots to leap on you if you use "anticipate" as a synonym for "expect." Anticipate them by knowing the rule. Though they are widely used as alternatives, to "expect" something is to be confident it's going to happen, whereas to "anticipate" is to act in advance of your expectation. A goalkeeper might anticipate a shot at goal by leaping to his right with his arms outstretched.

appraise; apprise. To "appraise" is to put a value on something; to "apprise [someone of]" is to tell someone something. "The pawnbroker *appraised* my mother's engagement ring and *apprised* me of how much I could expect to pawn it for."

beg the question. This technically describes a sort of circular logic where you assume your conclusion in the premises you set out from. A mocking example would be the Sir John Harington epigram: "Treason doth never prosper, what's the reason? For if it prosper, none dare call it treason." Now it's commonly more loosely used to mean "prompt the question," as in "The manager's abrupt departure *begs the question* of whether the Yankees' hopes of making the playoffs are at an end."

classic; classical. The distinction in usage is not absolute. But, in general, "classic" applies to something time-honored and impressive, such as a "classic album"; "classical" applies to periods or styles of art and civilization (specifically ancient Greece and Rome). A 1924 Bentley is a *classic* vehicle; a gladiator's chariot is a *classical* vehicle. Or, when it comes to schoolgirl practical jokes, compare: "We put a newt in Miss Trunchbull's jug of water! It was *classic!*" with "We crucified Miss Trunchbull on the Via Appia! It was *classical!*"

comprised; composed. Both words, in the sense in which they are usually confused, describe the relation of sum and parts. The first supplies the word "of" implicitly—"the search party *comprised* Shaggy, Scooby, and Velma"—and the second does not: "The search party was *composed* of Shaggy, Scooby, and Velma." "Comprised of" is the common muddle, and is safest avoided. "Consisted of" and "made up of" might make your life easier.

deny; refute; rebut. If you "refute" or "rebut" a charge, you disprove it. If you "deny" a charge, you simply claim it isn't true. A distinction is sometimes made between "rebut" and "refute"—the latter meaning a categorical disproval and the former emphasizing the mounting of an argument—but in common usage they are interchangeable. The *OED* defines "rebut" with the words "disprove" and "refute."

dilemma. Pedants will say that it describes a choice between two things, and not more, on the basis of its etymology (the Greek *di-lemma* meaning two propositions).

discreet; discrete. The former refers to tactful secrecy, the latter to separate things. "My wife and my mistress occupy *discrete* parts of my life. Fortunately my butler is *discreet* about it."

disinterested; uninterested. Often used to mean "not interested in," as in, "He was completely disinterested in what I had to say." "Disinterested" means "not having skin in the game"—i.e., "A *disinterested* observer would see the justice of Fred's complaint." "Uninterested" is what you say when you want to convey boredom.

enormity. This is an old-fashioned word meaning a moral abomination or wickedness—as in Ben Jonson's *Bartholmew Fayre*: "The very womb and bed of enormity." It is commonly now used to mean "enormousness," and the usage doesn't seem to have led to any great loss of life.

flaunt; flout. If you "flaunt" something, you're showing it off. If you "flout" something, you're showing contempt for it. "Kim Kardashian *flaunts* her curves in a daring peekaboo bikini." "The celebrity website's showbiz coverage *flouts* the decencies of a civilized society."

fulsome. This adjective, usually applied to apologies or praise, means "horribly over the top" rather than "generous and effusive." It's used so much in the second sense, now, that the sticklers look to be losing that battle. Oliver Kamm points out that the second sense of it predates the first, and that the *OED* contains an instance from 1325 meaning "plentiful" or "abundant."

hanged; hung. A criminal is "hanged" (as in, "by the neck until dead"); pictures and porn stars are "hung."

headbutt. This is, if you're going to be fussy, a tautology. You can't butt someone with any part of your body other than your head.* This is not a common stickler obsession, but it has a story attached. I was in an editorial meeting at the newspaper where I used to work when an ashen member of the news desk interrupted us. He told the editor that our drunken Scottish political reporter had headbutted a Scottish lawmaker in the Holyrood bar. Our then editor frowned. "Actually," he said, "I think you mean 'butted.'" No more, as far as I know, was said on the subject.

---

* Oddly, you can't butt someone with your butt.

hopefully. This is another usage that causes sticklers to weep sweet, sweet tears of anger. They will say that the word "hopefully" is an adverb meaning "in a manner filled with hope"—as in, "It is better to travel *hopefully* than to arrive." Therefore, they argue, to write, "*Hopefully,* I will finish my book before my deadline" is at best a dangling modifier and at worst a crime against the language. Where's the verb it modifies? The answer is that it's not modifying a verb; it's modifying a sentence. And as a sentence adverb—a role it's had since the first half of the twentieth century—it conveys the meaning that something is to be hoped for. It has, in other words, acquired a new meaning.* It seems to irritate people particularly because many sentence adverbs can be rewritten in their verbal forms—"it is sad that" for "sadly," "it is amusing that" for "amusingly," and so on—and "it is hopeful that" doesn't quite work the same way. Nor do "thankfully," "frankly," "regretfully," and any number of others. Sadly, pedants will keep going on about this. Mostly, they can be ignored.

imply; infer. If you "imply" something, you are putting a meaning across in a slightly oblique way. If you "infer" something, you are drawing a conclusion about the meaning.

invariably. I invariably catch myself using this to mean "most of the time" or "very frequently." Technically it means "without variation," i.e., unfailingly and all the time.

irregardless. Not a word, it's widely thought. In fact this awkward or jocular collision of "regardless" and "irrespective" does appear

---

* *The Economist Style Guide* has an intriguing theory as to how. It blames the Germans. German immigrants to America, it suggests, "found the language of their new country had only one adverb to serve for both *hoffnungsvoll*, meaning full of hope, and *hoffentlich*, which can mean let's hope so." The *Economist* offers no evidence for this, but it's an interesting idea.

in the *OED*—but more than half of the citations there feature the word in the context of doubting whether it's a proper word at all: "She tells the pastor that he should please quit using the word 'irregardless' in his sermons as there is no such word." Steer clear.

just deserts. Since "deserts" in its non-sandy sense is only ever used in the set phrase "just deserts," it frequently gets muddled with its pudding-meaning homophone. It means "what you deserved," and shares the verb's single *s*. Just Desserts would be a punning name for a restaurant. If you ate there all the time and got fat, that would be your just deserts.

lie; lay. "Lie" is an intransitive verb with the past tense "lay." "Lay" is a transitive verb with the past tense "laid." You *lie* on a bench. You *lay* wreaths. You *lay* on a bench yesterday. You *laid* wreaths yesterday. Dialect usage sometimes substitutes "lay" (usually in participle form) for "lie": "I was *laying* on the sofa when I remembered I had an appointment." That's not standard written English.

literally. This word traditionally means "not figuratively." "That soccer player *literally* has two left feet" would denote not clumsiness on the ball but an unprecedented birth defect or mutilation. Its use as an all-purpose intensifier—"I wouldn't kiss you, Piers, if you were *literally* the last man on earth"—has become so common that it has now come to mean "figuratively." It's a word that literally now means both one thing, and the opposite of that thing. Even the *OED* now includes among its uses (though as "colloq") the indication "that some [. . .] metaphorical or hyperbolical expression is to be taken in the strongest admissible sense." Fortunately, the context almost unfailingly tells you which sense it's being used in. If someone says "I literally died," they didn't.

mischievious. This is a misspelling (or if you insist, variant) of the word "mischievous." An online poll for the Oxford Dictionaries blog in 2014 found that 53 percent of respondents claimed to use the misspelling rather than the correct version. I suspect they were being, well, mischievous.

snuck. An unexceptionable variant past participle for the verb "to sneak"; chiefly (the *OED* says) an American usage. Gets some people riled. I've had grown men take time out of their lives to write me angry letters when I've written "snuck up on."

such as; like. These are very often used interchangeably. "Elite athletes like Giant Haystacks and Jocky Wilson were mainstays of Saturday afternoon television when I was a child." Sticklers will have it that you should say "such as" rather than "like" here, since you're not emphasizing a *resemblance* between the athletes on television and the people in question, but offering named examples of the people who were on television. "Such as," in those instances, is preferable. Compare: "Very fat men like Giant Haystacks and Jocky Wilson are a liability on the trampoline." Often, these senses will overlap, though. It's worth trying both out when you're not sure. What sounds right? If it's possible to replace "like" with "for example," you are probably best off going with "such as."

supersede. It means to replace something. "Supercede" is a common misspelling. "The spelling 'supersede' has *superseded* the variant 'supercede.'"

Wrong Notes

There are other, subtler missteps to watch out for when it comes to vocabulary. These have to do with style and tone. If your tone is arch, self-regarding, pompous, sneering, cutesy, or merely jocular you might score the odd snigger from the peanut gallery, but you do nothing to reach the more skeptical reader.

It's worth being particularly careful of boastful self-descriptions or, worse, boastful self-descriptions that appear to be neutral or even self-deprecating. It's the equivalent of giving yourself a nickname like "Dutch" or "Ace" and hoping it sticks. You are asking to be bullied. Some are obvious. If you describe yourself as a "maverick," a "cynic," a "reprobate," a "provocateur," a "wag," or similar, you are on a sure course for others to apply less flattering descriptions to you.

But others are subtler: "Skeptic," "realist," "radical," and "progressive" are all essentially boasts masquerading as statements of fact. "Skeptic" says: "I'm the sort of person who thinks critically about what I read or hear." Since everyone presumably aspires to do just that, you're trying to say you're cleverer than those around you. "Radical" means nothing at all, in this context, except that the speaker thinks that there's a particular disruptive bravery to his or her political persona—which is a judgment for others to make. "Progressive" is a compliment that the political left pays to itself: a near-antonym of "conservative" that smuggles in a vague sense that the right direction of travel is self-evidently forward, and that there's only one sort of forward that works.

At the other end of the political spectrum you should be likewise cautious about appeals to "common sense" or "right thinking," which arrogantly assume that a position is so obvious it needs no argument. If it did need no argument you probably wouldn't need to assert it in the first place. These and phrases like them are generally code for an unexamined assumption. If something stands to reason, you should make clear why.

Then there's the linguistic equivalent of the Christmas sweater or the revolving bow tie. Avoid jocularity. Jocularity is not the same thing as humor; it's the substitute for humor deployed by those incapable of the real thing. It's being asked what you do for a living and saying: "I'm a schoolteacher . . . *for my sins!*" It's arriving to meet your friends and announcing: "Gentlemen!" or "Ladies!" It's raising a glass of wine and announcing: "Ah, the true, the blushful Hippocrene . . ."

The showy or joking use of foreign words or phrases is often a hallmark of this style of language. *Weltanschauung* doesn't do much that "worldview" doesn't. And so on. Of course there's huge latitude for personal preference—some people will think *alfresco* or *esprit de l'escalier* pretentious, but the first is common enough (at least to my ear) to pass muster, and the second, like *Schadenfreude*, has no similarly economical English equivalent. But the more showily and often you drop a loanword or loan phrase into a piece of writing, the more likely it is that it will grate on the reader.

A handful of examples should give you the general idea. All are usages that tell the reader less about what he or she wants to know and more about what the writer thinks of him- or herself. They are, effectively, advertisements for a persona: semantic junk mail.

"Academe," especially preceded by "groves of." "Academia" or "the academy" don't have that awful archness. See also "Big Apple" and "Frisco" (unless you're Otis Redding or Sylvia Plath).

"The Bard" as an epithet for Shakespeare. Just about all right for a headline writer; terrible in speech or continuous prose. Likewise, Wilde is not "the divine Oscar" unless you're hoping to look horribly arch.

"Bibulous" or "convivial." "I should like to entertain you to a bibulous lunch." "The gathering promises to be convivial." "Drunken" will do just as nicely in both cases.

"Call out" as a synonym for "challenge" or "oppose." This popular expression grades its own homework—it implies that what you object to is ipso facto wrong, and that in speaking against it you're not expressing a different view so much as bravely speaking truth to power. The self-flattering *High Noon* implications are particularly embarrassing.

"Deconstruct" as a clever-sounding synonym for "analyze." It has a meaning in philosophy. That meaning is not "write a short commentary on something I saw on the internet."

"Embonpoint" and "décolletage" are prissy and usually slightly jocular euphemisms for the visible parts of a woman's breasts. "Breasts," "tits," "boobs," "cleavage," "puppies," or what have you all serve better in their respective contexts. "Bosoms" in the plural is technically a fault, and certainly a vulgarism—but it has passed (see also "bazooms" and, presumably by analogy, "bazookas") into fairly common use. "Derriere" is a criminally arch way of referring to someone's backside. The *Daily Mail*'s website, at the time of writing, contained 5,840 instances of the word "derriere," of which more than 2,000 collocated with the word "pert."

"Luncheon" is a perfectly good English word. But "lunch" is a better one.

"Tome" is a mimsy and arch usage. Try "book." And if you automatically reach for "slim volume" as the standard epithet for a book of poetry, you're reaching for a cliché.

Whenever I'm confronted by vocabulary of this type, I'm reminded of an old cartoon. It shows a man in a fancy restaurant saying: "Waiter: What's the *plat du jour*?" Waiter: "It's 'dish of the day' in French, sir."

In a word, if you catch yourself sounding like Frasier or, worse, Niles, think hard about your vocabulary choice.

8

Out into the World

Long-Form Structure

This might seem like a catchall category. In a way, it is. I mean, here, to paddle for a moment out of the shallows into the open sea to consider forms of writing that aren't constrained by the formal properties of, say, a memo or an email. Think of it as the big-chunk-of-prose section. Some of what I say here will apply to things such as letters and emails, too.

An essay is, as its name suggests, an attempt. It can—when you write it at school—be an attempt to answer a question or marshal a set of ideas. But there's something tentatively implicit in the premise. It's a piece of writing that will want to find its own form, or whose form will be dictated by its material and by the movement of thought. But form of some sort, it will need to have. A piece of prose is not just a collection of sentences. It needs to arrest the reader's attention, draw them through the argument, and end with a sense of resolution that, ideally, throws the reader forward toward action or conviction.*

PLANNING

First: Don't panic. If you can't write down a perfectly lucid abstract of what you intend to say, and in what order, that's normal. Most writers learn what they mean in the process of writing it; they come to feel how points and ideas flock together. Transitions will suggest

---

* One of the more withering critiques of a piece of writing I've had is that it "doesn't so much end as stop." For good examples of the pitfalls of this see page 252.

themselves. That's what I mean by the material suggesting its form. Further clarity will come in the process of revising.

That's not to say you shouldn't plan at all. If you're arguing from a set of premises to a particular set of conclusions, order your thoughts. Get clear, not just in your head but on a piece of paper, what those premises and those conclusions are. Try putting them in order of importance. You might find that two or more of them belong together—or that one is a subcategory of another.

You can afford to free-associate a little bit on the page. What you're looking for at this stage is a set of units of thought. My notes often look like a collection of spider plants viewed from the air: A theme in block capitals will be linked to relevant quotations or subthemes by a set of lines, and these clusters in turn will be linked by longer lines to other clusters. Don't think of these as essay plans so much as preliminary maps of your ideas.

These clusters might end up as groups of paragraphs, as subsections, as chapters, or as bullet points, depending on the genre you're working in. When you set about assembling your piece, you'll consider how to fit them together in the linear order that continuous prose demands. You can't say two things at once, so when you have two or more things to say, you'll need to prioritize. You may find that the logic of the argument leads you one way and that the impact it needs to make leads you another.

How you prioritize will depend on what sort of thing you're trying to do. In most situations you're caught between wanting to end strongly (because readers will remember the end best, according to the so-called "recency effect"), and wanting to begin strongly, because if you don't, they won't reach the end anyway. The compromise is usually either to deliver the material in decreasing order of importance, as per the inverted pyramid on page 205, and then deliver a recapped essence of it as the payoff; or to build steadily up to a high-energy conclusion.

Think of a graph shape. In terms of energy and importance, your composition will either start strong then drop to a low level, and build back up, or start strong, dwindle down, and then spike back up at the end. That shark's-tooth shape may structure your broad argument, but it will also be seen section by section and paragraph by paragraph. Something more academic or meditative—where you're arguing up from premises to conclusions—might take the first model; something more object-oriented and practical—where you're stating a case and then offering the supporting evidence—the latter.

Say you're making the case for your company buying the old toothpaste factory on the edge of town. You'll probably start by saying (headline news) that you need to buy the old toothpaste factory. Then you might say that there are four reasons: the attractive price; the need to diversify into toothpaste; the tax write-downs available; the knowledge that your competitor is planning a toothpaste operation. Each of these reasons will command a little section. You'll put those sections into order of importance, probably with the most important first. Each one will begin with the reason you're giving, and then the evidence in support of those reasons.

So a plan might look like this.

We need to buy the factory

We need to diversify into toothpaste
The bottom is falling out of the acne cream market
Our pharmacists already know how to make toothpaste
Toothpaste is performing strongly because of the world mouthwash shortage
If we don't make toothpaste our rivals will get out ahead of us
Our spy at EvilPharm says they are planning on making toothpaste
They can outcompete us if they have a wider range of products
The price is good

*The factory went bust and creditors are disposing of its
assets in a hurry*

*A similar site sold earlier this year for $150,000 more than
the asking price*

We can claim the cost against tax

At this point in the tax year a big capital expenditure will help

So to recap: We need to buy the factory

That's a great big shark's-tooth Z-shape, with a series of smaller shark's-tooth shapes embedded in it.

As I said above, every situation will ask for a different structural solution. But enough of them map onto each other that there are general remarks you can make, and—indeed—ideas that have endured through history. A few are to be found below. Think of them as a nonexclusive selection of techniques, rather than using any one of them as a rigid template.

STRUCTURAL TRICKS

Say It Three Times

The classic, and the simplest, piece of advice is: Tell people what you're going to say, say it, and then tell them that you've said it. First, you cue your audience up to receive your message. Then you deliver it in detail. Then you recap in brief.

Exposition

Argument

Recap

Classical Structure

There are various classical schemes for the arrangement of a piece of persuasion, but most of them are simplifications or elaborations on this one, from the first-century rhetoric handbook, originally attributed to Cicero, called *Ad Herennium*.

> ***Exordium****: Your introduction, where you grab the attention.*
>
> ***Narration****: You set out the facts of the case as generally agreed.*
>
> ***Division****: You make clear where the areas of disagreement are.*
>
> ***Proof****: You make your own argument.*
>
> ***Refutation****: You offer your case against any counterarguments or objections.*
>
> ***Peroration****: Sum up; forcefully state your conclusion or recommendations.*

Fascinating AIDA

An orthodoxy in modern marketing is that customers can be herded down a "purchase funnel" toward buying a product. If you think of your argument as that product, you can see how the purchase funnel maps onto communications in general.

The notion of AIDA describes a movement through different stages.

> ***Awareness*** *or* ***Attention****: Make the consumer aware of what you're selling.*
>
> ***Interest*** *or* ***Information****: Make the consumer want to find out more.*
>
> ***Desire*** *or* ***Direct Benefit****: Make clear why this personally affects the consumer.*
>
> ***Action****: Close the deal.*

So, for instance:

A: Have you heard about our revolutionary new bandage for corns?

I: They use patented nanotechnology to clear up corns 60 percent faster than our rivals.

D: If YOU have corns, they will remove them in ten days flat—or your money back.

A: Call 1-800-CORNPLASTERCON now to take advantage of our limited-time discount offer!

More soberly and at greater length, this rough structure does service for an intellectual selling situation, too. It has audience awareness baked into it. It asks you to grab the attention, to set out the facts, to explain the relevance to the audience at hand, and then to make a call to action at the end. Not so different, when you consider it, from the classical structure.

Such is the popularity of this sort of acronymic scheme that you'll come across many others. The *Oxford Guide to Plain English*, for instance, offers SCRAP (Situation, Complication, Resolution, Action, and Politeness) and SOAP (Situation, Objective, Appraisal, Proposal).

The former is good for apologizing for a mistake or snafu.

Situation: It's Chinese New Year.

Complication: Your Chinese-built window shutters will be delivered a week later than advertised.

Resolution: We'll knock 10 percent off the price by way of apology.

Action: Do let us know if this is acceptable or if you'd prefer to cancel the order.

Politeness: Sorry again for the inconvenience. We look forward to hearing from you.

The latter, which again echoes the classical scheme, is good for making a case for action.

Situation: Our pension fund is in a failing bank.

Objective: We need to ensure the safety of our capital.

Appraisal: If we diversify our portfolio it's less vulnerable to market crises.

Proposal: Let's seek permission from the trustees to withdraw it from Failbank and place it in a DiverseFinance fund.

What these and schemes like them have in common is that they follow the movement of thought. You start by setting out a situation, move on to an analysis, and end with a call to action.

Inverted Pyramid

This is the classic structure of a news report. It's useful in all sorts of situations and contexts, particularly when the material is urgent and the attention of your readership is not guaranteed. Essentially, you deliver the vital information and then unpack it.

The very first paragraph of a news report tells you the *who*, the *what*, the *where*, and the *when*. American hacks call this the "nut graph"; it's the core of the story.

The vital information is at the top, and the farther down the news story the less informationally rich the story is. You can skim the paper, read the first few paragraphs, and get the essentials, but the longer the reader invests in the story, the more information he or she will be supplied.

It should be obvious that headlines as often as not function as a pre-nut-graph nut graph. The headline is a crunched-down version of the first sentence, which itself is a crunched-down version of the second sentence, and so on. So, that's the inverted pyramid. Read down and you'll get—in the average news story—background information about the events in the nut graph, then quotes (often extensive quotes, if the story's importance is deemed high enough that it runs prominently and at length) from the participants, and so on.

A company report or an email to a colleague may use just the same structure. You'll announce the headline news about this year's profits, or the impending takeover, or what Gloria heard Fred say at the coffee machine—and with the attention engaged you then expand on the detail.

Indeed, this is usually how we deliver news in conversation. "I'm having a baby!" comes first; the due date, gender, etc. wait till afterward. That means that, as ever, talking it out can help you get a sense of what comes first. If you have something complicated to say, and you're struggling to plan a piece of writing on the subject, try—without much premeditation—telling a friend (or an imaginary friend) what you're writing about. What comes out first will probably be your way in.

A variation of the inverted pyramid can be seen in the slightly more leisurely style known in my trade as the "drop intro." Here the first paragraph or even two whimsically walk you into the story. My old mentor Peter McKay, who learned his trade in local papers in Scotland, used to delight in recalling the formulaic drop intro that he had occasion to use every Tuesday morning: "What began as a quiet Friday night drink with friends yesterday had its sequel in the Aberdeen district magistrate's court . . ."

Knock the drop intro off, and paragraphs two or three will usually supply the traditional *who what where when* sentence. If you do decide to use a drop intro, it needs to have, as with McKay's wan humor, something to grab the attention. The main thing with an inverted pyramid is to get the vital information up top.

Ready for Your Close-Up?

In a more expansive context, you can afford to be less telegraphic. Think about camera shots. Let's say you're writing a long speech, a blog, an essay, or a report on a civil war in a faraway country. You may be needing to capture both the feel of the action on the ground and the geographic or historical overview. Is there a way of navigating easily from one to the other?

Starting with a close-up seldom lets you down. Perhaps you have an anecdote, a bit of personal reportage, or a quote that will give the material a human face or, better, exemplify your bigger theme. Whack it in first. That will immediately engage the attention and it will boost the ethos of your writing: It brings to it the authority of firsthand material.

> *Mohammed leaned his motorcycle on its kickstand and pulled his keffiyeh up against the rising dust. The AK jounced on his back. He spat.* Tomorrow, he told me, he would rescue his wife from the raiders or die trying.*

Then you can afford to pull back and take the bigger view.

> *The civil war in Otherstan has been going on for nearly ten years now. Fighters like Mohammed are typical of the young men whose lives have been caught up in it. After the collapse of the government in 2004, fighters spilled across the border from the neighboring state of Interferia, and this three-hundred-square-mile area, once farmland, is now a lawless zone of kidnapping, banditry, and sectarian warfare. Since its founding after the civil war of 1964, Otherstan has been a troubled republic. Three-quarters of its people are Otherish,*

---

* On rereading this, I'd have him spit before pulling his keffiyeh up rather than afterward. A good advertisement for paying attention.

like Mohammed, but it has been governed for thirty years by the minority Samians.

And so on. Here is the prose equivalent of a now much-parodied movie trope: We start in medias res with, say, a teenager in his underpants carrying a huge bowl of popcorn and running for his life from a skateboarding grizzly bear; then there's the sound of a record scratch; freeze-frame on the boy's face; and the voice-over comes in. "Yup, that's me. And you're probably wondering how I ended up in this situation..."

Playing with camera angles is a vital tool of the fiction writer's craft. It makes a huge difference whether something is written in the first, second, or third person, or in the shoulder-cam-like free indirect style (where an omniscient narrator in a third-person narrative inhabits the thoughts or feelings of the character: "It was agony. How could she just stand there and look at him that way?"). You have a more restricted palette as a writer of most sorts of nonfiction, but if you can control how you move between the wide arc of an argument and the detail, and how you address your audience, you control how that audience receives your writing.

Callbacks

In stand-up comedy, you'll often see sets structured with "callbacks." As the comedian makes his or her way through their monologue, they start to refer back to jokes they made early on, weaving a reference to the initial joke back into a new one. Done skillfully, this builds rapport with the audience and, delighted by the familiarity, that audience will give a bigger laugh each time the material reappears. It's a primal feature, too, of narrative; motifs, images, and ideas reappear in different forms. In political communications, a message is strengthened by repetition; catchwords that encapsulate a message recur. Remember Donald Trump banging on about "law and order."

A writer is not a stand-up comic. But you can give a piece of writing thematic coherence by using an approximation of this technique. If there's a central theme or set of themes to what you're writing about, it's a good idea to keep them front and center. Show how each new development of the argument bears on them. To take a very obvious example, if you're writing an SAT essay titled "Religion Is the Opiate of the People: Discuss," you will likely want to thread what you understand by "religion," "opiate," and "people" through the argument that follows.

Writing gets messy when it turns small circles: point A, then point B, then—oops—a bit more of point A, then point C, and so on. Fiddly or uncontrolled little eddies of thought damage structure. So your callbacks need to be under control—echoes rather than clumsy full-scale reprisals of your earlier sections of argument. Each one moves the whole thing on. Think of the leitmotif in music.

A grand version of the callback is what I call "loop the loop," below.

Loop the Loop

One of the most useful tricks in journalism—and it works just as well in other essayistic situations—is to tie things up with a bow. That is, find a way in your closing paragraph to refer back to the beginning. So, for instance, you might start with a particular quotation, an anecdote, or an image. And at the end you circle back to close on the same thing; not, ideally, an exact repetition, but a twist on it. You might answer a question that you asked in the opening; you might return to a scene from a different angle; you might tease out a new meaning in a quotation.

Giving a speech in the White House at the turn of the millennium, for instance, the Holocaust survivor Elie Wiesel opened by describing how "fifty-four years ago to the day, a young Jewish boy from a small town in the Carpathian Mountains woke up, not far from Goethe's beloved Weimar, in a place of eternal infamy called

Buchenwald." That boy was, of course, Wiesel himself, and he used that image as a launchpad for a speech about the history of the twentieth century. In his conclusion, he said: "Once again, I think of the young Jewish boy from the Carpathian Mountains. He has accompanied the old man I have become throughout these years of quest and struggle."

That's a particularly elegant instance of the circling structure, and it draws its emotional force from a shift in camera angles. The boy in the opening of the speech is, as it were, over there—separated from us by a continent and fifty-four years. When we reencounter him he's in the room with us. The speech has made the journey from Buchenwald in the mid-1940s to Washington at the tail end of 1999.

You don't have to be Elie Wiesel to use this technique. I once wrote a column about Christmas carols, for instance, after the newspaper I worked on had done a poll to find the readers' favorites. I started out by pouring scorn on the winner (insult the readers: always a good attention-getter), which was "Hark! The Herald Angels Sing." My argument for the purposes of the piece was that the best Christmas song of all time was not a carol but "Fairytale of New York" by Kirsty MacColl and the Pogues. I banged on about the emotional content of the song for a few hundred words—the love, the loss, the anguish, the affirmation, the nostalgia—and ended by asking: "What's that if not the hopes and fears of all the years?" By quoting "O Little Town of Bethlehem" like that I brought the whole thing back to Christmas carols. It was the cheapest of tricks, but it made a piece that would otherwise have been a rather clunky two-part cut-and-shut job ("Hark!" is bad; "Fairytale" is good) look more elegant than it was.

Closing where you opened doesn't cost much mental energy, in other words, and the payoff can be considerable. Even if what's in between is a bit of a ramble, the sense of closure it brings will leave your readers with the impression of something neat and well-made.

Letters

Old-fashioned old things, letters. Who now sends them—other, of course, than credit card companies and the IRS? In a paperless age, this section of the book in your hand may well seem like the most nearly redundant. Nevertheless, the essential rules and courtesies that apply to snail mail letters apply, in large part, to those you send electronically. The email is a development of the letter, not a new thing entirely.

Also, there are many circumstances, still, in which the dead-tree letter is the best or the only thing to send. Certain business situations demand them—particularly legal ones. And when it comes to condolence, congratulation, or giving your lover the old heave-ho, there's nothing like handwritten script on paper.

BUSINESS LETTERS

The rules around these are pretty straightforward. The ethos you are seeking to project is one of professionalism. And a lot of the work of projecting that ethos—particularly in terms of first impressions—will be done not by what you write but by how it's set out.

In *American Psycho*, Patrick Bateman, who as well as being a serial killer is an excellent judge of professional ethos, agonizes over the tastefulness of his business cards. "That's bone," he boasts to his colleagues, "and the lettering is something called Silian Rail." He's mortified when he's one-upped by someone whose cards have "raised lettering" and a "pale nimbus white" tint.

We can't all be Patrick Bateman, but weight of paper, style of letterhead, font choice, and layout will make an instant impact on your reader. Be anal. If a wonky printer means that your letterhead is at a slight angle to the body of your text, it'll be noticed.

Likewise, better no letterhead than a badly homemade one.* If you have forgotten—or not bothered—to sign your name in pen between the sign-off and your printed name, again, it'll make a small but significant impression. That is, if anything, even more important when the letter is a mass mail-out. Don't underestimate the value of making clear that you have paid personal attention to each one.

Also, start from the assumption that it's better to sound a bit stiff than to sound presumptuous. Addressing people you've never met by their first names will strike the more old-fashioned of them— and there are still a few of those—as rude and unprofessional. If you're involved in a correspondence and the person starts signing off with his or her first name, you might take that as an invitation to begin doing so—but don't presume familiarity.

In terms of register, that goes for the whole thing. Be formal without being pompous. Be brisk and clear—businesslike, in fact— and set your points out in order, one to a paragraph. The quicker your letter is to read and digest, the greater the courtesy to your readers. Show them that you value their time.

The most common style nowadays—and the one that to my eye looks most professional or official—is block format. That is, each paragraph begins flush with the left-hand margin, and paragraphs are separated by a line break. In that case most often everything— address, date, reference number if applicable, and sign-off at the bottom—will be left-justified.

You put your address at the top (a letterhead will often cover this); then the recipient's name and address; then the date. The date usually looks best written out in full. It can also be handy to give a letter a heading—the equivalent of a subject line for an email. This would usually go between the salutation and the body of the letter.

---

* I used to see pitches to newspaper feature desks from people calling themselves professional writers that—I kid you not—came accompanied by a clip-art image of a quill pen dipped in an inkwell.

So, for instance:

Ping-Pong Paddles Ltd.
Ping-Pong House
2404 Table Tennis Way
Baltimore, MD 21216

Frank Johnson
Services Manager
William Henry Harrison Youth Club
320 Dexter Street NW
Washington, DC 20007

November 20, 2016

Dear Mr. Johnson,

Ping-Pong Paddle Catalog

I enclose as requested an up-to-date list of all the Ping-Pong paddles our company currently supplies, with prices and details of availability.

Should you wish to order more than two boxes, I'm happy to advise you that a 10 percent discount is available for bulk orders. You can also find details on our website, ping-pong-paddles.com, where an online order form is available for download.

Yours sincerely,

P. Pong
Customer Service Director

An indented style might be appropriate for a slightly less formal letter. Perhaps you're writing personally to offer someone a job, thanking someone for a piece of work, or congratulating someone on forty years of service. Stylistically, it moves slightly in the direction of a personal letter and the format may reflect that. In this case you'd indent the first line of each successive paragraph.

When you get to the text, as I shouldn't have to say, make damn sure that you have checked the grammar and punctuation. That care is a courtesy to the reader, and one that will be noticed if it isn't there.

It is equally important to get forms of address right. Traditionally, a letter addressed to "Dear Sir/Madam" should be signed "Yours faithfully"; one addressed to a named recipient "Yours sincerely." If you're dealing with members of one or other titled aristocracy, academic or medical doctors, and what have you, you need to get their form of address right, too. Don't "Miss" a Mrs. or "Mr." a professor. It just looks sloppy.*

And for goodness' sake, above all other things spell the person's name, and get their job title, right. Fouling that up is the one-on-one equivalent of sending a mass mailing headed "Dear [Insert Name Here]." As a journalist, I get endless press releases where it's clear the sender has lifted my name off some database and is spamming me (and a million others like me) at random. The sender has no idea, or doesn't care, that I don't and have never written about knitwear, that I'm not a section editor on *Country Life*, or what have you. Those releases are very easy to throw out.

JOB APPLICATION LETTERS AND CVS

Here, as with a business letter, the absolute priority is to look professional. Proofread that sucker into the ground. If at all possible address it to a named person—you'll get brownie points for having

* See "Forms of Address," page 247.

troubled to find out who to apply to. "Dear Sir/Madam," in the age of LinkedIn and Google, looks lazy.

The other thing to remember is that, in most cases, the recipient is going to be looking for a reason—any reason—to cut down the pile on his or her desk and file your application in the wastepaper basket. You'll no doubt remember the old gag about the CEO who randomly tossed out all the job applications he was sent on the grounds that he only wanted to recruit candidates who were lucky.

Brevity and clarity are more than usually vital. I'd hesitate to send a cover letter that strayed onto a second side of the page. The same for a CV. So: One side for the cover letter; one side for the CV.

And as ever, apply the baiting-the-hook principle: You need to think not of what the company can do for you, but of what you can do for the company. Find as much out about the job as you can in advance, and highlight those aspects of your experience that best answer its specific needs. Identify key words in the job notice you're responding to, and find a way of using them appropriately in the letter of application.

Avoid cliché. Describing yourself as a "team player" or a "highly motivated self-starter" simply signifies that you've absorbed a certain amount of business cant. Nobody's interested in your "passion" for this or your "vision" for that. Sorry. And as a rule your hobbies and interests will be of very little interest to a recruiter.

There are many different schools of thought on how you design a CV. But as with the letter it accompanies, it needs to be waffle-free and it needs to be tailored in each case to the specific job you're applying for. If you were a "senior facilities executive at Tent Solutions Ltd.," make plain—crisply—what that involved; job titles often don't speak for themselves.

Again, you're looking to give someone with limited patience as much useful information as possible as quickly as you can. Professional headhunters, when surveyed, claim to spend four or five minutes reading each CV that crosses their desk. But when a jobs site called Ladders put the claim to the test—using eye-tracking software—they found that the real figure was six seconds.* Yup. Six.

This means that the most sensible way to arrange a CV is according to the inverted pyramid structure of a newspaper article. The important stuff goes up top: your name and contact details first of all. Then put your recent career history in *reverse* order.

The eye-tracking study I mentioned above also discovered that recruiters spend 80 percent of their time focusing on six data points: name, current job title and employer, previous job title and employer, the start and end dates for the last job, the start and end dates for the job before, and the candidate's education.

So think about how far you want to go back. The CV at this stage is a marketing tool rather than a life history. It gets you (with a bit of luck) through the first stage of the recruitment process. If the company then wants more detail, you can give it to them further down the line.

They'll want to know what you did most recently before they want to hear about your test scores or your glittering collection of school sports trophies. In fact, once you have one or more real-world jobs under your belt, you can probably dispense with any academic history beyond (if applicable) your university degree.

I'd suggest job title, company, and dates (in brackets) in bold followed by no more than a sentence or two of explanation in ordinary type. For instance:

* Will Evans, "You Have 6 Seconds to Make an Impression: How Recruiters See Your Resume," Ladders, March 12, 2012, theladders.com/p/10541/you-only-get-6-seconds-of-fame-make-it-count.

Senior Facilities Executive, Tent Solutions Ltd. (2014–16)

I managed a team of five workers, and was responsible for running the invoicing system, dispatching orders to customers, and maintaining stock levels in the warehouse. I'm familiar with Tentware and Tentcel as well as standard financial and accounting software.

Use a clean, well-sized font (I'd recommend twelve-point) and use white space plentifully. A CV that makes you squint and strain your eyes isn't one that's going to be attractive. Whether you center or left-justify the text is up to you, but experiment with what looks cleanest, easiest to read, and least gimmicky. Wacky fonts, multicolored text, and random capitals will make your CV stand out—but not in a good way.

Unless you're applying for a job as a model, you can do without attaching a photograph of yourself. That goes even if you're super-hot; in fact, it goes especially if you're super-hot. That eye-tracking software I mentioned earlier discovered that recruiters would spend fully a fifth of those all-important six seconds looking at the pretty photographs rather than reading the CV.

LETTERS OF COMPLAINT

The most important thing to remember when writing a letter of complaint is that you want its recipient to be on your side. You may be utterly enraged, but if you want to achieve something without recourse to the law, you vastly help yourself by being courteous and reasonable.

Particularly with large corporations, the person who gets your letter of complaint will not, usually, be the one who has wronged you. At least to start with, they have no skin in the game. They may even be sympathetic to your situation. That sympathy evaporates when you begin slinging around words like "incompetent" and "farcical," demanding people be fired, or making empty threats of legal action. It makes you feel good to bluster and rage, but it's how the recipient of the letter feels that will actually matter. As ever, the trick is to go to where your audience is.

Try to picture how the first draft of your letter might go over if Dave in Customer Relations reads it out to Jane at the next-door desk. The thing to remember is that Dave almost certainly doesn't give a monkey's. The more bloodcurdling the letter, the more likely that he and Jane will have a good giggle over it and start thinking up ways to raise your blood temperature further. Start from the assumption that you are entertainment. And then work to countermand that assumption by being reasonable. In an ideal world, if Dave reads your letter to Jane, Jane will go: "Yeah. You have to admit that person has a point . . ."

Your task is to make irresistibly plain how you've been inconvenienced, and then propose what will seem to your correspondent a reasonable and proportionate redress—and one that is within their power to make. In an ideal world, they will come away feeling good about themselves and you'll come away having obtained satisfaction.

So a letter of complaint needs to be forensically clear. First, get your ducks in a row. What are you complaining about? What do you want to happen? Let's say you got your dry-cleaning home only to discover a giant iron-shaped burn mark in the lining of your favorite suit. The guy in the dry-cleaning shop claimed it was nothing to do with him. Now you're writing to the head office.

Enclose the evidence you have. Include relevant photographs or receipts. Be precise about what happened when, and in what sequence. If you had an argument in person with the man in the shop, you might want to mention it—but keep your eyes on the prize: Your concern is with getting your suit mended. Don't get diverted into he-said-she-said. Rudeness is seldom subject to concrete redress, and your correspondent might well assume that you gave as good as you got.

If your previous five letters have gone unanswered, patiently enumerate the dates on which you sent them. If this is the latest in a long correspondence, again, make sure you identify the date of the last one they sent you for their ease of reference. If there's something relevant in a contract or the terms on the dry-cleaning ticket, point it out clearly.

And when you're proposing redress, "I demand" is—oddly—a lot easier to ignore than, for instance, "In the circumstances it seems reasonable to expect . . ." Remember the exchange between Harry Hotspur and the bombastic Owen Glendower in Shakespeare's *Henry IV, Part 1*? "I can call spirits from the vasty deep," Glendower brags. "Why, so can I, or so can any man," laughs Hotspur. "But will they come when you do call for them?"

You're trying to take your correspondent gently but firmly by the elbow, rather than bashing heads with them. Once an exchange gets to be oppositional or abusive, it will tend to stay that way. I've been let off parking tickets by writing politely and apologetically to explain the circumstances. I've never got anywhere by calling someone a fool.

The tweet of complaint—which is rapidly taking over as a means of complaining to large organizations—is a special case. I'll discuss that in the section on writing for electronic media.

LETTERS TO FRIENDS

Here we are in more or less uncharted territory, and I don't propose to try charting it. A letter to a friend is an unbridled exercise in voice. And almost nobody—now we have emails and Facebook messages and DMs on Twitter—writes them these days. It's a shame. They should. There are no rules. You can be as informal as you like. You can include sketches and doodles. And your letters will be a lifelong conversation. One day a trove of them will spill out of a box and give you unimaginable happiness.

One of the saddest things for me as a literary journalist is the realization that the collected letters, as a genre of published book, is almost certainly dying out. But if you read the great epistolary friendships—Robert Lowell and Elizabeth Bishop, say, or Kingsley Amis and Philip Larkin—you will see what we have lost. In our letters we are doing what has been called "writing to the moment": The quick of life is in them, and all its absurdity.

That sense of a lifelong conversation comes poignantly through in the last letter from Larkin to Amis. Dictating from his deathbed, Larkin ended his last letter to his friend: "You will excuse the absence of the usual valediction, Yours ever, Philip." Every letter that he'd sent Amis for decades had ended in the word "bum." But out of consideration for the sensibilities of the woman who'd be transcribing his tape, Larkin omitted it. Eleven days later he was dead.

Always remember that your job, writing to a friend, is to entertain. That can mean reveling in the odd pratfall. In *London Fields*, Martin Amis offered the best postcard-writing advice I've ever read: "The letter with the foreign postmark that tells of good weather, pleasant food and comfortable accommodation," he warned, "isn't nearly as much fun to read, or to write, as the letter that tells of rotting chalets, dysentery and drizzle. Who else but Tolstoy has made happiness really swing on the page?"

THANK-YOU LETTERS

If someone has treated you to lunch, sent you a card on your anniversary, or—in an instance that occurs about as often as a Higgs boson presents itself spontaneously to a physicist—remembered their godchild's birthday, you cannot but cover yourself in glory by writing a proper thank-you with a pen on a piece of paper.

Sitting down with pen and paper to write and thank them, in the manner of a Dickensian scribe, and then locating a stamp, and an envelope, and their postal address, and a zip code, will seem like an extraordinary pain in the neck. That's exactly why it's worth doing. You're demonstrating your appreciation by exactly that effort—and you increase considerably thereby the chance that they'll treat you again.

LETTERS OF CONDOLENCE

There's little that paralyzes the average person more than writing a letter of condolence to a friend who has lost a loved one. You feel awkward and embarrassed. That's fine. But the act of writing is in itself what will be valued; however awkward the letter, someone grieving will want to hear from you rather than not. You are extending respect and friendship. Write quickly, and write—I'd strongly suggest—by hand.

You'll want to calibrate what you write to your relationship both with the recipient and with the deceased. The whole point of this letter is that it's personal. If you knew the deceased well, sharing a couple of warm memories—even funny ones—will let the recipient of your letter feel that there's a shared bond. If you didn't know the deceased, you will very likely be able to make some respectful reference to what you knew of them.

And take care. Julian Barnes's 2013 book *Levels of Life*—which includes a memoir of his loss of his wife to an aggressive form of cancer—describes with unusual candor how the grieving can feel anger toward friends "for their inability to say or do the right things, for their unwanted pressingness or seeming *froideur*. And since the griefstruck rarely know what they need or want, only what they don't, offense-giving and offense-taking are common."*

Use tact. Don't be bossy. Don't tell the recipient how they should be feeling. If you're finding it hard to know what to say, you can acknowledge that; but don't harp on it. "I'm finding this a hard letter to write,

---

* Barnes includes a positively scalding anecdote about how not to do it: "Someone suggested I rent a flat in Paris for six months or, failing that, 'a beach cabin in Guadeloupe.' She and her husband would look after my house while I was away. This would be convenient for them, and 'we'd have a garden for Freddie.' The proposal came by email during the last day of my wife's life. And Freddie was their dog."

butIwantyoutoknowthatallmythoughtsarewithyou," or something
like it, is fine. Absolutely to be avoided are operatic, or competitive,
expressionsofgrief.Don'tfocusonhowthepersondied.Acknowledge,
butdon'tbelabor,thedreadfulgriefandpainthattherecipientmustbe
feeling.You'retryingtofocusontheindividualexcellenceoftheperson
they've lost rather than the consequences of the loss itself.

And everything I've read by or heard from people who've experienced serious bereavement is that bland, open-ended offers of
help are as little use as no offers at all. "Let me know if there's anything I can do" may make you feel better, but it puts the burden of
thinking of something for you to do on someone who has enough of
a burden already. A letter of condolence shouldn't demand a reply—
though it may get one.

Also, a respectful tact with regards to matters of religion is
advisable. If you write to the widow of a die-hard atheist—even if
you yourself are a believing Christian—saying that you're certain
he's in heaven right now crosses the line from condolence to troll-
ing. It's not about you.

LOVE LETTERS

It is not my place here to dabble my inky fingers in the stuff of people's souls. There are as many potential love letters as there are lov-
ers. The fact that you can't propose a boilerplate way of doing it is
exactly the point. This needs to be particular to the addressee, and
particular to you.

On the other hand, I can't quite resist. As Cyrano de Bergerac
showed us (which most of us will know via the Steve Martin movie
Roxanne), the right words can win the girl even when the boy's nose
is disfiguringly enormous and she would totally swipe left on Tinder.

What makes a love letter work? Above all, the lover wants to be
seen. The letter is about attention. I've sometimes heard it said that
what makes a relationship work is not how you feel about the other
person, but how the other person makes you feel about yourself.

Here is the essence of the performance: You are making clear how you feel about the other—how enveloping and alive your attention to the person is—and at the same time you're demonstrating a particular quality of attention. That is, you're being your best self—most alive to the world, most engaged with the other—so that the attention you're paying to them becomes a fantastic compliment: They are the prime focus of a consciousness that flares and sparks.

So moaning on about how miserable you are and how they're the only one who can save you from the awfulness of your solitude—true though it may be—makes you a burden, not a catch. Likewise waxing lyrical about moonlight and roses and whiskers on kittens is unlikely to work, except on a dullard; you're supposed to be intoxicated with your lover in his or her particularity, not intoxicated with your own prose style or with a collection of hackneyed literary gestures.

When William Godwin was courting his future wife Mary Wollstonecraft, he made just this mistake. He sent her a stilted love poem. She responded sharply. She said she didn't want an artificial composition but a "bird's-eye view of your heart." She told him not to write to her again "unless you honestly acknowledge yourself bewitched."

And there's no harm in a bit of filth. Sex is intimate communication, and so is intimate communication about sex. Here is Ted Hughes to Sylvia Plath during an enforced separation early in their marriage.

Above all, save every whisper until Saturday, save every little bit of you. I can hardly remember you without feeling almost sick and getting aching erections. I shall pour all this into you on Saturday and fill you and fill myself with you and kill myself on you....

I love you

Your husband, Ted.

One essence of the love letter is risk. It is a form at once self-concealing—in that you are shaping your self-depiction through words—and self-exposing. As countless works of literature from *Clarissa* forward bear witness, a letter can fall into the wrong hands.* It cannot be "taken back" or spun in quite the same way that a moment of drunken sincerity can. So the further you can go into intimacy, the more directly you expose yourself to the attention of the other, the more you place yourself in his or her power, the greater the trust you imply and the greater the confidence you instill.

DEAR JOHNS

Dorothy Parker wrote a short poem we could all do with taking note of.

> *By the time you swear you're his,*
> *Shivering and sighing,*
> *And he vows his passion is*
> *Infinite, undying—*
> *Lady, make a note of this:*
> *One of you is lying.*

Sooner or later, if it's not for keeps, you're going to be either a dumper or a dumpee. There are, again, no rules for this. But there is an elementary consideration you can pay. That is, have the conversation face to face. And if the written word does enter into it, write personally and try not to do so in anger. Dumping people by text message or email, or abruptly changing your Facebook status to single, are ways of adding insult to injury. Why would you not want even an ex to feel okay about themselves—or as okay about themselves as it's possible to be? As Kurt Vonnegut, whom I regard as an infallible moral authority, said: "God damn it, you've got to be kind."

Plus, self-interest enters in. Acting ungallantly when your

---

* The same goes for sexts, as Anthony Weiner knows to his cost.

relationship breaks up—particularly now that we live so much of our lives in public—will mark your card with others. The Genesis drummer Phil Collins was reported to have dumped his second wife by fax after twelve years of marriage. That is so much of a dick move that—even though Collins firmly denied it and nearly a quarter of a century has elapsed—it's still one of the main things people remember about him.

Writing for the Screen

I don't mean screenwriting. I mean writing for digital technologies, from websites to social media. Much of what I say here will have to be tentative—because the rules and conventions governing online interaction are still being set.

Linguistic change, as I've said before, is brought about by social relationships. Language encodes those social relationships. We learn language in the context of families, schoolyards, and communities, and we tend to stigmatize usages—be they regional or class variations—that are seen to belong to an out-group.

From the contact pidgins that are formed when two linguistic communities rub up against one another to the "creoles" that emerge from them as the first generations grow up who speak those pidgins as a native tongue, from the jargons of academic specialism to the vernaculars of different youth subcultures: All of these are artifacts of communities and identities. They are social.

Any number of linguistic and ideological tribes mix and clash in cyberspace. So it is no surprise that the internet in general and social media in particular (the clue, as the cliché goes, is in the name) are great laboratories of language change.

Imagine, if you like, the difference between patiently studying human evolution back through the fossil record, and then moving laboratories to start work on *Drosophila melanogaster*. A fruit fly generation is not much more than ten days long. Suddenly, you can study evolution in real time. So it is with something like Twitter.

Usages will pass in and out of fashion in a matter of a few months.

Similarly, orthodoxies in website design come and go—and each will be, as per the baiting-the-hook principle, specific to an audience and its style of engagement. To take an example from my world, that of newspapers, it tended to be conventional wisdom about ten years ago that a paper's website should be primarily navigable by clicking through. You'd be presented with a landing or home page that would (usually) take no more than a single screen. Arranged on it would be an array of headlines and teaser quotes and photographs that you'd click on to read the stories. Menus would also lead you to different sections, each of which would have its own landing page and its own submenus. Everything would be stacked like a Russian doll. You could call it a form of visual hypotaxis. You might click on the *Guardian* home page; click through to its review section; click through from that to its books section; and click through from that to the particular book review or feature you were attracted by.

Then the mid-market tabloid *Daily Mail* went online, and it more or less dispensed with all that. Instead of stacking everything behind a neat and well-organized landing page, it simply offered a seemingly endless torrent of stories stacked up on top of each other according to no obvious logic. Hard news, internet memes, gossip, paparazzi shots of actresses on beaches . . . you could scroll down indefinitely through this potpourri. And it's now one of the most viewed and most "sticky" news sites on the World Wide Web.

Its purpose isn't to dispense news in an orderly way. It's to provide a moreish experience in which—much like the way we browse the rest of the internet—the curious reader will click between the absurd, the dismaying, the titillating, and the trivial in no particular order.

That mashing up of genres and categories seems to go through the way we read online now. We are frequently distracted. Even when we're concentrating on reading a serious essay online, we might well have several other windows open. We'll be checking our phones, alt-tabbing over to Twitter, idling through someone's party photographs on Instagram . . . The experience of continual attention to a particular genre of thing and a particular tone (what, for the sake of argument, you might get while reading a book in a quiet library) is rare in the networked world.

So digital writing is above all about getting and retaining attention. You want your readers to click in the first place, and you want them to stay there once they have. You're aiming for clickiness and stickiness.

And we do know—roughly—what travels online. Pictures go further than text alone. And emotional content, or content that has a social logic, is particularly effective. Anger and outrage, humor, curiosity, astonishment, and tribal "virtue signaling": All of these will cause a posting to go further and faster online. That is why set phrases like "will astound you" and "you won't BELIEVE what X looks like now" have demonstrated their crude effectiveness in ads and promoted content; likewise why "secrets" so often feature in that content; and why "listicles"—"24 Continuity Errors in *Star Wars*" or what have you—so effectively gain our sense of curiosity.

When a few years ago I interviewed Jonah Peretti, the founder of BuzzFeed, he argued that memes and web culture in general are "organized by a sort of social logic. What kind of things do people like to do together? What kinds of things do people relate to? We organize our site by these emotional responses." Sure enough, shock or curiosity, sentimentality, amusement, and anger are the staples of viral content, and if you go onto BuzzFeed you'll find "sections" marked not "News," "Arts," "Comment," "Gossip," and so forth but "LOL," "win," "omg," "cute," "fail," and "wtf."

Hyperbole and emotive language come to the fore. The landing page for BuzzFeed at the time of writing was long on items that promised to be "hilarious" or "insanely clever," on lists of things that "sum up" a particular phenomenon or mistakes that "everybody makes." Headlines challenge the reader directly to engage. "Can You Pass This Basic German Test?" it wonders. "Can You Guess the Disney Princess?"

Here's a language that is informal, amped up, compressed, and maximalist. That is the default, though not the only, language of online engagement.

EMAIL

Email is a slippery form of communication. It runs the gamut from a digital version of ordinary letter-writing to something much more like a text message or an instant message, so getting a sense of the correct register requires a moment of thought. If you're sitting at your desk all day firing off emails—one to your husband one moment and one to your boss the next—it can be easy to let the registers blur. That fretwork of kisses with which you sign off is fine to a friend; is probably inappropriate with a colleague unless you know them well; and (in certain contexts) can stray into the realm of the ditzy, flirtatious, or even creepy if used with your manager or a subordinate. Remember, as Hillary Clinton didn't, that copyright in emails you write in the office will almost certainly belong to your company, and that the company (and its ISP) will archive those emails indefinitely. Before you hit send, think about the worst-case scenario: How would this email chain look if printed out and left on the CEO's desk, or raised in evidence at an employment tribunal? Better safe than sorry.

Emailing strangers, particularly in a professional context, asks for the same level of formality as a paper-and-ink letter. You won't need to supply a date or a return postal address, but the greeting and sign-off ought to be in place as usual. And even if you have an automatic digital signature, you look more courteous if you take the trouble to type your name at the end. As your exchange of emails turns into a conversation, the register might well move toward more informality. But, at least to start with, treat it as a formal exchange. You wouldn't open a written letter to a stranger with

"Hi Bob!"; and some if not a majority of Bobs will receive an email that opens that way with irritation. Friendly is fine; presumptuous runs a risk.

Flagging emails "urgent"—which many clients give you the option of doing—may well make sense within a company if it's part of your corporate practice. For emails to outside contacts and strangers, though, it looks as if you're presuming to jump a line. There'll be exceptions to that, but out-of-the-blue offers, press releases, business pitches, and so forth are not usually among them. The great pleasure of email is that it combines immediacy of communication with the courtesy of letting people respond in their own time. When the telephone was first invented, many people were horrified at the idea that complete strangers would be able to make a bell ring in the privacy of their living rooms. We got used to telephones, but that instinct is worth bearing in mind. If someone feels you're forcing yourself on their attention, they won't like it.

Requesting a read receipt will also almost always play badly. Put yourself in the recipient's shoes. Before they've even considered what you have to say, you're demanding something of them. A read receipt is a jabbed finger in the chest. I straw-polled Twitter on the subject and—though my Twitter followers obviously don't count as a scientific sample—the responses were pretty unequivocal: "I always, in every situation, make a point to decline to send a read receipt"; "blind rage"; "def. not fine by me"; "REVOLTING." If even 10 percent of your recipients respond that way, it's something to avoid.* If you absolutely need a response in a specific time frame, make it courteously clear in the email itself.

There are a number of practical as well as tonal concerns when it comes to email.

The first is spam filters. An all-caps subject line, as well as

---

* Actually it's likely to be a lot more than 10 percent. The Twitter poll I ran got 654 votes, of which fully 95 percent considered asking for a read receipt a "bloody cheek."

looking ugly and shouty, can be a one-way ticket to the junk mail folder. Likewise, obvious trigger words such as "free," "win," "sex," "Viagra," "cash," and "gold" and excitable punctuation marks along the lines of "!!!!!!" Most of us, it's true, won't have much occasion to send a professional or even a personal email with the subject line "FREE VIAGRA!!!!" but spam filters are dumb. You could imagine some of the words "cash," "gold," "free," and "win" appearing in a careless commodity trader's subject line, and it would go the worse for that email if they did. Other spam flags include unusually big or small font sizes, a high proportion of hyperlinks to ordinary text, and lots of big images rather than text (spammers sometimes try to get around filters by sending their messages as image files). If you're sending a legitimate attachment, make sure that your email makes reference to it in the text. A link or attachment in an email with no body text, even if it navigates the algorithmic filters, often signifies to the recipient that the sender has been hacked.

The second is our old friend the attention span. The many studies that have been done on how people read email agree on one thing: They don't read it very carefully. At least half of them won't bother scrolling down an email, and a very large number will read emails only in the preview pane, meaning that (depending on the configuration of their email client) they'll see only the first few paragraphs of the content, if that.

So the subject line and greeting are important. Make them easy to understand, personal to the recipient, representative of the email's actual content, and interesting enough to hold the attention.

And, as ever, put the most important material in the first couple of paragraphs of the email. Don't spend your first four paragraphs summarizing the situation as it stands, and only then get around to offering your proposals for changing it. That may be logically impeccable, but it's badly geared to the human attention span.

Dear Ed,

For several weeks now the staff have been complaining about the stodgy meals in the staff canteen. Yesterday the cauliflower curry was sent back uneaten by 40 percent of the workers. Earnings are down 20 percent, and morale is, at least anecdotally, low. Did you taste that fish the other day? It was like soggy toilet paper! Not only that, but we only just scraped through the last hygiene inspection. In light of all this...

Ed might enjoy your grousing, but if he's in a hurry he's going to put this in the TL;DR (too long; didn't read) file and leave it for later.

Rather, begin with: "I think we should sack the caterers. Here's why . . ."

BLOGGING AND WEBSITES

Keep it brief. If the internet had a catchphrase it would almost certainly be the four letters TL;DR. We are, in the words of T. S. Eliot, "distracted from distraction by distraction." So if you want anyone other than your mom to read your website or your blog, it pays to bear that in mind. Search engine optimization (SEO) is a specialized discipline, and beyond the scope of this book, but businesses building websites do well to be aware of it. SEO professionals recommend keeping page titles short so they will appear in full on search engine results. Depending on the search engine and the format of the title, you'll get a limit of between forty and seventy characters. Err on the safe side.

An eye-tracking study conducted in 2006 by a web design consultant, Jakob Nielsen, suggested that people don't just read distractedly when they read online; they read *differently*.* He

---

* Jakob Nielsen, "F-Shaped Pattern for Reading Web Content (Original Study)," Nielsen Norman Group, April 17, 2006, nngroup.com/articles/f-shaped-pattern-reading-web-content-discovered.

discovered that, typically, people scan a page of online text in a sort of rough F-shape. ("F for fast," he warns.) First their eyes track horizontally across the top area of the text. Then they again track horizontally—reading a bit less far across—a little farther down the page. Then they move their eyes vertically down the left-hand margin.

Nielsen drew three sensible conclusions from his study.

1. "Users won't read your text thoroughly." That means that you can't rely on word-for-word digestion. Punch up the stuff you really need them to notice.

2. "The first two paragraphs must state the most important information." We're back in inverted-pyramid territory. Get across what you need to get across in the crossbars of the F.

3. "Start subheads, paragraphs, and bullet points with information-carrying words." What this means, crudely, is that the left-hand side of the page is where the action is. So, particularly in a business document or website, concentrate the important stuff there. And make use of design features such as bullet points and subheads to capture the reader's attention as his or her eye wanders down the left-hand margin.

The bad news, too, is that the average web page attracts ten seconds or less of attention; fewer than one website in ten gets two minutes or more of attention. You might be able to bank on a bit more, of course, depending on what sort of page it is; if the user has navigated there deliberately, he or she is expecting to invest some time. But don't take attention for granted. The more words there are on a given page the more time a reader will spend on it—but that's subject to the law of diminishing returns. Nielsen used a different, large data set to consider this problem and concluded that for every extra hundred words on a site, it attracted only 4.4 seconds more of attention. That's less than twenty words at average reading speed.

A blog isn't a single sort of thing. Some blogs are essays; some are diaries; some—if you include in the blogging category profiles on platforms such as Pinterest or Tumblr—might be more like a curated collection of artifacts. Each will have its own special qualities and formal structure: An essayistic blog will want to advance well-set-out arguments; a diaristic one will tend to major on tone of voice, a feeling of intimacy, and/or an eye for the evolving event or the deft name drop.

The thing that can be said about all of them in general is that knowing your audience is the key to their success. There's no shame in deciding that the audience is you, or you and a small handful of friends; by all means write about what you ate for dinner or how fed up you are with your homework. But if you hope for a wider audience (and you presumably do, if you're posting it online), you need to give that audience a reason to read.

Blogs are personal. What's your selling point? Is it your particular expertise or authority? Or is it your taste and style and tone of voice? A blog, one way or another, needs a USP (unique selling point). It's notable that, within reason, a successful blog will tend to specialize in one particular thing. If people come to your blog expecting to read about food, and for two weeks solid you write only about knitting patterns, you probably won't take those readers with you. Readers will come back for that one particular thing. That thing might be you yourself; but more often it will be something you know or something you do.

Take a couple of examples. British journalist Eliot Higgins began as a web-savvy amateur who in 2012 became interested in the weapons that were being used in the Syrian civil war. He started blogging under the pseudonym Brown Moses and, using sources available on the internet and social media, became very good at identifying which weapons were being used where. His growing expertise and ingenuity started to furnish him with scoops—he busted the Syrian regime's use of barrel bombs against civilians and went on to establish the presence of Russian troops in the 2014–15 conflict in Ukraine. He got good at a particular thing—and his "citizen journalism" has had considerable political impact. If you want to know what's going on in Syria, Higgins—who founded the citizen journalism collective Bellingcat—is an indispensable source.

Another blogger who has used expertise to draw a following is the lawyer David Allen Green. Originally blogging as Jack of Kent, he uses a drily forensic style to analyze the legal issues involved in major political news stories. His attractiveness to his readers, including me, is his precision and his narrow specialism: You can get ideology here, there, and everywhere online. But someone who knows the difference between a tort and a Sacher torte, and can explain it with clarity to non-lawyers, commands attention. He's able to bring something particular to the analysis of the news.

Brooke Magnanti, who blogged as Belle de Jour, had a different sort of selling point. She was a professional sex worker. Readers went to her blog because it gave them a window into a world that they would not otherwise have had access to. It helped that she wrote stylishly and that she had a wide and intelligent range of interests outside her job. People came out of curiosity or in the hope of titillation—they stayed for her voice and personality.

Then, of course, there are the tone-of-voice blogs. Neil Gaiman is well known for his work as a writer of novels, children's books, and comics. He was early to the blogging world and built up a large following because he wrote well, had interesting things to say—and because people *really* wanted to know about Neil Gaiman. He had some good, if wryly admonitory, advice to those who hoped to emulate him. "People come to me and they ask, how do I get 1.5m people reading my blog?" he said. "And it's like, you need to start it in 2001 and try not to miss a day for the first eight years . . ."*

SOCIAL MEDIA

Social media presents particular perils and opportunities to the persuasive writer. The opportunities are that it has a potentially limitless reach. You really can, with a well-crafted Facebook post or a lucky tweet, reach around the world from your back bedroom.

On the other hand, it also provides for things to go viral in the wrong way. You need to bear three things in mind.

1. Tone often fails to travel online.

This is the killer. Irony, self-mockery, or dark humor can easily be parsed as bigotry. A question can be parsed as a sneer or an act of aggression—hence the rise of the defensive formula "genuine question." You only have to look at the so-called Twitterstorms that descend on quite innocent individuals to see the hazards. In his book *So You've Been Publicly Shamed*, the writer Jon Ronson used the example of a PR executive, Justine Sacco, who tweeted a bad-taste joke just before climbing on a plane: "Going to Africa. Hope I don't get AIDS. Just kidding. I'm white!" A tweet designed to mock a racist attitude was taken to be endorsing it, and by the time Sacco's plane had landed it had been retweeted more than two thousand times and picked up by mainstream outlets. In less than twenty-four hours Sacco had become a public hate figure, and she lost her job as a result.

2. You have multiple potential audiences.

Your potential overhearers may not be as sympathetic to you as your friends or followers. This point is closely allied to the first. But it means thinking about what certain behaviors might look like

---

* Tom Chatfield, "Interview: Neil Gaiman," *Tom Chatfield* (blog), tomchatfield.net/portfolio/interview-neil-gaiman/.

if spread more widely. The safest assumption to make is that even ostensibly closed social media sites such as Facebook or a locked Twitter account are essentially public forums. In 2016 the writer Nicholas Lezard joked in his private Facebook feed about wanting to crowd-fund a political assassination. Those hostile to his politics affected to have taken this as an incitement to violence. He was widely pilloried online and the newspaper for which he worked came under pressure to fire him. No joke for him at the time.

3. Stuff never, ever disappears from the internet.

It really doesn't. You can delete a tweet or take down a Facebook page or edit an Instagram post, but some bastard will have it screen-capped. Drunk texting can be a mistake; posting on social media drunk—and/or in anger or self-pity—can be a catastrophe. Post in haste; repent at leisure.

There are certain other lesser principles to bear in mind. None is an infallible rule, but all are worth thinking about before you put thumb to smartphone.

• Don't always be on transmit; social media is set up for conversation. If all you do is post links to your own self-published books, or invite people to "like" the Facebook page you've set up in tribute to yourself, people will see you as an advertising bot. Ask questions. Respond to people. This goes just as strongly for corporate accounts as it does for personal ones.

• The tone of voice you use will set the tone of the conversation. Fury tends to invite fury. Reasonableness tends to invite reasonableness. On the whole social media communication is far more informal than offline communication, and it has its norms of style. Labor to get the hang of them, but feel free to investigate the comic potential of the odd violation of decorum. The writer Saul Wordsworth has a spoof

Twitter account @nazihunteralan, purporting to be the thoughts of a Bedfordshire retiree called Alan Stoob who searches the English countryside for Nazis. Being old, Alan doesn't quite get Twitter so he frequently signs his tweets, "Regards, Alan." I mention it because it shows how most of us have so internalized the norms of social media that when someone writes a tweet like an old-fashioned letter it sounds comically odd.

• Be funny, if you can. If you make somebody laugh, you have them for life. A few years back the not-especially-well-known English novelist David Whitehouse* tweeted: "Lance Armstrong should be applauded for being able to ride a bike so well on drugs. I tried it once. Hit a dog and fell into the canal." It earned him nearly ten thousand retweets. What worked so well there? In the first place it was topical. Also the way it was worded. The detail of the dog—the fact that two accidents befell him rather than one—gave an awful extra vividness to the image. Plus people falling into canals on their bicycles is funny. His publisher replied to his tweet to congratulate him: "Your Lance joke retweeted 9249 times. Good going. If only *Bed* [Whitehouse's first novel] had sold that many!!"

• Reposting praise for yourself will turn people off. My advice would be to repost only insults and abuse. People enjoy reading those more in any case.

• Use hashtags judiciously. As I mentioned briefly in my chapter on punctuation, the hashtag does more than one thing. It is primarily an organizational tool. Where it indicates the subject matter of a social media post, or the debate to which it is a contribution, it makes it

---

* I describe him thus not to be rude but to make the point that he doesn't get thousands of retweets just for being him. You can't draw that many conclusions about social media success from a J. K. Rowling tweet that has done well.

possible to follow a particular thread of conversation through the tapestry. It also gets used to mark something as a comment. Facebook, Instagram, or Twitter posts that end in a thicket of hashtags tend to look gauche. #fail #lol #dadadvice #whodoyouthinkyouare-kiddingmisterhitler

• Think about who you're including in the conversation, and whether you're doing so with their consent or not. Facebook users will be familiar with those friends who add them to groups without asking them. That's bad manners. It's especially irksome if you aren't a regular Facebook user and struggle to figure out how to remove yourself from the lively "Bring Back Birching" or "Send Them All Home" communities. Likewise, if you respond to someone's tweet and then get into a six-hundred-tweet dustup with some third party, @-ing the original tweeter into every single one of your replies is a colossal pain in the mentions. If someone isn't actively participating in a discussion, untag them. Also there's a world of difference between @-replying to someone you disagree with—so that only people who follow you both will see the tweet—and either quoting their tweet below your response or putting a little period at the beginning so that your reply is visible to the world. The latter is the equivalent of writing an open letter. It's often an act of aggression, inviting a potential pile-on from your followers. It more often than not looks pompous and high-handed in any case.

• The two points above—about hashtags, and about who you include in the conversation—mesh when it comes to the interaction between individuals and corporations in the public spaces of social media. Corporations like to "engage" with their public. That's a good thing. But you make yourself vulnerable. The Facebook pages of unpopular companies can get swarmed with negative comments. And when you set up a hashtag you need to think hard about whether and how it might be used against you. In October 2016, the English train company Southern Railway was frustrated by a forthcoming strike by the Rail, Maritime, and Transport Union. So @SouthernRailUK tweeted: "Time to get back on track. Tweet @RMTunion & tell them how rail strikes make you feel. #SouthernBackOnTrack." It was a huge mistake. They got thousands of replies and hashtagged posts supporting RMT workers, ridiculing their service ("When people waited three hours at Brighton last night, was that because of strikes?"), and objecting to the company apparently encouraging its followers to demonize its own employees. The onslaught forced the company to ditch a planned poster campaign—the memos about which were, of course, immediately leaked onto social media.

A similar dynamic can be seen when individuals complain to companies in public in an effort to apply public pressure to alter their behavior. You might tweet: "Hey @GenericFriedChicken, I found this rat tail in my Cluck-O-Burger. What you going to do about it?" In the best-case scenario, your tweet will go viral (especially if you include a photograph of the offending food) and your apology and compensation will be faster and more groveling than had you written a polite private email. This works, naturally, especially well for celebrities with millions of followers. Corporations hate bad PR. The worst-case scenario is that you'll look whining and entitled and someone will point out that your "rat tail" is actually a piece of fried onion. Choose your battles.

• Think before subtweeting. The practice of bitching about people behind their backs—"subtweeting" is the name given to saying rude things about someone on social media (not just Twitter) without mentioning the person's name—long predates the internet. But it has especially toxic potential online. They may not notice. They may notice, recognize themselves, and be hurt or angry (sometimes the intended effect). And onlookers may judge you more harshly than the subject of your subtweet. Done elegantly, subtweeting can be a witty joke or a scalding rebuke. Done clumsily, it . . . which takes me onto my next point.

• Remember that—whether you live in a country blessed with the right to free speech or not—the laws of libel apply to you, and that repeating a libel is itself a libel. If someone posts a juicy-sounding rumor about a celebrity threesome, a government cover-up, or some appalling corporate malfeasance—especially if they name names and make concrete allegations—to share the post or link to it is effectively to adopt the allegation. "Interesting if true," or "I wonder what X has to say about this," or "*innocent face*" do not make you immune to being sued. If you don't know whether something is true, and you post it anyway, the consequences are on you. Being "in the know" makes you feel good. Being sued, not so much.

• Remember that there are as many different ways of "doing" social media as there are people doing it. Social media has tribes. People talk about "Weird Twitter" or "Black Twitter." Know the tribe you're tweeting to; get the hang of its private languages and conventions.

• Above all, respect the first rule of the internet: "Don't be a dick." Unless that's your express purpose, in which case knock yourself out. But be prepared to take the consequences.

Linguistically, as I've hinted above, the smart social media poster will be aware of the speed with which a popular usage hardens into cliché and then is discarded. If you don't want to look like your dad dancing disco at a wedding, you'd be wise to use caution when it comes to repeating a style of post you see being used by others on the site. Internet language changes fast.

President Trump was much mocked in 2017 for signaling sarcasm by adding the exclamation "Not!" to the end of a tweet; the movie *Wayne's World*, which briefly popularized the usage, came out twenty-five years before. Likewise, the former UK prime minister David Cameron was teased rotten for thinking, apparently, that "LOL" stood for "lots of love" (rather than "laughing out loud"). "LOL" itself has since changed its meaning in any case. Now it's more often deployed lowercase, either as an all-purpose unit of punctuation or semi-sarcastically, as if to say: "Yeah, sure. Funny." And do people still say "roflcopter" or "roflmao"? You'd have to doubt it.

There's an ever-lengthening list of these kinds of usages that have come into vogue and then have quickly turned into clichés, taking their place alongside well-worn words such as "trad," "groovy," and "tight" in the graveyard of redundant hipsterisms. Remember, to take a handful of examples, these?:

• "Wow. Just wow." (glossing something you appear to think is re-markable)

• "I can't even." (preceding something in response to which words, apparently, fail you)

• "This." (preceding a quoted tweet you agree with)

• "When you…" or "tfw…"* (preceding a reaction gif)

• "You're welcome." (preceding a post in which, by posting a picture of a hot celebrity or an unusual-looking cat, you deem yourself to have done the world a favor)

• "brb,† just…" (usually preceding a piece of news or a quoted tweet to which you are responding humorously, as in "brb, just killing my-self" in front of news of, say, the novelty boy band Hanson reforming)

• "[Town name], I am in you." (slightly smutty-sounding announce-ment of your movements that caught on briefly about five years ago but now seems mercifully to have withered)

---

* "That feeling when."
† "Be right back."

• "Burn!" (indicating that someone has said something withering to someone else)

• "DELETE YOUR ACCOUNT" (usually preceding a quoted tweet deemed to be so outrageous that death from shame seems like a sensible way forward)

• yolo (a general-purpose injunction to seize the day ["you only live once"], apparently used as punctuation by millennials)

• wtf or wtaf (meaning "what the fuck," or "what the actual fuck")

These are particular to their platform or platforms. They don't have much of a place in conventional prose but they (or whatever supersedes them) have a vigorous half-life on social media. What they have in common, I'd suggest, is a certain (albeit formulaic) informality and playfulness. Most of them indicate an emotional response.

Layout and Presentation

I am not a graphic designer or a newspaper copy editor. My concern here—and such expertise as I have to offer—is primarily to do with putting words together into sentences, sentences into paragraphs, and paragraphs into letters, emails, essays, reports, blog posts, chapters, and books. The question of typesetting and layout is one that admits a whole library of books from people with far more expertise in it than me.

But if for no other reason than to put down a marker that these things matter, I wanted to include a brief discussion on the design features of text. Some of the things we've already touched on—such as paragraphing and punctuation—have visual as well as semantic implications. These aren't trivial. A paragraph gives the reader a breather, as does a period. They allow the brain to catch up, consolidate what has gone before, and prepare to take in what follows.

Most design features, used properly, will do the same thing. Headings and subheadings in bold or a larger font size, bullet points, and indentations all help the reader orient him- or herself in the text. Generous spaces between paragraphs help, too; your word-processing package will tend to add an extra line or half line in between paragraphs, and it does that for a reason. White space is the reader's—and therefore your—friend.

Think, too, about what your eyes do when you read. They don't track continuously across a line of text, then return to the beginning of the next line and repeat. They move in what are known as "saccades"—little jumps of around ten characters every quarter of a second—between points of fixation. They haul a batch of letters into the brain, sometimes jump back to something they've already looked at, then on again.

When a line breaks, the reader is momentarily more energized and focused. Each new line is itself a sort of breather. Attention wanes progressively as the eye travels farther toward the right-hand margin. You could think of the reader's eye as a swimmer breaststroking across a pool: Little spurts of energy carry it from the left margin to the right, and each time it hits the side of the pool, it gets a bit of a boost as it kicks off the edge.

Things that make it hard for readers to concentrate on a text include the following.

Very close line spacing. The spaces between lines of type— sometimes known as "leading,"* from the days when print compositors used strips of lead to increase the vertical separation between lines of text—have a strong effect on its legibility.

* Pronounced "ledding."

When authors submit manuscripts to publishers, or students send essays to their teachers, they are often encouraged to do so "double-spaced." This is a hangover from the days of the manual typewriter, when the only way of increasing the line spacing was to whack the carriage return lever twice. This is especially useful if the reader is expecting to make comments, or proofreading corrections, in between the lines.

Most printed text won't need double-spacing, and leading—in a sensible proportion to font size—will be taken care of by your word-processing program automatically. But you do have the option to change these, and latitude to do so much more precisely than with a manual typewriter.

These defaults will mostly do the trick for a letter, memo, article, or what have you printed on a side of white printer paper. But they're not a universal rule. Web pages and blogs often use more generous leading—making it easier to skim down them quickly.

Small type size. It's not only those with poor eyesight who find tiny letters tricky to read. Small print makes reading harder work even for those with perfect vision. Also, it has implications for leading—because as I mentioned above, there's a natural relationship of proportion between the size of the letters and the spaces between the lines. That means that if your font size is tiny, your lines will also appear squished up.

The other relationship of proportion to consider is the size of your page. Typographers tend to agree that the optimal number of characters per line is between fifty and eighty, spaces included. This takes maximum advantage of the refreshing effect of the eye returning to the left margin, without that happening so often that the reader's rhythm is broken.

On a page of printer paper, the average font in twelve-point type will give you something around the right line length. If the font is set in eight-point, you have 100 or 150 characters per line. Not only will readers' concentration tend to flag, but by the time they reach the right-hand margin, they may struggle to find the beginning of the next line on the left-hand side.

Overlong paragraphs. Here, again, is the principle of paragraph as mental breathing space. A paragraph is a sort of super-line-break. The reader benefits from it. So though you can get away with only one paragraph or two per page, you will make your text less attractive.

The same goes with long sections. If you can break up a body of text into coherent sense-units (assuming they are appropriate to the genre of what you're doing) you do the reader a favor. Bait the hook.

Tiny margins. One of the instant turnoffs for a reader is a block of text that's so large and dense it's forbidding. Generous margins (though not so generous that the text is stranded like a postage stamp on a pool table) give a much more appealing visual appearance. And, again, they help to keep the number of characters per line within the fifty-to-eighty ballpark.

Justification. This is the term used for when the text is spaced so that it's flush with both left and right margins. It gives you a sort of oblong of text on the page. Its advantage is that it looks neat. Its disadvantage is that it leads to some words being hyphenated as they "turn" over line breaks. The usual alternative is what's called "flush left" or "ragged right," where the spaces between letters are regular, and where a word that won't fit entire on the line simply moves over to the next.

Most printed books, such as the one you're reading, are justi-fied. Documents on letter paper, on the other hand, often look better with body text ragged right. Again, consider proportion on the page; a book's page is much smaller, and the eye travels vertically much more quickly. It gets to the edge of the pool more easily. Therefore it's worth trading off the soothing white spaces that ragged right gives you for the neatness of justified text. For the same reason, there's seldom an extra line space between paragraphs in a book, but your word processor will default to putting one in when you're preparing a letter-paper document.

Most word-processing programs will also offer "flush right" (where the text is flush to the right-hand margin) and "centered" (where the middle of each line of text is exactly aligned with the middle of the page). Neither is any use at all for body text. Imagine the reader's poor eye seeking the anchoring safety of a regular left-hand margin, and finding none to fix on. But titles and chapter heads will be set center, and some special text—photo captions, or the sender's address on a letter—may be set flush right.

Typographical porridge. It should be obvious that mixing up type sizes and font too much makes a document look zany and amateurish. As a rule, stick to one font for body text. If you use a different font for titles, captions, and what have you, make sure it's close in style to the body text. Try not to have any given page contain four different fonts in three different sizes. Where you use italics or bold—say, in section headings—try to have a consistent scheme.

FONTS

Fonts stir strong feelings in a small minority of the population. Zealots have set up an extensive website—http://bancomicsans.tumblr.com/—dedicated to expunging a single typeface, Comic Sans, from public life. A whole documentary was made about Helvetica. My publishing stablemate Simon Garfield dedicated an excellent book to the pleasures and sorrows of different typefaces.[*]

---

[*] Simon Garfield, *Just My Type: A Book About Fonts* (New York: Penguin, 2011).

The point I want to make here is that fonts may stir strong feelings in some, but they also stir weak feelings in the very many people who may not think of themselves as having a view on fonts at all. The feelings they stir may be subliminal, but they are there.

Typefaces are like lighting design in the theater, the soundtrack to a film, or the wallpaper of a hotel room. They shape the experience, though they may not be consciously noticed at all. That makes them important. Garfield goes so far as to argue that Barack Obama's 2008 presidential campaign was helped along by the fact that all its posters were set in Gotham: "There are some types that read as if everything written in them is honest, or at least fair."

A font, therefore, feeds into the question of register and decorum; it shapes your ethos appeal. Are you a go-ahead advertising firm using a lot of sans serif* italics? A coffee shop full of people with man buns whose short toast menu of artisanal sourdoughs calls out for typewriter-like Courier? Or a solicitor of long standing who communicates in sober Times New Roman?

Truth be told, if you're not in the business of designing a logo or an advertisement, you're best advised to stick to a font that doesn't scream and draw attention to itself, but that is light, legible, sober, and well spaced. Still, it doesn't hurt to play around a little and see how the feel of your document is changed by putting it into a different typeface.

Forms of Address

There are a number of rules in standard formal English for how you should address and identify people, in both the second person and the third. The rules on all this are far too baroque for me to reproduce here in full—so I sketch out only a couple of the basic ones.

It pays to get them right, though; if you ever do find yourself writing about or to a senior academic, an archbishop, a hereditary

---

* Without the twiddly bits.

earl, or a Warden of the Cinque Ports, check that you are doing so correctly. Here's an instance in which there are right and wrong ways to do things; these are specific and fixed conventions rather than random mutations of language, and it doesn't compromise your egalitarian principles to get it right.

But it will take you a moment or two of Googling: What you write on an envelope, how you begin a letter, what you'll say when introduced face-to-face, and how you'd describe them when writing *about* them will all be slightly different things. Wikipedia has extensive material on the ins and outs. Do bother to look these things up. In the US, you are blessed by the absence of an old-fashioned aristocracy, but you do have presidents ("Mr. President"), ex-presidents ("Mr. President"), members of Congress and the military, academic and medical doctors, and so on.

Ordinary civilians—whether you're shaking them by the hand or addressing an envelope—will take "Mr.," "Mrs.," "Miss," or "Ms." Unless you're both sure of the marital status of a female correspondent and certain that she has no objections to that being brought into her form of address, good manners these days is to use "Ms."*

If you're feeling old-fashioned and/or a little affected, and you're writing to a man, you can put "Dave Smith Esq." on the envelope. Don't for Pete's sake put "Mr. Dave Smith Esq."; it's either/or. In any case the letter inside should begin "Dear Mr. Smith."

"Master" and "Miss" for children, these days, also sounds affected. I might address a letter to my goddaughter "Miss Mila Arbuthnott," but when I do so I'm being arch. Old-fashioned usage stipulates that when you write thanking a married heterosexual couple for a weekend at their house you write to the wife rather than the husband, or that if, in other circumstances, you are writing to

---

* An analogue of this is the tendency to replace gendered terms such as "chairman" with "chair." Whatever the letters page of the *Daily Telegraph* thinks about it, this mild and courteous eruption of political correctness hasn't yet brought about the end of Western civilization.

both of them you'll say: "Mr. and Mrs. Dave Smith." All that is on the way out.

Transgender people often choose their own pronouns and titles. There's nothing approaching uniformity on this, so it's easiest just to ask. If in doubt the stickler-horrifying "they"/"them"/"their"—as in "Not long after I met them, Dave Smith asked me if I would like to read their thesis"—does inoffensive service as a gender-neutral pronoun. If addressing a letter, just go First name Surname; if saying hello, jump in and use the first name until enlightened otherwise.* Good manners, here, probably trumps any fixed ideas you might have about traditional grammar or correct form. As I've said many times in these pages, language is a social instrument.

Overall, what I hope to impress on you is that to get someone's form of address right is an important courtesy. It shows, quite literally, that you know your audience. And finicky though it may be, you have nothing to lose by it and—especially if your correspondent is someone who does mind about these things— everything to gain.

* * *

It's worth keeping a particular eye out for a journalistic usage that seems to have bled into the wider culture. News reporters like to identify people in a compressed way, with a job description before a name.

Apprentice yoga instructor Carol Smith was shopping on the main street when the bomb went off.

Here you're treating the subject of the sentence—"apprentice yoga instructor Carol Smith"—as one unit, as if it were a compound word.

---

* Or there's always that old fallback, beloved of those of us who forget people's names at parties, "Hey you."

That's why it doesn't work if you attempt to separate the parts of it with a comma.

Apprentice yoga instructor, Carol Smith, was shopping on the main street when the bomb went off.

This makes "Apprentice yoga instructor" the subject of the sentence, and nobody would write "Apprentice yoga instructor was shopping."

So you need an article: "*An* apprentice yoga instructor" or "*The* apprentice yoga instructor." The former introduces her from scratch. The latter presupposes that we've already been told that an apprentice yoga instructor was on the scene, in which case her name is a fresh tidbit of information thrown in parenthetically.

And you will need to punctuate differently depending on whether you're using a definite or indefinite article. Unpacking this apparently simple phrase is a little complex. Consider the following variations.

i. "The apprentice yoga instructor Carol Smith was shopping on the main street when the bomb went off": Grammatical but odd—it implies that she is a well-known apprentice yoga instructor. ("The pop star David Bowie was shopping . . ." poses no problems.)

ii. "The apprentice yoga instructor, Carol Smith, was shopping on the main street when the bomb went off": This is grammatically fine, but its shade of meaning is peculiar. It implies, as I say, that we've already been introduced to an apprentice yoga instructor. It would read naturally only if, for example, the previous sentence had been: "Yesterday's explosion was witnessed by an apprentice yoga instructor."

iii. "An apprentice yoga instructor Carol Smith was shopping on the main street when the bomb went off": Not grammatical. Carol Smith needs to be lodged between a pair of commas if she's being introduced with an indefinite article.*

iv. "An apprentice yoga instructor, Carol Smith, was shopping on the main street when the bomb went off": This is faultlessly grammatical but a little weird. Why emphasize her (irrelevant) profession? Had she been a bomb-disposal expert or an emergency triage nurse on her day off, it might be a different story; you might be wanting to make the point that a professional was on the scene. Perhaps your next sentence will be, "She immediately helped several survivors into the downward dog pose," but I doubt it.

v. "An apprentice yoga instructor, Carol Smith was shopping on the main street when the bomb went off": This, grammatically, just about works. Effectively you're putting her profession in parentheses—Carol Smith is the subject of the sentence—but putting it before the main clause. It's grammatically cognate with my preferred version vii, below. But it seems to imply that her profession has something to do with her presence on the street. "A shoe collector in possession of a platinum credit card, Carol Smith was shopping on the main street . . ." might support that single-comma construction.

vi. "The apprentice yoga instructor, Carol Smith was shopping on the main street when the bomb went off": This doesn't

---

* This applies to the article-free version, too. As I was writing this I received an email that opened: "*The Ethical Carnivore: My Year Killing to Eat* by former environmental journalist, Louise Gray publishes September 22nd." Without that comma, the sentence would be ill-made but grammatically tolerable. As it stands it's just wrong.

work. It not only falls into the trap of the previous one-comma version, v, but it has the problem of other definite article variants such as ii, of implying that we've already been introduced to an apprentice yoga instructor.

vii. "Carol Smith, an apprentice yoga instructor, was shopping on the main street when the bomb went off": This is more natural. Carol Smith was the witness to the event, and the reader gets her profession as a secondary detail.

It also bears saying that anywhere but in the pages of a newspaper, the original article-free usage looks very awkward. It's journalese. Hence the grating opening of Dan Brown's novel *The Da Vinci Code*:

> *Renowned curator Jacques Saunière staggered through the vaulted archway . . .*

This may be the first novel in which the ineptitude of the writing declares itself not from the first sentence or even the first word, but *before* it. There's a word missing before the book even begins. Golf claps for Dan Brown.

Acknowledgments

I'd like to thank all at Profile Books—with especial props to Andrew Franklin, Ed Lake, Penny Daniel, Valentina Zanca, and the late John Davey—for their encouragement and (especially) patience. Caroline Wilding for a witty index, my favorite bit of the book, done fast. Also, all at Rogers, Coleridge and White, who are more like a family than an agency.

I'd also like to commend my US editor Nick Cizek, at The Experiment, for his good humor and tact—and his ruthlessly brilliant colleague Anne Horowitz, who copy edited the manuscript to within an inch of its life.

Thanks, too, to the many sensitive writers on language and usage I cite here, whether to usurp their authority, steal their insights, or blacken their good names; I am a dwarf standing on the shoulders of giants (and the odd dwarf).

Finally, all my love and thanks go to my wife Alice (who puts up with a lot when I'm writing a book) and my three domestic dwarves, Marlene, Max, and Jonah.

Index

About the Author

S am Leith is a literary editor at the *Spectator* and columnist for the *Financial Times, Evening Standard,* and *Prospect.* His writing has also appeared in *The Times,* the *Guardian,* and the *Times Literary Supplement,* among others, and he is the author of many books, including his most recent, the critically acclaimed *Words Like Loaded Pistols: Rhetoric from Aristotle to Obama.*